AFTER THE EURO

Pg 169
Pg 25

After The Euro

Shaping Institutions for Governance
in the Wake of European Monetary
Union

Edited by
COLIN CROUCH

OXFORD
UNIVERSITY PRESS

OXFORD

UNIVERSITY PRESS

Great Clarendon Street, Oxford OX2 6DP

Oxford University Press is a department of the University of Oxford.
It furthers the University's objective of excellence in research, scholarship,
and education by publishing worldwide in

Oxford New York

Athens Auckland Bangkok Bogotá Buenos Aires Calcutta
Cape Town Chennai Dar es Salaam Delhi Florence Hong Kong Istanbul
Karachi Kuala Lumpur Madrid Melbourne Mexico City Mumbai
Nairobi Paris São Paulo Singapore Taipei Tokyo Toronto Warsaw

and associated companies in Berlin Ibadan

Oxford is a registered trade mark of Oxford University Press
in the UK and certain other countries

Published in the United States
by Oxford University Press Inc., New York

British Library Cataloguing in Publication Data

Data available

Library of Congress Cataloging-in-Publication Data

After the Euro : shaping institutions for governance in the wake of European monetary
union / edited by Colin Crouch.
Includes bibliographical references and index.
1. Monetary unions—European Union countries.   2. Monetary policy—European Union
countries.   3. European Union countries—Economic policy.   4. Economic and Monetary
Union.   I. Crouch, Colin, 1944–
HG3942.A35 2000   332.4'94—dc21   99–059038

ISBN 0 –19–829639–8

3 5 7 9 10 8 6 4 2

Typeset by Graphicraft Limited, Hong kong
Printed in Great Britain
on acid-free paper by
Biddles Ltd
Guildford and King's Lynn

Acknowledgement

This book is the result of a workshop organized in May 1997 within the 1996–97 Forum on the Political Economy of an Integrated Europe, of the European University Institute, Florence. The editor and authors are grateful for the opportunity afforded by the workshop in helping to develop this project.

Contents

List of Contributors

Robert Boyer is a member of the Centre National de la Recherche Scientifique, economist at CEPREMAP, and Directeur d'Etudes at the Ecole des Hautes Etudes en Sciences Sociales, Paris. His research is focused upon the macroeconomic impact of institutional change. His publications include *States aganist Firms: The Limits of Globalization* (with Daniel Drache (eds), Routledge, 1996); *Contemporary Capitalism: The Embeddedness of Institutions* (with Rogers Hollingsworth (eds), Cambridge University Press, 1997). He is active in the development of *régulation* theory that has been presented in *The* Régulation *School: A Critical Introduction* (Columbia University Press, 1990) and *Régulation Theory: The State of the Art* (Routledge, 2000). Member of the Conseil d'Analyse Economique, he has co-ordinated for the Commissariat General du Plan a report on the Future of the euro *Le gouvernement économique de la zone Euro* (La Documentation Française, 1999).

Stephen Clarkson is Professor of Political Science at Toronto University. He specializes in the study of Canadian politics. His recent works include: *Canada and the Reagan Challenge: Crisis and Adjustment, 1981–85* (Lorimer, 1985, 2nd edition); and *Trudeau and Our Times*: Vol. 1; *Magnificent Obsession*; Vol. 2; *Heroic Delusion* (with Christina McCall, McClelland and Stewart, 1994).

Thomas Christiansen is a Lecturer at the Centre for European Studies, University of Wales, Aberystwyth. He specializes in the study of European integration within international relations theory and with reference to regional politics.

Colin Crouch is a Professor in Sociology at the European University Institute, Florence. He is also an External Scientific member of the Max-Planck-Institute for Society Research at Cologne. He is currently working on a project with colleagues in France, Germany, Italy and the UK, studying local production systems of small firms in various European countries. His recent books include *Industrial Relations and European State Traditions* (OUP, 1993); *Are Skills the Answer?* (with David Finegold and Mari Sako, OUP, 1999); and *Social Change in Western Europe* (OUP, 1999).

Gabriele Tondl is an economist at the Researach Institute for European Affairs, University of Economics and Business Administration, Vienna. Her research and publications are mainly concerned with European economic convergence and regional development.

Jonathan Story is Professor of International Political Economy at INSEAD. His latest book, is *The Frontiers of Fortune: Predicting Capital Prospects and*

Casualties in the Markets of the Future (*The Financial Times* / Prentice Hall, 1999). He is co-author, with Ingo Walter, of *Political Economy of Financial Integration in Europe* (Manchester University Press, 1997), and his chapter 'Monetary Union: Economic Competition and Political Negotiation', appears in *The Franco–German Relationship in the European Union*, edited by Douglas Webber and published by Routledge, 1999.

Leila Talani is a Lecturer in European Economics at the European Institute of the London School of Economics and Political Science. She is the author of *Betting for and against the Euro: Who Wins and Who Loses in Italy and the UK from the Process of European Monetary Integration* (Ashgate, 2000).

Christopher Taylor is a senior economist with the National Institute for Economic and Social Research, London. In recent years his research and publications have been focused mainly on questions of European economic integration.

Amy Verdun is a Lecturer in the Department of Political Science, University of Victoria, British Columbia. Her publications are mainly concerned with the policy-making processes of European integration, including the role of epistemic communities among European policy-making elites.

List of Figures

List of Tables

1

Introduction: The Political and Institutional Deficits of European Monetary Union

COLIN CROUCH

Most discussions of European Monetary Union (EMU) are concerned with the structure of the monetary and other economic institutions, and their likely economic implications for the countries involved. Political analysis has been largely limited to details of the past—to processes leading to and surrounding its introduction; and to broad future speculation—the implications for national sovereignty of its long-term functioning. It is time to shift attention to more detailed discussions of the future—the implications for a wider range of institutions and policy areas than the grand but nebulous arena of sovereignty. My reference to political and institutional deficits is a deliberate echo of the well-known theme of 'democratic deficit' which has coloured European Union (EU) debate for some years. There has been concern that basic political institutions of democracy—parliamentary power, executive accountability—taken for granted in their nation states by populations in the advanced societies, have not developed at EU level in pace with mechanisms of economic integration and European level regulation (Verdun 1998*a*). But we also need to look beyond the purely political to other institutional contexts. The monetary arrangements of nation states are embedded in a range of other institutions to which they might respond and which respond to them: in addition to the whole apparatus of democracy there are, most prominently, the interest group organizations of the economy, various territorial levels of social organization, and also entrenched cultural beliefs about the functioning of the economy. The EU in contrast has a distinctly thin layer of such institutions.

From some perspectives an institutional deficit of this kind might be considered an important positive achievement, such institutions being regarded as deleterious interferences with the market processes that otherwise characterize the economy.[1] The contributors to this collection write

I am grateful to Amy Verdun and Christopher Taylor for comments on an earlier draft of this chapter, though neither can be considered responsible for the final outcome.

[1] The market is of course an institution, and in fact a particularly complex, subtle and finely constructed one. However, for the purposes of this discussion we are using

from different perspectives on this issue, and no attempt has been made to reconcile them. Our book is therefore not a joint report but a series of approaches, and as a result there is no chapter of conclusions. But whatever views we might variously take of the subject of institutional deficits do not prevent us from examining the questions raised by the contrast that the level of the Union presents here with that of all individual member states. The core questions are as follows.

First, what implications is EMU having for the diversity of forms of capitalism within Western Europe? More specifically, will it favour the development of a distinctive European model as envisaged by Jacques Delors, or will it contribute to the triumph of the Anglo-American form of capitalism (Delors Report 1989)? This is considered from different points of view by several authors in this book. Robert Boyer makes a general assessment of the relationship of EMU to the 'diversity of capitalism' debate. Jonathan Story argues that French and German leaders have chosen to transform their financial systems into those of the Anglo-American type. Leila Talani analyses the difficult relations between EMU and the City of London (the principal embodiment of the Anglo-American model within the European economy though not yet within EMU). Finally, Stephen Clarkson contributes the particular perspective of relations between Canada and the USA within the North Atlantic Free Trade Area (NAFTA).

Second, does the establishment of the European Central Bank (ECB) mark a new stage in the extension and thickening of the structure of the European Union, or will it remain an isolated body? Amy Verdun and Thomas Christiansen consider problems of the imbalance being created among European institutions by the particular form of the ECB. Christopher Taylor uses his analysis of this same issue to make some practical proposals for embedding the ECB into European political structures.

Finally, there is a number of questions concerning the implications of monetary union for social policy. At one level this is a simple issue: through the bias against public expenditure built into the criteria of the Maastricht Treaty and subsequent Stability Pact (Artis and Winkler 1997), the erection of EMU exerts a downward pressure on all elements of public expenditure. However, in so doing it only reinforces many other general tendencies of contemporary public policy. We have therefore not included a general chapter on the issue of welfare state decline. There are, however, two areas of social policy where there are some highly specific questions related to EMU, in particular relating to the heterogeneity of the territories to which the

'institutions' to mean 'institutions other than the market', because there is no doubt about whether the EU's programme is about the construction of markets. Were we to be discussing Eastern Europe, we could not make the same assumptions, as there the growth of a certain type of capitalism has not necessarily been accompanied by a development of a real market, which it would then become important to study in any account of economic institutions.

common monetary policy is being applied. Gabriele Tondl considers taxation policy and the scope for fiscal federalism to offset some of the tendencies to geographical inequality likely to be induced by the single currency, Colin Crouch considers the question of wage determination and the possible role of industrial relations institutions.

European Monetary Union and the Diversity of Capitalism

The rise of a globally integrated capitalist economy has raised the issue of the scope for diversity in the institutional forms that can be taken by that economy. Some accounts (most popularly Albert 1991) saw the issue in Manichean terms as a conflict between an essentially European 'Rhenish' form embedded in a wide range of associations and regulations and an Anglo-American free-market model. Others (Berger and Dore 1996; Boyer and Hollingsworth 1997; Crouch and Streeck 1997; Hollingsworth, Schmitter, and Streeck 1994) saw a wider variety. All, however, tended to agree that the Anglo-American free market favoured by the current neo-liberal orthodoxy in economic ideas represented the main challenge to the viability of the others, however these were conceived.

The new European currency is part of this same puzzle. In many respects it can be interpreted as an attempt to establish a rival to the US dollar and therefore a potential challenge to the US global economic domination which is fundamental to the power of that state's preferred model of capitalism. On the other hand, in order to construct the currency the European economies have embraced many of the neo-liberal assumptions fundamental to the US model. In fact, the main choice seems to be between two forms of economic liberalism. One is the American form, where limitations on capitalist freedom mainly take the form of civil law remedies for aggrieved parties, particularly consumers. The other is the German *Ordoliberalismus* model where the capitalist order is guaranteed by a number of statutory institutions, of which the Bundesbank and its elaborate banking regulations are a major example. One can see elements of the tension between these ostensibly similar forms of capitalism in the conflicting perspectives of the institutions of the City of London and the Bundesbank-led rules of the European Central Bank (Talani, Chapter 4). While from the perspective of German social democrats and the West European left in general the Bundesbank is an epitome of the dominance of free-market orthodoxy, from the point of view of the City of London its approach is riddled with regulation and restrictions.

Another, closely related, formulation is the contrast between pure and embedded neo-liberalism proposed by Van Apeldoorn (1998). The former is the familiar deregulated form of capitalism that regards most action by governments and other social institutions as distorting interferences with pure markets. The latter sees a need for markets to be embedded in certain wider institutions if they are to receive infrastructural support and social consent, though the aim remains as little actual interference with markets as possible. European neo-liberalism tends to take the *Ordoliberalismus* or embedded form, if only because at the European level institutions are still being designed and forged which a primarily national, institutionally well-entrenched capitalism of the US kind is able to take for granted.

On the other hand, there is a strong tendency for European policy-making to shift towards the purer, Anglo-American neo-liberal approach under the pressure of the globally dominant orthodoxy of a 'new constitutionalism' (see Ryner 1998 for a direct application of this to the construction of EMU). It is the current prevailing belief of what Verdun (1996) has called the epistemic community of world policy-makers that matters work best when markets are most free and when governments and other social interests have least capacity to have any influence over them. According to this originally American theory, the post-war Keynesian economy became entrenched in a mass of welfare and pro-labour interferences in the economy by the polity, which has confused the clarity of the separation between state and economy fundamental to the concept of the capitalist economy. From this perspective, which is pessimistic about the capacity of public policy to achieve anything constructive other than to reduce its own role through deregulation, the central strategic aim of the movement for deregulation, privatization, welfare state reduction and tax cuts is to untangle the entire process of the post-war welfare state economy. Identification of an 'institutional deficit' in the European architecture becomes an achievement of institutional deconstruction to be celebrated rather than a problem over which heads should be shaken.

Many of the provisions of the Maastricht Treaty concerning the preparation of countries for EMU, the Stability Pact agreed for governing their subsequent conduct, and the behaviour to date of the ECB can be seen as part of this master project: insistence on the reduction of public-sector deficits and rejection of the Keynesian argument that deficit public expenditure can constitute infrastructural investment rather than simple debt. The most appropriate image of the contemporary state is not Hobbes's *Leviathan* containing within himself all members of the society, but the biblical Samson, blinded, shorn of his strength, able to destroy his enemies only by crushing himself to death at the same time. At the start of the Second Millennium the state, emasculated by a sense of its past failings, lacking any confidence to believe that it can itself see what policies are needed, destroys its own capacity to act any more by tearing down the regulatory frameworks and institutions that surround it, and which it has come to see as hostile to its own main purposes.

As Boyer argues (Chapter 2), the entire monetary union project is an ambitious political programme designed to seek such an economic determinism over politics, this core paradox producing a host of other paradoxes. As he puts it, in some ways markets and democracy have been trading places: financial markets are monitoring national and European policy, while politicians are seeking to promote economic efficiency. Such is the logical outcome of the accepted sovereignty of economics and loss of self-confidence within the state.

Jonathan Story demonstrates (Chapter 3) how the French and German governments and their associated banking elites, the main protagonists of the single currency, seem quite consciously and deliberately to be using monetary union to dismantle the institutional structure of their mutually distinctive national financial systems in favour of an Anglo-American model. To some extent this is simply a necessary cost of the priority given to the single-currency goal. As the whole history of the creation of the EU demonstrates, negative integration that takes the form of stripping away market impediments is far easier to achieve than the construction of an 'institution-rich' model. (See Scharpf 1996 for a full discussion of this theme.) This results from the lowest common denominator requirement of joint decision-making. To agree to strip away a set of institutions requires a certain consensus; then to reconstruct a new set requires further agreement on which alternative to adopt. This is already a tougher decision requirement. If the new set is that associated with a particular country, other countries will object; if it is associated with no country, it is regarded suspiciously as an untried model. Negative integration is therefore likely to dominate as the main form of agreement that is feasible, quite apart from any ideological preferences. This therefore implies convergence by default on a pattern that requires least beyond liberating markets, and thus the so-called 'Anglo-American' model.

It is however mistaken to see this model as merely the result of clearing away impediments to a set of free markets. Anglo-American financial markets are in fact institutionally very specific; their individual structure did not, *pace* Hayek, simply grow that way because that is how institutions grow in a kind of state of nature if governments do not interfere with them. Both are indeed the product of a good deal of past regulation and rather specific, different, national circumstances. In particular, the British and in turn the Americans developed systems of this kind during epochs when they have dominated, not only world trade but world power in the more straightforward military sense too. Today, shorn of this kind of power, the British model shares the role of a dominant system only through its association with the militarily still dominant USA. Also, these are all highly complex systems, and French, German and many other European financial managers are placing themselves at some disadvantage if they really are replacing their systems with one of a kind in which the British and the Americans (though also the Dutch and the Swiss) are considerably more experienced.

It is also ironic that one feature of the US system is that the Federal Reserve Bank operates in a far more relaxed, quasi-Keynesian manner than the European Central Bank is permitted to do. In a financial world where future expectations, second-guessing, and a competitive edge based on discounting future changes are more important than current known realities, the financial markets take it for granted that US monetary management will follow a strict regime; therefore it does not have to do so. The markets' stereotypes of the Europeans is that they cannot be trusted to be strict; therefore they have to be. As a consequence, the Fed is able to pursue more relaxed policies during a period of rapid growth than the ECB is during a recession.

In fact, the elaborate, *Ordoliberalismus* structure of the ECB and its associated monetary regime is far from being a simple negative integration structure. Something far stronger than a lowest common denominator motive has been at work in producing the EMS. This returns us to the argument at the outset concerning the collapse of confidence of politics, the state and indeed most other non-market institutions by elites which have come to see their institutions as tired and overloaded.

We can see this most clearly, if extremely, in the Italian case. Salvati (1997) has spoken of a 'Copernican revolution' needed in the changes of perspective of Italian business and political elites in entering the euro. One might however also, returning to an image used above, call it a Hobbesian revolution. The Leviathan on whom Hobbes's hopelessly embattled individuals call is an outsider, not endogenous to the society, not suspected of having an 'interest' of his own. This reflects the preoccupations of the England of Hobbes' time, wracked by civil wars and eventually looking to elsewhere in Europe for a new ruling dynasty. This resembles a particular Italian concern in the 1990s. Partly for deeply rooted historical reasons which are not our subject here, partly because of the chain of corruption scandals that engulfed most of the political class throughout the decade, Italians had become disillusioned with their endogenous politicians. Europe has become the Italians' Leviathan. The Italian public was prepared to accept sacrifices and welfare reductions in the name of making the country fit to join the EMU.

In turn, Italian politicians had begun to despair of a society that never produced decisive majorities, and which reproduced at the top level of one of the world's seven leading industrial nations a system of clientelist and particularistic relationships more appropriate to the *padrone* system of a small agricultural town. They were happy to have the justification of the Maastricht criteria and the constraints of the ECB to free themselves from the morass of popular demands. Italian public and politicians alike sought a liberation from each other in 'Europe'.

The Europeanist response of the Italian public was unusual; it is difficult to imagine another country in which conformity with the demands of the EU could be urged as the reason to make sacrifices that would not be made for internal national purposes. But the response of Italian politicians was less so: a political class seeking through an external constraint to liberate itself from demands for spending, for subsidies, for special measures, may well be typical. French and German political and economic elites have, as Story shows, sought to impose on themselves a financial regime that is different from those that have given them past (though less so current) economic success; is more expertly practised by some of their competitors; and which removes from them major policy instruments. This can be understood as being similar to the reaction of Italian elites: the desire to escape the demands of at least some elements of the national public, combined with lack of confidence as the nation state Leviathan becomes Samson.

For the economic part of European elites the motive is more obvious. In lightly regulated global capital markets, a monetary system of the Anglo-American kind gives far more opportunity to choose locations for economic activities. To acknowledge this is not to deny the importance of sunk costs which make most industrial (and much service) capital less mobile than the globalization rhetorics of both left and right claim—indeed sometimes less mobile than labour. In practice, in these situations there is often interaction between industrial employers and labour concerning the risks of uncompetitiveness and the range of solutions available, and labour's adaptations can be negotiated and worked through in a reasonably civilized manner. Nor should one reject the possibility that, once all factors have been considered, investors might sometimes prefer a location in a country with a strong infrastructure and skilled if inflexible labour markets. The point is, however, that investors want the chance to choose. They are prepared to risk much for that freedom, even if, like the Swedish firms which dabbled inexpertly and therefore disastrously in the London property markets in celebration of their capital liberalization in the 1980s, they have to learn how to manage such markets the hard way.

Further, European firms are reluctant to take too much notice of arguments which stress sunk costs and stability. They fear that to do this means being left with the slower moving and therefore less dynamic forms of capital. Hence the complaints about the slowness of German, Austrian, and Scandinavian social dialogue processes and the rejection of associational networks, even those of firms themselves, which necessarily involve discussion and interaction with the workforce. Business elites therefore increasingly see the essence of competitiveness as being to attract rapidly moving, footloose capital, which is by definition more dynamic than stable local capital. Hence the convergence on a belief in the superior capacity of the faster moving, short-term oriented Anglo-American forms of capitalism over the more heavily investment-oriented German or Japanese forms. Significantly, the European Round Table of Industrialists, arguably the most important business lobby within the EU, has tried to redefine competitiveness to mean 'capacity to attract footloose capital' (ERT 1997; Van Apeldoorn 1998).

The wisdom of this can be challenged. It leads to the conclusion that there is some inherent superiority in investments favoured by 'footloose' capital over those that require long-term commitments. At the end of this road is the argument that investment in retail outlets for T-shirts is always superior to that in a new pharmaceuticals concern. It is interesting that, in moving to this input-oriented measure of competitiveness, rather than an output measure, such as capacity to achieve a positive trade balance in open markets, the ERT is using redefinition to short-circuit a serious economic argument. If by definition it is not possible to achieve competitiveness by routes other than making a country as attractive to footloose capital as possible, it is no longer possible to argue that slower-moving quality investments requiring considerable social infrastructure support might in the longer run lead to superior economic performance. For example, the German economy has continued, despite unification, to achieve positive trade balances in manufactured goods: the sector where trade has been most deregulated but where labour regulation and trade unionism are usually at their highest. The UK and the USA continue to run deficits in manufacturing. This might be deployed to argue that the Anglo-American model is not necessarily the most competitive. However, if competitiveness is redefined to mean having a system with certain characteristics, rather than having certain outcomes, the 'battle of the systems' has been won by definition.

In general, the issue is not yet fully resolved in favour of the new constitutionalism. The strains towards *Ordoliberalismus* or embedded liberalism have powerful support in the traditions of most Continental liberalisms and the continuing task of institution-building at the European level. Significantly, and in complete contrast with the new constitutionalism model, it has been political rather than purely economic criteria which have shaped the entire question of the single currency. As Boyer notes (Chapter 2), although the theory of optimal currency zones totally disconnects its analysis from any political considerations, membership of the EMU was never decided by what might comprise a theoretically optimal zone, and that theory is quite useless in defining the EMU zone. And it continues to be political criteria ('What will the markets think about our commitment to stability if we take such and such an action?') which dominate the actions of the ECB rather than economic ones (e.g. 'What does the future health of the European economy indicate that we should do?'). This became evident early in 1999, when the position of the then Finance Minister of Germany, Oskar Lafontaine, became impossible, because the fact that he argued that a cut in interest rates was required by the European economies became the reason why the ECB could not implement such a cut. So much for the dominance of economic theory over political arguments.[2]

Also striking is the response of British Conservatism, the political strand within Europe closest to current American notions of the limited state; Conservatives have in general opposed EMU precisely because of the challenge it poses to the sovereignty of national governments, and hence to politics. Or is this so straightforward? Talani argues (Chapter 4) that the fundamental reasons for British hostility to EMU during the years of Conservative government were the preferences of the financial institutions of the City of London. The UK is unique in the world in having dominant over its economy a financial sector which has little involvement in the rest of it. The other two leading financial centres, Japan and the USA, are different. First, the financial sector is proportionately larger within the UK economy than in these cases. Second, the City has a set of privileged connections to the British state which no other part of the economy can begin to emulate. In Japan the large corporations of the industrial sector not only have privileged access to the state, but are also far more integrated with financial institutions than are their opposite numbers in the UK. The US financial sector does not have the same political connections as in the UK; it is not possible for any sector of the US economy (except the centrally important armaments and aerospace industries) to have privileged linkages to a unified and powerful executive of the British kind, if only because the USA has no unified and powerful executive.

It becomes almost facile to ask whether British society as a whole shares the interests of the City of London. Rather, other groups in that country have to define their interests so that they are compatible with those of the financial sector.[3] The City is sometimes seen, and often sees itself, as a kind of offshore island in relation to the UK. However, unlike other offshore islands, it has a hegemonic role within the larger society off whose shores it metaphorically lies. As matters stand at present, entry of the UK into the single currency would represent a major setback for the City, and therefore,

[2] Even though price stability certainly has been a major motive in the development of the common currency, by itself the mere creation of the currency was not felt to guarantee such an outcome, and there were even fears that it might produce a high-inflation zone (Verdun 1998b). Therefore the Delors Report (1989) on implementation of the currency added the concept of the stability pact to support and undergird the price stability objective (Artis and Winkler 1997).

[3] On two occasions (in the 1930s and the 1970s) anxiety about the effect of the City's global role on the availability of funds for UK firms led to the establishment of government committees of inquiry. On both occasions prior criticisms of the financial sector by industrial firms came to nothing. Because of the City's dominance it was essential for major industrial firms to hold many of their assets in financial instruments. As a result, they were not able to speak of any conflict of interest between finance and industry, since the latter had become involved in the former even if this was less true the other way round.

so argues Talani, the UK remains outside the single currency zone. For as long as it does so, capitalism retains some of its internal diversity: the continental economies are separated from the biggest single source of Anglo-American influence on them, while the British economy retains its curious dominance by the financial sector which is different even from the US model itself.

The more general question of the role of currency autonomy in protecting economic policy distinctiveness is raised by Clarkson (Chapter 5), the only contribution to this collection to give a perspective from outside the EU. He discusses the Canadian position in relationship to North American economic integration and that country's debate over tying the Canadian to the US dollar. NAFTA is nothing like as well developed as the EU and contains major asymmetries consequent on US domination of the subcontinent. Canada's economic relationship to the USA resembles that of Austria or the Netherlands to Germany, or that of Ireland to the UK, even though the Canadian economy is itself part of the G7 group of leading economic nations. In the European cases—admittedly involving far smaller countries in world terms—the smaller states had in fact tied their currencies to those of their dominant partners since well before the initiation of EMU.[4] Nevertheless, Clarkson points to the value of scope for flexibility in the currency relationship. European governments who have lost all room for manoeuvre over their local currencies need to take stock of their other political and social institutions, to ask what scope these might offer for flexibility. Also, to the extent that some scope for distinctiveness of national policy is being lost, for which other model is it being exchanged?

The European Central Bank: An Embedded Institution?

One of the explicit objectives of a neo-liberal political philosophy is to produce economic institutions which are as far as possible disembedded from other institutions in the surrounding society. What are the meanings and implications of embeddedness and disembeddedness in the case of the European Central Bank?

By the embeddedness of an institution we mean the interactions that it has with other institutions, and the ways in which they shape their behaviour in relation to each other, even if they are, both formally and informally, autonomous (Granovetter 1985). A pure model of a non-embedded institution would be one, the performance of which was entirely independent

---

[4] The link between the pound sterling and the Irish punt was eventually formally severed.

of either the specific social context in which it was implanted, or the responses of other institutions in the society to its behaviour. One might explain the difference with an analogy. A non-embedded institution can be treated as a mechanical spare part: it can be moved to any motor system of the appropriate type, and, provided it is fitted properly, the motor will start working without difficulty. An embedded institution is more like the transplant of human organs: the reactions to the new organ of all other organs has to be watched very carefully.

Where central banks are concerned, this issue seems to be about the question of independence, but as we shall see it is really something quite different: it is possible for a central bank to be embedded but independent. The prevailing insistence on the need for total autonomy of the ECB is based on assumptions about the place of the Bundesbank within the Federal Republic of Germany and of the Federal Reserve Bank within the USA. These are both regarded as highly successful examples of central banks, owing their success in large part to their autonomy from surrounding political structures. The former has of course been the more influential model in discussion of the European currency, since the Bundesbank is obliged by the new arrangements to lose its role, and this makes both it and large parts of German public opinion anxious unless its mode of behaviour is to be reproduced at a European level.

It is therefore a useful point of departure for our study to consider the plausibility of this basic assumption: to what extent was the Bundesbank independent of the surrounding German polity and society? Was it so autonomous as actually to be 'non-embedded'? And how does the position of the ECB compare with it on these points? Taylor (Chapter 7) argues that the position of the European Central Bank within the European Union is in fact quite different from that of the German, US, or any other nation-state bank. However autonomous the latter might be, they exist alongside powerful political and wider institutional forces: democratically elected governments with powerful heads; national organizations of different business sectors capable of articulating their problems and needs to national mass media. Even if central banks have both a formal and real autonomy, they have to take some note of the other powerful institutions around them. It is only possible to understand the Bundesbank's eventual support (or at least failure fully to oppose) European Monetary Union by assuming that it was somehow sensitive to the strong preferences of German state and industry.

The institutions of the EU do not present the same challenge. The Commissioners have little democratic legitimacy. The Council of Ministers is mainly concerned with political matters affecting the various nation states; and there is no way that the rotating-term chairman of the Council of Ministers can stand as a counterweight to the president of the ECB in the way that Helmut Kohl was a counterpart for Hans Tietmeyer. Only at the point of geographical representation does the ECB begin to resemble a national central back in its social embeddedness: just as the Bundesbank has representatives of territorial banks on their boards, so the ECB has its supervisory board of national central banks.

Legitimacy is no minor point of public relations appeal, but of fundamental importance to the capacity of institutions to act. As Verdun and Christiansen argue (Chapter 6), legitimacy is not only weak among EU institutions, but highly uneven. In that context, the ECB is one which simply must have legitimacy, or the currency of which it is guardian will be in severe difficulties. All involved in the project at both national and European level therefore seek to promote this legitimacy. There is far less concern to secure that of the other, more political European institutions, and national politicians in particular often have good reason to undermine their claims. This contributes an autonomy of a subtle kind to parallel the explicitly entrenched institutional autonomies of the ECB's constitution.

Similarly, for good or ill, national central bank members and research staff are vulnerable to influence, contacts, exposure to non-banking perspectives by being located within their national societies, where they will feel at least the responses to their actions of fellow elite members and mass media. Against this, ECB personnel will live in a world of their own, even more remote from any surrounding society than the inhabitants of the Commission's various buildings in Brussels. There is no European society located in Frankfurt; and if they were to become unduly responsive to the German society surrounding them, the problem could be equally problematic.

Against this it can be convincingly argued that in the short term the Bank is deeply embroiled in a popular political concern: ECB members and staff will be anxious not to become targets of resentment among European populations in these difficult early years when they lack widespread acceptance and will be subject to far more scrutiny than is usual among central banks. This might offset some of the extreme sensitivity that the Bank is likely simultaneously and for the same reasons to show to the global financial community, the priorities of which are likely to be the opposite of the endogenous populations and governments of the EMU area. In the longer term, however, assuming an eventual stabilization of the euro, ECB personnel are likely to disappear into their private community of bankers, which will develop far more rapidly and easily than any wider and more inclusive European politico-economic community of discourse.

In an important sense the ECB is a deeply embedded institution in that its outline very much reflects the preoccupations of the circumstances of its construction. The most important implications of this will be considered below, but one aspect needs discussion now. The German Bundesbank was established in a country defeated in war which had a desperate need for industrial reconstruction; where there was a new and untried combination of liberal market forces alongside both the delicate edifice of democracy and well-established institutions of economic self-regulation through institutions; and at a time when the outcome of class conflict and the battle of the systems between Soviet communism and American capitalism was not only uncertain but being waged on German soil. The bank was unequivocally part of the market-liberal term in the social market equation that tried to balance these various forces, but existing in an environment comprised of the others, which were expected to be strong and unpredictable in their financial pressures. This was after all the first attempt at German democratic policy-making since the Weimar inflations.

The Bundesbank had to restrain what were seen, in the light of pre-Nazi German history, as powerful inflationary forces, and to counteract the market-interfering tendencies of the corporatist economy, both in the labour market and among firms. However, these elements were not to be abolished by the social market regime; the trade associations were needed for industrial recovery; labour market corporatism was needed to overcome class conflict and also to mark a complete break from Nazi intolerance of labour's right to organize. The Bundesbank was to stand as the *counterweight* to these other crucial and equally integral ingredients of the new democratic German experiment, not as their *conqueror*. Similarly, interest rates always distinguished between ordinary borrowers and those borrowing for vital industrial investment, who paid lower rates even at times when the Bank was exercising its eventually legendary deflationary capacities.

As I argue in my later chapter on the wage bargaining system (Chapter 8), in subsequent decades the Bank and the social actors developed in relation to each other, but in a very one-sided way. It was not that wage bargainers could do deals with the Bundesbank; far from it. They knew that it would be uncompromising, and therefore usually anticipated its responses in their own bargaining behaviour, rarely risking inflationary moves. In turn, the Bank was protected from a need to be fully deflationary by the fact that wage bargainers anticipated it in this way. This mutual accommodation was possible, not only because the Bundesbank was constitutionally uncompromising, but because the particular structure of German wage bargaining organizations was such that they were capable of strategic behaviour. It is doubtful whether either the Bank or the social partner organizations ever actually saw things that way, but standing back one can see that one of the only ways in which the paradox implied by a social market economy can be resolved is if the opposed forces are required to coexist.

It may well be true that eventually the organized interests of German business life become a series of protective cartels unable to adapt rapidly to change; but during at least the first three decades of the Federal Republic, the years of the *Wirtschaftswunder*, they behaved strategically and adaptively in a manner consonant with a national economic interest. To ignore the role of the associational structures in either anticipating the Bundesbank or pursuing strategies which mitigated its tough stance and the non-Keynesian position of German economic policy in general, is just as distorting as to speak only of the role of institutions in German economic success and ignore the role of the Bundesbank in restraining the tendencies to inflation (Matzner and Streeck 1991).

The European Central Bank came into being at both a time and a place that were very different. Both inflationary tendencies themselves and the demand management policies that are believed to have perpetuated them have been squeezed out of existence in all participating countries. Within many nation states, certainly within Germany itself, the trade and employer associations and chambers which enabled employers to achieve a rare degree of cooperative strategic action have been in disarray and no longer attract the support of their member firms. The labour movement that in the post-war years needed to be placated has now almost everywhere been pacified instead. As Story argues (Chapter 3), the battle of the systems between communism and capitalism has been replaced by that between shareholder and stakeholder forms of the latter, with the less compromising shareholder version increasingly dominant.

Meanwhile, the 'place' Europe is not yet either democratic or institutionally rich. There are no institutions at European level, and precious few at individual national levels, which can either stand effectively for alternative economic approaches or, probably more important, strategically anticipate the Bank's actions. The Bank has been girded with enormous armaments against putative social forces pressing for inflationary expansion and government economic involvement; girded, in effect, for fighting the individual national societies of Europe of the 1970s. But it was launched in the thin institutional space of Europe as such (not the national societies) against the pacified populations, restricted welfare states, and neo-liberal public finances of the 1990s. Just as generals are often said to be equipped to fight the previous war, it may well be that the ECB has been embedded into the European economic priorities of two decades ago.

A final aspect of the contrasted birth contexts of the European and the German monetary institutions relates more specifically to the euro and the Deutschmark (DM). The latter acquired an extraordinary record for stability and for being a 'hard' currency, which came to mean a currency that was slightly overvalued in terms of purchasing power parities (PPP), imparting a deflationary effect to prices and wages in the exposed sector of the economy and therefore a tough regime on domestic producers as opposed to importers. This was not however the situation in the initial decades of the *Wirtschaftswunder*—the crucial *Gründerjahre* during which the Bundesbank and German society learned to understand each other. For a lengthy period the DM enjoyed the happy and rare situation of being stable but somewhat undervalued. This resulted from the circumstances of its origin as the new-born currency of a nation and economy wrecked by war, and carrying a prior record of massive monetary instability. It was at that moment that the Bretton Woods regime of virtually fixed exchange rates was established. Although the DM was repeatedly revalued upwards during the period of that regime until its collapse in the early 1970s, the revaluations were always running behind the DM's continuously rising PPP value. It was only after the collapse of Bretton Woods and the regime of floating exchange rates that the DM acquired the true attributes of a hard currency.[5] Soon after-wards began the various experiments with snakes and exchange rate mech-anisms within Western Europe designed to contain movements and prevent the DM rising too rapidly in relation to the currencies of its main trading partners.

The central lesson to emerge from this is that the institutions of German society had their opportunity to learn how to cope with a highly autonomous central bank during an unusual period of a currency that was strong while being undervalued. This considerably reduced pressures on do-mestic producers, and in fact served as a useful *de facto* protection against imports at the expense of domestic consumer interests, while the German economy moved out of its earlier protectionism into a true free-trading position.

The euro has not had a similarly fortunate start in life. Expert opinion is divided over whether this is likely in the medium term to be a weak or a strong currency. However, in the short term it has been weak, since it and its central bank are unknown quantities on the international scene, and certainly less reliable than the DM bloc which they have replaced. This resembles the early days of the DM. However, there has been no system of fixed exchange rates, but a deregulated and computerized global financial market which, as occurred several times during the 1990s, can inflict enormous damage on even major currencies like the yen or the pound sterling if it lacks confidence in them. In these conditions it is very difficult for a currency to remain, like the young DM, 'stably weak', which is what would in fact constitute the ideal condition for European economic recov-ery. The infant ECB has therefore had to prove itself by tough deflation-ary action, even more so than has been imposed on the better known and understood national banks whose currencies have undergone crises. At the worst the euro might become 'unstably strong', the very reverse of the *Gründerjahre* of the Deutschmark and the very worst conditions for

---

[5] These had been the attributes of the Swiss franc for a much longer period, but it is not-able that this economy had previously been strongly protectionist, and in the post-war period developed its extraordinary characteristics of a high (at times over 30%) proportion of the labour force being immigrants on temporary residence permits based on employment.

European social and political institutions to learn how to come to terms with their new currency.

Under a more optimistic scenario, the currency, having started as relatively weak (undervalued in terms of PPP), will gradually find that speculators will not risk gambling on its decline—partly because of the same relative unpredictability that makes it vulnerable, and partly because it is simply too big to talk down. When the pound sterling was left on its own in 1992, it collapsed; but when shortly afterwards the French franc came under very similar pressure, the Bundesbank declared that for the purposes of this episode it and the Banque de France were one (i.e. a very temporary bipartite monetary union). The speculative pressure receded. The euro will be bigger than the franc and the DM combined. Under this scenario the early history of the DM could well be repeated: stable (because too dangerous for speculators to play with) but undervalued (because an unknown quantity). This will provide a valuable breathing space for European governments, social partners, firms and others, but in the absence of a global currency regime of the Bretton Woods it is highly unlikely that it will last the quarter century that the DM enjoyed. Soon the euro will become a true hard currency.

One must, of course, differentiate among prospective national experiences here. For Germany, Austria, and the Netherlands the currency will for a period continue to be undervalued in PPP terms in comparison with the immediate past record of their national currencies. Already in anticipation of monetary union these currencies declined in relation to the US dollar and sterling. This provided useful relief to producers in these countries. Italians and Spaniards, whose currencies already increased in value in relation to the DM in anticipation of their EMU entry, entered a harder currency than they had previously experienced, with major adjustment challenges. Their export producers face a far more difficult prospect than did Germans in the 1950s, though the currency's relative weakness during its first year of operation proved a considerable help.[6]

We must now add to the equation the likely implications for the monetary system if the UK eventually joins it. Following Talani's arguments on the strength of the financial sector within the British polity, it is not likely that this would happen in a manner that really hinders City concerns. Rather, the rules of the EMU will be amended to suit the City's preferences. For as long as the UK remains outside the single currency zone, the euro fails to have one of the world's three leading financial centres within it and

---

[6] It has, however, been argued by observers that the protected domestic sectors of these countries (e.g. property development, construction, distribution) may well be favoured by the appearance of the single currency, since they will benefit from measures that governments are likely to introduce to offset the burdens being borne by manufacturing, without having to share those burdens.

remains at a disadvantage in relation to the dollar and the yen. For Europe to have a major autonomous currency and financial centre is a central aspect of the whole drive to monetary union, but it cannot come about without co-opting sterling. The alternative, to build up an Amsterdam–Frankfurt axis that might become a fourth international financial centre, would be a lengthy and difficult task, with no success ensured. This is likely to mean that when a British government seeks to enter the single currency, not only will various rules about waiting times and entry criteria which the founding nations had to meet be waived, but various amendments to the euro regime demanded by the City will probably be met. Talani (Chapter 4) indicates what these are likely to be: for example, the relaxation of reserve requirements.

Before long therefore we are likely to see an EMU regime which is a hybrid of German and British models. This means a combination of a form of central bank autonomy modelled on the Bundesbank, with City of London concepts of offshore status for a financial sector—a degree of disembeddedness, and consequent considerably greater degree of disengagement from the surrounding society, than in either of these individual national cases. The banking system around the DM was deeply integrated with borrowing firms (as Story describes in Chapter 3); while until early moves for preparing to enter the EMU, British governments had not accepted an autonomous Bank of England.

As noted, however, the ECB is thoroughly embedded in the particular policy preoccupations of the contemporary politico-economic epistemic community. The fact that deficit financing is now seen in a very different light from the 1950s and 1960s does not mean that the context that has produced such a view will not change again. The fact that all advantages now seem to lie with those economies which prioritize the short-term maximization of shareholder values does not annul the experience of previous periods (i.e. until the 1980s) when certain advantages seemed to lie with economies which stressed long-term investment, relative managerial autonomy from shareholders, and personnel policies which accorded labour certain rights in the business.[7]

---

[7] To some extent this is a question of technological and other forms of creative advance. At present much advance is taking place in sectors of the economy which do not require massive long-term and stable investments—computer software, retail services, the arts. It is tempting to see this as a once-and-for-all shift towards post-industrialism and, more dubiously, post-materialism. However, the industrialization of Eastern Europe and many other parts of the world imply a continuing role for capital goods industries; many of the growing services sectors (e.g. distribution, travel), require major inputs of transportation equipment; and much new intellect-based development also takes place in sectors requiring long-term investment plans (e.g. pharmaceuticals).

Monetary Union and the Geography of Social Policy

Analogies between Europe of the single currency zone and nation states break down at the point where the 'real' nation states re-enter the European scene. In a completely different way from federal contexts like Germany or the USA, the level of political authority below the level at which the European Central Bank is located is the one at which both the practice and public expectations of economic policy will continue indefinitely to be concentrated. And among Western European states this level is far from institutionally 'thin'. The establishment of the EMU and the ECB is not leading European electorates to stop pitching their expectations for economic improvement at their national governments. Electorates punish or reward these governments for the state of the national economy; in doing this they are not particularly concerned with exactly how much governments deserve praise or blame, and (depending on whether it is praise or blame that is at stake) either governments or oppositions encourage them to behave in this way. In many countries even local government elections are determined by the so-called economic performance of the relevant parties in national government. If anything these tendencies have increased in recent decades, as electorates which are more volatile in their support and less rooted in value-based political identities are more likely to vote according to perceived efficiency performance. While the economy is not the only issue at stake, it is the biggest single one and affects most others. Even if a democratically elected government at EU level were to exist, it would take some time for national electorates to shift their attention to it in this way; but such a government is not in prospect.

Therefore, within the single currency area electorates continue to treat national governments as being in some way responsible for their fates, even though these have lost many of the instruments which they might use to anticipate these electoral judgements. And it is generally agreed that one consequence of monetary union, at least in the medium term, will be to produce considerable divergence in the economic progress of different regions, with consequent variations in the kind of political pressure to which governments will be subjected. There is therefore an interesting two-level game, in which governments, having surrendered important areas of policy control to an inaccessible transnational central bank, find that is they, and not the bank, which carries blame or praise for the outcomes of the bank's actions.

This leads us to something more important. In considering institutional deficits we should not just look at the level of the EU itself, which will remain thin for a considerable time to come. We must also consider the capacity of national societies—or even more local, regional constituent elements—to respond to the challenge presented by a disembedded hard currency regime at a supranational level. This is not at all just a matter of governments, but we should start with an analysis of their capacity.

Governments are well rid of some of the policy instruments which they have relinquished with the advent of the euro. This is principally true of devaluations—the policy option most obviously and completely excluded. While very occasional devaluations of currencies that have become seriously out of line make good economic sense, anything beyond this usually serves no one's interests. It is primarily a means of externalizing to trading partners an incapacity to contain endogenous wage costs; as such it often only postpones adjustments and invites retaliation. In turn, a series of retaliatory or competitive devaluations serves only to damage the group of countries involved and becomes self-defeating. Meanwhile, frequent recourse to devaluation creates a lack of confidence in the currency, producing an undesired instability.

Restriction of the capacity to vary interest rates is a more serious consequence of monetary union, as these can be perfectly reasonable market means of seeking economic adjustments, though differential rates are not excluded by monetary union, merely restrained. Access to such negative devices as protectionist measures and subsidies is being progressively removed, through the Single Market programme, competition policy, and the wider context of the General Agreement on Tariffs and Trade (GATT) system. With all these instruments unavailable the interesting question becomes whether, attempting to respond to their electorates' pressures, governments will replace them with new and innovative ways to deal with shocks and emerging internal weaknesses? Or will market liberalization be the only policy chosen?

In the pure neo-classical model, if countries or regions have a problem of competitiveness within a single currency zone, they solve it by a combination of reductions in labour costs and migration of population. However, European population movements are 'sticky', and this is unlikely to change in the medium term. But even if Western Europeans could be persuaded to move around their subcontinent in the way that US citizens do, and even if the public could be persuaded not to care about the resulting pattern of over-crowded cities, there remains a further immovable constraint. Even at its peak of capacity for mobility, labour can never be as mobile as financial capital, especially under current conditions. Capital therefore has a capacity to respond to any deterioration in the competitiveness of a given local labour supply far faster than labour could possibly respond to capital's movement by a similar mobility. This leads most commentators to argue that all adaptations must be made by reductions in unit labour costs—whether directly through reductions in labour costs, or indirectly by labour improving its productivity.

This imposes an enormous burden on labour. Until now the process has been somewhat restrained, in that some countries have deregulated both labour and capital more slowly than others. Those who deregulated first have gained two advantages. First, they have secured the advantage of winning the game of *competitive* deregulation, which is quite different from any gains from being deregulated as such. Second, they were able to win that game before it really began, because most of continental Europe was slow off the deregulation mark. This spared the front runners the unpredictable and destabilizing consequences of a true competitive deregulation by the fact that it reduced the extent to which any one country had to go in order to gain a competitive advantage. This placed a floor under what could otherwise be a bottomless downward spiral of worsening labour conditions and, in its wake, rapidly diminishing mass consumer demand (Campbell 1998). This is now changing. European labour markets are becoming deregulated, and the competitive pressure of the single currency is strengthening these tendencies considerably.

One response would be to call for global measures for the re-regulation of capital flows. These calls are unlikely to be successful. It is unlikely that international agreement could be secured while some governments see an advantage in sustaining unregulated capital markets. Further, it is often argued that, since financial capital has a capacity to escape regulation, it is pointless trying to capture it; therefore the burden of all adjustment must be borne by the labour market.

The Scope for Labour Market Adjustments

If adjustments have to be borne primarily by labour costs with only small assistance from labour mobility and with no other forms of action being possible, sometimes in response to exogenous shocks, there can be considerable social strain. It is for this reason that many neo-liberal economists oppose the concept of a European single currency. This is paradoxical, because the rules of the currency zone are almost textbook neo-liberalism. However, since neo-liberals believe more than others in the incapacity of any form of non-market intervention to achieve positive outcomes, they are left contemplating the full extent of adjustments needed by the labour market. For many, this leads to the conclusion that the possibility of national-level devaluation has to be retained to avoid major social dislocation from time to time in certain regions.

If one moves outside the neo-liberal paradigm it becomes possible to ask some different questions. Is it possible for labour markets to find alternative means of adaptation to either sudden and unanticipated cost reductions through massive deflations or devaluation? If one is able to take seriously the capacity of organized labour market actors to act strategically, then it is possible that within at least some sectors within some individual nation states voluntary wage restraint and other forms of concession bargaining might enable labour forces to make anticipatory adjustments, saving the need for inappropriate deflationary policies by national governments (see Chapter 8).

For these purposes the absence of an EU-wide industrial relations system is not a disadvantage in the medium term, in that diverse national institutional systems can provide an adjustment capability at national level in compensation for the loss of the devaluation and other instruments at the national political level. It should be noted that, even if these arguments are accepted, they are not offered as universal remedies; they are devices that are available where labour market institutions take a certain form. Those who are unable to construct strong representative and co-ordinated labour market associations, and those who have deliberately destroyed them because they are not consistent with the Anglo-American model, do not have these possibilities open to them.

Local Institutions and Scope for Adjustment

More generally, one can also consider other means, not necessarily involving organized labour, whereby actors in a region or country might take action beyond simple cost reduction to improve competitiveness. Seen in this way the single currency simply becomes a special case of the more general phenomenon of geographical areas within a global economy. After all, regions within a country have in modern times never had the possibility of making a currency adjustment.

We here immediately encounter another of the ways in which the Bundesbank always existed within a broader institutional context than is the case with the European Union. From the outset the post-1949 Federal Republic had a powerful mechanism for an egalitarian allocation of financial resources across the *Länder*, so that there would be no such thing as poor and rich regions. This was the *Finanzausgleich*. So successful was this policy that the original *Länder* came to have very few major economic inequalities among them, until the crises of the older industrial regions began during the 1980s. There was far less interregional inequality in Federal Germany than in France or the UK, even though both those nation states were far more centralized, far better established as unified nation states, and with far longer histories of sustained national government. To replicate something of this kind on a European scale would require a true fiscal federalism. At present, there is instead the set of structural funds and cohesion funds representing only small sums of money, likely to become smaller still as the regime of reduced public spending spreads. These funds are also subject to a political lobbying process whereby increasing numbers of regions become defined as eligible as each national government tries to ensure it receives more back from the European Union than it contributes. As a result, a rather small amount of money is spread increasingly thinly and is able to achieve relatively little.

Gabriele Tondl, in her contribution to this volume (Chapter 9), demonstrates what true fiscal federalism would look like. It is clearly technically feasible and could operate similarly to the German *Finanzausgleich*. Is there, however, the political will to effect fiscal transfers of this huge scale, across national boundaries, at a time when public spending is under pressure from the very integration process which itself both requires and makes necessary fiscal federalism? As in some other policy areas, some measures stipulated for the achievement of European integration make difficult other measures that are necessary for that integration. Again, the contrast with German federation-building after 1949 is stark. At that time there was a will to effect such transfers, even though the electorate that supported these decisions was far poorer than today's European voters. Within Germany, where today the challenge of redistribution to incorporate poor *Länder* is again a major part of the political agenda following the unification of 1990, one finds a complex situation. Large transfers are certainly being made within the new Germany, though there has been a reluctance to accept their full fiscal cost. As a result the Bundesbank imposed a deflationary regime at a time when other indicators suggested a need for some expansiveness. This is not an encouraging precedent, especially when one recalls that German unification is a more powerful appeal for solidarity than European integration.

Another area of action where some capacity might exist to slow capital flows from areas in difficulty concerns the capacity of regions to develop competences that make them attractive. This has been discussed in the large literature which has developed in recent years over regional and local economies (e.g. Amin and Thrift 1994a; Trigilia 1991). The central thesis is that certain kinds of institutional structure enable firms in particular geographical areas to build up specific competences, what Trigilia calls 'collective competition goods'. It is possible that these competences may, in Amin and Thrift's (1994b) colourful term, enable localities to 'hold down the global'.

Conclusion

For many purposes an analysis of the weakness of political and other institutional capacities at the European level, together with a lively debate over whether the erection of such institutions would serve well or ill, is the most important response to the institutional deficits and lack of embeddedness of European monetary union, and several of the authors in this book consider these questions. However, the later arguments in the above discussion suggest that, so long as much economic policy and most popular expectations of that policy remain nation-bound, these deficits may bring certain compensatory advantages—where particular nation states or even regions possess certain types of proactive, competition-friendly institutions. Nevertheless, it must also be noted that, for countries and regions that lack such institutions but which are also likely to be among the losers in pure market terms, the outlook seems just as bleak from this perspective as from many others worried about the lack of real economic convergence.

As signalled at the outset, no united conclusions emerge from the following chapters, as the authors take very different views on many of these issues. We hope, however, that the different contributions will advance debate on a number of issues: the political and institutional questions posed by the introduction of the euro; the imbalances in the roles of political and monetary authorities within Europe; the scope for new institution construction at European level to counter these imbalances; the scope for recognizing continuing national differences through such devices as fiscal federalism or the industrial relations system; an understanding of the diverse dynamics that are directing the approaches of different national political and business elites to act in different ways towards the EMU concept and its development.

2

The Unanticipated Fallout of European Monetary Union: The Political and Institutional Deficits of the Euro

ROBERT BOYER

Throughout the 1990s, discussions of European Monetary Union (EMU) focused on the rationale of the convergence criteria set by the Maastricht Treaty, the likelihood of each specific country being part of the first wave, the opportunity to postpone its launch, or the degree of flexibility in interpreting the convergence criteria. But after the European Summit of May 1998 and still more after the launching of the euro in January 1999, all these issues ceased to be relevant; analysts began to raise the neglected but fundamental issue: does the Amsterdam Treaty design a viable configuration for European integration and national policies? This chapter proposes a structural analysis of the viability of the current phase of monetary integration.

The Seven Paradoxes of European Integration

For the key actors promoting EMU, success depends on the clarity of the objectives pursued and steadfastness in meeting the convergence criteria (de Silguy 1998). 'On parvient toujours à ce que l'on veut quand on le veut avec persévérance pendant quarante ans' is the quotation from Marguerite Yourcenar in the front page of the book on the EMU by the commissioner in charge of the euro. Conversely, other analysts express gloomy pessimism about this innovation and point out the lack of political will of national governments to abandon a large fraction of their sovereignty. A second distinctive feature of this chapter is to deal simultaneously with these two opposite visions of EMU. Pointing out a series of paradoxes about the current integration process might be a convenient starting point.

1. A Political Project Disguised as an Economic One

A brief historical retrospect suggests that the European project launched by Jean Monnet was clearly a political one. In order to prevent the repetition

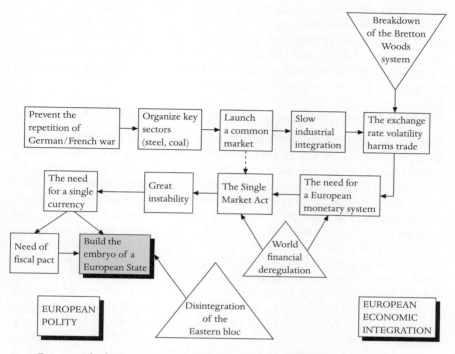

FIG. 2.1. The long march of European integration: from polity to economy . . .
and back to polity?

of the dramatic German/French conflicts, why not organize and co-ordinate
economic activity of the key sectors such as coal and steel? Given the success of this first initiative, the project was extended by the creation of the
Common Market by the Treaty of Rome, which in turn has been triggering a slow process of economic integration among the founding members (Fig. 2.1). The breakdown of the Bretton Woods system brought
much exchange rate instability among European currencies, hindering the
ongoing process of economic specialization across national borders. The
European Monetary System (EMS) was precisely designed in order to
remove this source of discrepancy, but success was difficult to achieve given
the huge move towards financial deregulation. The dramatic 1992 and 1993
episodes brought a confirmation of the project contemplated by the
Maastricht Treaty:(a single common currency would be a definite solution
to the recurring instability among European currencies. This project was frequently presented as a purely economic strategy, whereas it is clearly a political project, put forward by France and Germany after the collapse of the
Soviet empire and especially German reunification (Vernet 1998). This is the

first paradox: (the euro is presented as a purely functional device reducing transaction costs and removing exchange rate uncertainty, whereas it is basically a political enterprise.) During the early years of the European project, economics was a means and political integration the objective, whereas today the political will is assumed to be applied to purely economic, not to say monetarist, objectives. A paradox indeed!

2. A Daring 'Constructivism' in the Epoch of Free Market Beliefs

A second paradox relates to the relations between states and markets. A priori, the euro is a quite exceptional process of monetary integration. Usually, a new currency is backed by an emerging leadership over a territory, with few countervailing powers of private agents such as banks or financiers. After all, US monetary unification was made possible by the victory of the North over the South, the emergence of a unified political power solving previous conflicts of interests (Boyer and Coriat 1985). An opposite configuration prevails at the end of the 1990s: the euro is the outcome of an intergovernmental treaty, without any clear hegemonic power. To the contrary, most governments expect thus to mitigate the initiative and power of the Bundesbank and the hegemony of the Deutschmark. The potential conflicts of interests among European countries are not solved but postponed until the implementation of the Amsterdam Treaty. Furthermore, financial markets have acquired such power that they assess in real time the credibility of any economic policy, and especially such a daring experiment as the euro. Back in the 1970s the Werner Report had already proposed monetary integration, without any success, but at a period when the limitations to capital mobility would have allowed such a creation. In the 1990s, governments no longer have full control of their policy, but now wish to create a common currency. In other words, *governments could have created the euro when they were not convinced of its usefulness, but now they wish to do so but do not necessarily have the power to implement it*, and 'beat the market'. Briefly stated, the euro is an ambitious example of constructivism—in the sense of Friedrich von Hayek—at the very time when a vast majority of agents operating on financial markets seem to adhere to a rather naive free-market ideology.

3. A Euphoric Presentation of a Complex and Contradictory Project

A third paradox opposes the selling of a bright future and getting mediocre results. Such a disappointment had already taken place with respect to the Single Market Act in the mid 1980s. The European Commission (EC) had taken this initiative in order to overcome the crisis of European integration, and actually it changed a rather pessimistic mood into a much more optimistic one. But a series of economic studies were launched and used, showing that European growth would be 12 per cent higher, with job creation by millions. Nearly ten years later, an *ex post* assessment shows far more modest achievements of the single market Act: only 1.5 per cent of extra GDP growth could be attributed to this structural reform, of course largely partial and limited to some key industrial sectors (Monti 1996). The EC seems to have reiterated exactly the same process for the single currency: early research delivered a quite optimistic message (EC 1990); but as soon as the euro had been agreed, a much more balanced view was proposed, stressing the need for difficult structural reforms, without which the benefit of EMU could not be reaped (EC 1998*a*). In the age of the rational expectations revolution, *it might be risky to oversell the merits of a quite complex and contradictory innovation.*

4. Integrating Europe . . . but Exacerbating Domestic Social Conflicts?

A fourth paradox derives from the previous one. On one side, the politicians and civil servants engaged in European integration, along with the most privileged groups in each nation state, tend to adopt a quite positive assessment of the consequences of the euro. The official statements present this innovation as Pareto-improving (i.e. benefiting everybody without hurting any single individual agent). For instance, in a recent published book, the European representative Yves-Thibault de Silguy presents a very appealing picture of the consequences of the euro: it will reinforce the single market, stimulate growth, alleviate public budget deficit, enhance innovation and the profitability of European firms; and last but not least, it will speed up job creation (de Silguy 1998: 74–118). Why should anybody be against such a wonderful scenario? The paradox is precisely that on the other side, many social groups perceive EMU as a threat to their previous position or privilege. This is the case for small entrepreneurs, retailers, low skilled workers, retired people, and more generally any group strongly related to the national welfare system (see Table 2.3 p. 59). The dilemma is therefore the following: a project, which is supposed to be unanimously supported by the citizens, is actually generating strong and sometimes new divisions within most societies. Incidentally, the dividing line between pro- and anti-euro frequently crosses each party, be it leftist, conservative, or even centrist. For instance, in France, both the Gaullist party (RPR) and the union of conservatives (UDF) have a majority in favour of the euro, but a vocal minority against the Amsterdam Treaty. Therefore, the very political architecture built after the World War II is challenged by EMU. Will the sharpening of domestic social and political divisions be the cost to be paid for unifying Europe?

5. Enthusiastic Southern Europe, Reluctant Northern Europe

A similar paradox can be observed when one compares the respective support of EMU by various national public opinions (Table 2.1). In general,

TABLE 2.1. A hidden paradox: Countries expected to suffer more from EMU have the most positive attitude (Spring 1997)

Positive Southern Europe	Sceptical Northern Europe
France 70% have a positive view on EMU 58% consider that the benefits overcome the required sacrifices	*Germany* 60% are anti-EMU
	UK 58% are anti-EMU. But 56% UK businessmen wish to join
Spain 70% have a positive view on EMU	*The Netherlands* The change in positive view on EMU:
Portugal 53% are prepared for financial sacrifice in order to have their country in the first wave of EMU	1995: 73% 1996: 46.3% 1997: 34%
Italy 70% have a positive view on EMU	

Source: Le Sondoscope (1997), No. 129, April: 70–73.

Southern Europe is generally quite enthusiastic about this new phase of European integration: in France, Spain, and Italy for instance, in early 1997, 70 per cent of citizens had a positive view of EMU, while in Portugal, 53 per cent were ready to bear financial sacrifices in order that their country be part of the first wave. In contrast, Northern Europe is rather reluctant, and the fraction of the population rejecting it seems to have increased as the deadline set by the Maastricht Treaty approached. Is it not surprising to note that the very countries that require the more drastic structural reforms experience the most support by the population for EMU, whereas the already integrated countries are facing a somewhat sceptical, if not opposed, public opinion? Italy is a good example of the first configuration, Germany and Netherlands of the second. The cases of the UK, Denmark, or Sweden are different again, since political leaders have followed public opinions in not joining Europe, given the large costs to be born in order to adapt national structures to the requirements of the Maastricht Treaty. Nevertheless, this fifth paradox opposes the general political assessment of the desirability of EMU to the economic costs of the transformations it requires for some countries.

6. Unifying Europe at the Risk of Balkanization

This leads to the next paradox. Clearly, the Single Market Act, then the Maastricht Treaty, and ultimately the Amsterdam Treaty do aim to promote European integration and unification. But the conditions for adhesion to EMU, as well as the challenging requirements for national autonomy in order to harmonize diplomacy, defence, and security, are bound to restrict the number of countries able and willing to join such an ambitious and novel project. Therefore, the very process intending to unify Europe is likely to trigger a multiple-tier Europe, with potentially diverging forces. By enforcing strong criteria convergence, EMU would actually split the previous integration process, either according to the opposition between core participants and new members, or by multiplying a *Europe à la carte* (i.e. separate agreements including a variable number countries for each domain of competence, CEPR 1995; Dehove 1997). For instance, after the European Summit of May 1998, the eleven countries elected for EMU have to organize their monetary and financial relations with those remaining outside; this may provoke new and difficult problems in the institutional architecture of the EU. Should the outsiders be admitted to the Euro-X Council designed to co-ordinate national budget policies? Will some countries stay out of EMU forever, or are they supposed to join as soon as their public opinion is ready for and/or satisfy the convergence criteria? Paradoxically enough, for unity's sake new divisions have been brought into the EU, and they will not be easy to overcome.

7. Democracy and Market: Trading Places?

A final paradox concerns the interpretation to be given to the current phase of European integration. For some politicians, the final objective is to recover one form or another of collective control over exchange rates, interest rates, and more generally the ability to monitor a large continental economy in the epoch of globalization. For other politicians or analysts, the objective is strictly the opposite: to unleash the forces of the market in order to redesign the institutional forms which are now outdated, confronted with the internationalization of production, high unemployment, and the new technological paradigms. This opposition is evidence of a still deeper paradox. For a decade markets and democracy have been trading places. During the 1960s governments used to make strategic decisions, whereas underdeveloped and highly regulated financial markets were playing a quite minor role, even in allocating capital to alternative sectors or individual firms. Taking charge of the long run was the task of the state, adjusting short-run disturbances the role attributed to the markets. Nowadays, the highly sophisticated financial markets scrutinize any government initiative, in order to check its long-run viability and sustainability. Conversely, governments try to have an efficient short-run management that meets the criteria set by the bond markets, which have built a large autonomy with respect to public authorities, including international organizations such as the IMF, World Bank, WTO, or OECD. In a sense, the launching of the euro does not dissipate this ambiguity: will a tentative control of the European currency be a step in the direction of a victory of collective interventions over market forces; or conversely, will it be the hidden strategic device invented in order to bring the forces of globalization into the inner domestic space of each member state?

An Integrated Framework to Capture the Complexity of 'Europeanization'

The current debate is polarized by strong opposition between the supporters of EMU and its opponents (i.e. a black and white picture with few nuances). Analysts should recognize the complexity of the issues at stake and develop original frameworks able to illuminate some of the major political choices, both at European and domestic levels. In order to do so, one has to recognize how contradictory the current phase of European integration is and how detrimental is the division of academic research between economics, political science, and law.

A Challenge to Conventional Economic Theory

Actually, all these paradoxes boil down to a central feature present in all the arguments in favour of EMU. They derive from an economic theory which considers that markets are the more adequate mechanisms for managing modern economies. Thus, the role of public authorities is to reform existing institutions so that they resemble more and more the ideal of pure and perfect markets. In this world, the polity *per se* is non-existent, since its only function is to move the economy towards a pure market equilibrium, which is supposed to be a Pareto-optimum. This vision is in line with the general trend of macroeconomic theorizing, which considers that markets are self-equilibrating and that the unique rational objective of governments is to adopt pro-market reforms. This is at odds with the Keynesian vision adopted by most governments until the 1970s. During this period, it was quite common to assume that markets are unable to deal with uncertainty, externalities, and even the simplest co-ordination problems. It is notable that this old framework is rarely used to assess the impact of EMU, whereas its impact on effective demand is frequently discussed.

More precisely, the conventional arguments in favour of the euro run as follows (EC 1990; de Silguy 1998). The irrevocable fixing of exchange rates among the participant countries removes the basic uncertainty which was hindering the deepening of the single market. Simultaneously, transaction costs are reduced, which enhances both external trade among countries and the profitability of firms. The clause about excessive public deficit benefits the credibility of the euro, still enhanced by the large independence granted to the European Central Bank (ECB). Therefore, all members should benefit from lower interest rates, which is particularly important for countries which used to experience high inflation, such as Italy or Spain. Under the binding constraints of the Amsterdam Treaty, each nation state faces strong incentives to rationalize and modernize its tax and welfare systems.

Similarly, labour markets are made more flexible, in order to cope with the loss of the exchange rate as an adjusting mechanism, when a loss of competitiveness has to be compensated. When all these mechanisms are added up, the European Union would benefit from a renewed dynamism under the new common currency: more innovation, faster growth, more employment, higher profit, and even real wage increases. This is the charm of any Pareto-improving reform.

But this is a drastic idealization of the consequences of the euro. Many arguments can be opposed to it, the more so since the European Summit of May 1998: now many analysts and even the experts of Commission recognize at last the costs associated with the implementation of the euro (EC 1997b, d, 1998a, b). This chapter is devoted to the investigation of the costs and benefits of the euro, which are contrasted according to each scenario. Before doing so, it is important to discuss some methodological problems, which are at the origin of conflicting assessments of EMU.

First, optimism about the deepening of the Single European Market is built on a very naive conception of the creation and functioning of any market. It is assumed that a common currency makes easier price comparisons across national borders and therefore that the law of the single price will prevail all over Europe after the completion of EMU. But, for instance, price formation in the car industry clearly shows that the very same product may have quite different prices according to the system of retailing, taxation, the relative strength of the national producers, and of course, the tastes of domestic consumers (Monti 1996). Basically, markets are social constructions (Favereau 1989), not the outcome of any 'natural' economic process, and they may take contrasted configurations (White 1998). Furthermore, modern economies combine markets along with private hierarchies, state interventions, communities, associations, and networks, and their performance is not related to the purity of market mechanisms but the coherence of the institutional arrangements combining all these co-ordinating mechanisms (Hollingsworth and Boyer 1997).

A second objection relates to the concept of money. The proponents of EMU exhibit a strange schizophrenia. On the one hand, most theoretical models, such as real business cycle ones, postulate a complete neutrality of monetary creation in the medium and long term. If so, the management of any currency may only have transitory effects. Thus, the euro would not be important at all and one may wonder why governments have accepted abandoning a fraction of their sovereignty against such minimal and transitory gains. On the other hand, official statements (de Silguy 1998: 110–18) argue that job creation will result from the euro, as was previously mentioned. But then, money is no more neutral, neither in the short run, nor the long run, since monetary policy influences interest rates, credit, and capital allocation, the direction and the speed of innovation (i.e. long-term growth pattern). This contradiction between the technical references and the popular presentation is quite damaging for the legitimacy of the euro. Last but not least, as soon as the Monetary Council of the ECB was appointed, its very first statement was to stress that national monetary policies followed during the second phase of EMU have had no responsibility for the level of European unemployment and that, in future, EMU will have no impact at all on job creation. The Council seems to confuse the theoretical model of a market economy with actually existing capitalism, and this discrepancy may hurt the realism and acceptance of the policy followed by the ECB.

Similarly, discussion of the objectives and tools of the ECB seems to consider that all national economies resemble one another, probably because they are supposed to be market economies, bound to converge towards an idealized Walrasian equilibrium. If this assumption were true, there would be no problem for the viability of a common European monetary policy. Unfortunately, many comparative studies, institutional, statistical, or econometric, confirm that the functioning of domestic economies remains quite diverse (Crouch and Streeck 1996; Berger and Dore 1996)—even for countries as closely linked as France and Germany, not to mention the considerable discrepancy between Northern and Southern economies, or the major differences between the UK and continental Europe in the conduct of monetary policy. Therefore, these major institutional differences show up in different adjustments on the product, credit, and of course, labour markets (Crouch 1993; Dore, Boyer, and Mars 1994). Consequently, the same monetary policy may have totally different outcomes for various countries: instead of homogenizing Europe as a continent, EMU may well exacerbate national heterogeneity—even if the common European policy may remove some of the previous idiosyncratic shocks associated with the autonomy of national economic policies (Calmfors *et al.* 1997: 312–24). Incidentally, this argument relates to real convergence, and of *régulation* modes, not to the typical nominal convergence of inflation and interest rates which has been achieved by the eleven countries admitted into the first round of EMU. This benign neglect for these institutional differences may be quite risky for the future of the euro.

A fourth limit of the conventional approach to the euro is to polarize the analysis over a very specific form of uncertainty, that related to exchange rate variability in the context of full capital mobility. No doubt the fixing of the rate of conversion of each national currency into the euro will remove definitively the repetition of the European currency crises which have been so frequent. But uncertainty is intrinsic to the very process of capitalist competition, and it is enhanced when financial markets are fully developed and sophisticated. Therefore, one may expect the shift from one kind of uncertainty (about exchange rate among member states) to others: uncertainty over the exchange rate of euro with respect to the dollar and the yen, the degree of cooperation or alternatively conflict between national budgetary policies, the credibility of the euro as a permanent feature of European integration, and so on. Will finally the degree of uncertainty be lower after the euro than before? The jury is still out. Any economic system reduces some type of uncertainty at the cost of a possible extension of another. In assessing the post-euro configuration too many analysts tend to consider that exchange rate uncertainty is the most detrimental (De Ménil 1996) and that therefore the stability of the EU will be enhanced. But a fully convincing empirical evidence is far from available: there is no consensus among economists about the effective costs of exchange rates variability (Calmfors *et al.* 1997: 19–39). To paraphrase a motto of the French historical school of the *Annales*, 'any economy displays the uncertainty associated with its structure'. Thus it would be risky to infer that the euro will remove any such uncertainty, since quite on the contrary it will create new sources of political conflict and economic crises.

A final, but fundamental, criticism may be addressed to the usual vision of economists about the significance and impact of EMU. The role of national governments would be to implement the reforms which are deemed necessary by European experts in order to adapt each economy to the requirements of the Maastricht and Amsterdam Treaties. Polity would be the direct expression of the economy—an economic vision indeed! Actually, the very tradition of political science and the recent resurgence of political economy convincingly convey the message that politicians deal with power relations whereas entrepreneurs are concerned with economic activity and capital accumulation. From a logical point of view, these two motives have no direct connection, even if *ex post* the economic and political spheres are indirectly linked (Théret 1992; Palombarini 1999). On the one hand, a stable constitutional order is essential for property rights enforcement. On the other, any state requires minimal material resources (i.e. a sufficient level of economic activity as a potential for tax basis). Therefore, any viable society has to combine these two requirements, which *ex ante* are not necessarily compatible. In many instances, this compatibility is the unintended outcome of structural crises, during which both polity and economy are in a sense synchronized again. If one adopts this vision, then the EMU project does not exhibit any clear viability, since the inner logic of both European and national political arenas is not taken into account. Will citizens accept this transfer of responsibility without countervailing power at the European level? If important decisions are taken by the ECB, a priori largely independent, who will control this new body? If the building of the credibility of the euro imposes some large costs, for instance in terms of slower growth, will public opinion accept such adverse outcomes, especially within the countries where EMU has been presented as a solution to the unemployment problem (Mazier 1997)?

All these questions relate to the issue of the political aspects of the euro and its impact upon institutionally rich societies, a problem largely neglected by most research on the consequences of EMU.

Integrating Polity and Economy

For conventional theory, economic policy is assumed to be the consequence of a rational calculus operating on purely economic variables: the evolution of consumption, a measure of welfare and the rate of interest. Basically, there is no autonomy whatsoever between polity and economy, the former being the direct expression of the latter. In a sense, the old Marxian theory had the same simplification, when it stressed that the state was operating to the benefit of the capitalist class, and not for the well-being of the society as a whole. As already mentioned, this is the implicit presentation of the Maastricht and Amsterdam Treaties by EC officials. It is a quite common vision in contemporary economic theory.

Of course, the validity of such a conception is highly problematic for the euro, which was decided after German reunification: the French government wanted to tie Germany firmly to Western Europe and proposed to launch EMU, whereas the German government was eager to develop a political integration of Europe, possibly along federal principles (Story, Chapter 3). This explains why both the Maastricht and Amsterdam Treaties display three pillars, not only the monetary side but defence and security aspects. Since German public opinion is highly attached to the Deutschmark as a symbol of monetary stability, strong requisites were imposed on the expected participants to the euro in order to preserve the same monetary stability as experienced in Germany. Clearly, the euro does not derive from a cost–benefit analysis about the reduction of transaction costs and exchange rate externalities, but it is the outcome of a political bargaining among nation states. Polity comes first, and the economy should follow—according to a second vision which is the strict opposite of the first.

But is it that certain that any decision taken by governments will be compatible with the inner dynamics of economic adjustments and their transformations—especially if the reform is as structural and far-reaching as EMU? Since the breakdown of the Bretton Woods system, exchange rates are no longer a purely political variable since they are formed in currency markets via the interactions of various expectations. Given financial globalization, these play a bigger role than governments. Therefore, the euro has to convince the international financial community of its relevance, viability, and long-term legitimacy. Consequently, neither the economistic vision nor the primacy of polity correctly define the future of EMU. A third vision seems much more satisfactory: the political innovation put forward by the Maastricht Treaty sets in motion a series of economic transformations, most of them probably unintended.

Just to take one example, analysts have paid much attention to the effect of the euro on the product market. In the early stages, the most dramatic impact seemed to bear on financial markets, banking, and insurance (Davies and Graham 1998). In turn, the related concentration will influence the governance mode of industrial firms, their investments, location, and finally employment and income distribution (Froud *et al.* 1998). By comparison, the completion of the single market for manufacturing goods may seem of minor influence. But in democratic societies, citizens are entitled to express their feelings about the conduct of domestic economic policy. If structural changes, triggered by the euro, end up opposing losers and winners, the political regime has to take this into account, and consequently revise its economic policy. The euro will define a coherent socio-economic regime only if it can make compatible the evolution of the *régulation* mode along with the transformations of the political regime.

A Complete Shift in the Hierarchy of Institutional Forms

Therefore, the current phase of monetary integration is not simply a 'rationalization' of previous national policies, nor an incentive to the deepening of the Single Market. Basically, it implements a major structural change in the way national economies operate and interact. It is quite partial to compute the welfare gains associated with the euro, as if it were a simple marginal reform around a well-established market equilibrium in order to reach a Pareto-optimum. Actually, the very adjustments governing credit, finance, capital formation, employment decisions, and even innovation will necessarily be transformed. Thus, not only are national business cycles possibly transformed, but the very growth pattern is likely to be affected. It is therefore important to adopt a long-term view and to reassess the specific impact of the euro along with other contemporary major transformations. *Régulation* theory might be useful in analysing this issue (Boyer and Saillard 1995), since it is particularly concerned with the institutional transformations of capitalist economies.

1945–73: The National Labour Compromise Rules over the Monetary Regime

It might be useful to go back to the origin of the post-war exceptional growth. The major political and social transformations which occurred at that epoch prevented a repetition of the dramatic events of the inter-war years (i.e. a major financial crisis, then a depression which led inevitably to World War II). Structural and diverse public interventions were at the core of this success. Paradoxically, this was contrary to the current conventional wisdom about what should be a sound economic policy. In most countries, the central bank was highly dependent on the ministry of finance, markets were severely regulated and controlled by public authorities. Capital mobility was very low, external trade limited but growing. Last but not least, labour contracts were highly institutionalized (e.g. minimum wage, indexing of wage with respect to productivity and past inflation, surge of internal labour markets). Nevertheless, economic performance was exceptional in terms of productivity, standard of living, full employment, and even business cycle dampening.

For *régulation* theory this a priori surprising outcome is the result of the coherence of the institutional architecture built on the central role of the post-war capital–labour accord. The implementation of productivity sharing allowed the development of mass production and consumption, which stabilizes the growth pattern by approximately synchronizing the extension of production capacities and the generation of effective demand, within societies where wage earners are the vast majority of the population. The state is transformed by the impact of this capital–labour accord since it then promotes the access to education, housing, health care, retirement funding. Clearly, the nominal wage is no more a price set on a typical market, but the consequence of a series of labour contracts, frequently implementing a seniority principle and a competition for internal promotion. Given this structural compatibility between the trends of supply and demand, the price of manufactured goods, specially durable ones, is set according to a mark-up principle, with minor influence of transitory market imbalances.

In this context, monetary policy used to be the 'servant' of the capital–labour accord and oligopolistic competition. Capital was not really mobile across borders, and international relations were stabilized under the hegemonic role of the USA and especially the institutions defining the Bretton Woods system. Given this international stability, the exchange rate used to be set by national public authorities and it was adjusted when the previous fixed rate could no more be sustained, mainly due to trade deficit, and after the 1970s the emerging phenomenon of flight of foreign capital. If one country experienced a higher inflation than the rest of the world, a devaluation allowed a return to external trade equilibrium, while mitigating the conflicts on income distribution. In a sense, national monetary policy had the role of alleviating tensions in income distribution, and the exchange rate was a discretionary tool when inflation became too important. This pattern prevailed in the vast majority of European countries. One exception, Germany, experienced a rather different hierarchy, quite similar to the one which is now embedded into the Amsterdam Treaty.

Therefore, an accommodating monetary policy was essential in preserving the cohesiveness of the national architecture of institutional forms and specially the primacy of capital–labour accord. This mode of *régulation* was very convenient for policy-makers, since it reconciled dynamic efficiency and social justice in the direction of wage earners. Why did this system come to an end?

Three Major Structural Changes since 1973

Basically, the very success of this style of economic management led to the endogenous erosion of its stabilizing properties. Three structural transformations explain its demise. EMU is partially a tentative answer to some of these transformations.

First, mass production techniques and organizations experienced a productivity slow-down, initiated in the American economy, but diffused to other industrialized countries after the two oil shocks. Therefore, the conflict over income distribution became more acute, and inflation tended to speed up, triggering significant financial instability. In a sense, the monetarist counter-revolution is a response to this potential threat, whereas the shift towards flexible exchange rate takes into account the significant heterogeneity in inflation rates. After two decades, new productive organizations are emerging and tend to replace the Fordist ones, but until now total factor productivity has not recovered the previous trends. Again, this has an impact on industrial relations, which have to take into account a slow-down in real wages, as well as more decentralized wage bargaining in order to cope with sectoral changes and new sources of competitiveness.

Second, the significant slow-down in growth rates, especially in Europe, affects previous political alliances, according to which even rather conservative governments had pro-labour policies. The surge of unemployment weakens the bargaining power of unions and workers, whereas a new wave of organizational and technological innovations destabilize job demarcations and hierarchy of skills which were at the core of the post-war capital–labour accord. Furthermore, the great freedom granted to productive and portfolio investment gives a premium to internationalized firms, which tend to look for markets and production sites far from their domestic space. Again, this destabilizes the capital–labour accord, and the wage–labour nexus has to be adapted to the new conditions for competition. This is further evidence of the shift in the hierarchy of post-war institutional firms. Last but not least, governments themselves, whether conservative or social democratic, tend to adopt pro-business legislation, taxation, and welfare reforms.

But the most relevant transformation is without any doubt the growing disconnection between the space on which economic activity takes place and the territory controlled by public authorities. Since a larger fraction of production is exported and a significant part of investment may come from abroad, the domestic circuit of mass production and consumption opens up and tends to be replaced by an export-led regime, at least for some countries (Bowles and Boyer 1995). Last but not least, the dynamism of financial innovation, the creation of world financial markets, and the difficult curbing of public debt totally change the conditions and objectives of national monetary policies. Since 1982, financial markets have promoted anti-inflationary policies via high interest rates, and have pushed and extended such a strategy all over the world. National central banks today emphasize price stability, whatever the costs in terms of growth and unemployment. The exchange rate is then a pure market variable, with fewer and fewer controls from national or supranational public organizations. Simultaneously, the financial markets diffuse rapid changes in the formation of expectations, and they usually overreact to public statements and budgetary policies.

The EMU project, already present in discussions in the 1970s, awoke renewed interest in the 1980s, because it was an attempt to restore a minimal control over monetary policy, at the European level rather than at the national one. Speculation among European currencies is by definition forgone, whereas the density of intra-European trade tends to synchronize the cycle of the core countries, but not necessarily that of the more recent member states. The overall exposure of the EU to external trade is similar to the level in North America and Japan. Consequently, a common monetary policy could have the same relative autonomy as that enjoyed by the Federal Reserve System or the Bank of Japan.

This historical retrospective helps in correcting a frequent misperception about the euro. For most of those opposed to EMU, it is the main culprit for all the evils borne by European countries, from financial concentration to mass unemployment. Actually, a common European currency is a response to already existing structural problems, which of course are transformed—for better or worse—but not created by its launching. Any scenario with the euro should always be compared to alternative possibilities, built on different attempts to overcome the (same) current European problems.

The Current Primacy of Monetary Regime and Form of Competition

Nevertheless, the euro is a component of the complete shift in the hierarchy of institutional forms which differs drastically from the configuration of the Golden Age (Fig. 2.2). Basically, a national territory is now inserted into dense international relations, in such a way that competition at world level permeates nearly all other institutional entities. The considerable freedom

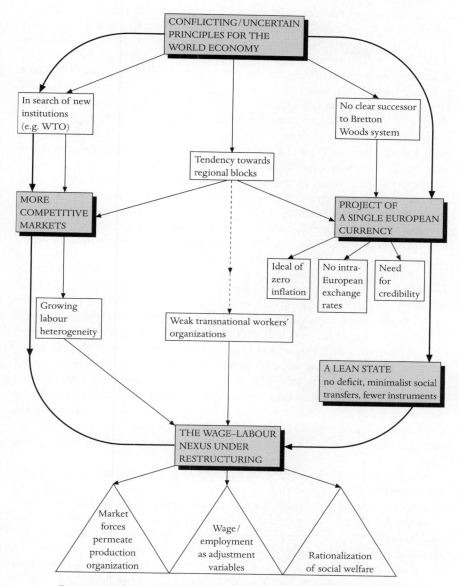

Fig. 2.2. Implications of the euro: a new hierarchy and architecture of European socio-economic regime.

of national competition policy is now restricted by international treaties extending the GATT to the WTO: a government may object to a fusion or absorption of one company by another, even if this concentration takes place far from its domestic territory. This process is sometimes called the globalization of competition. It takes another form within NAFTA or the EU, where a transnational organization is in charge to check the legitimacy of any concentration, under the general principle of fair and open competition. Therefore, price competition is more acute in the 1990s than during the 1960s, even if price wars are limited to a small number of sectors. Clearly, workers have to take into account this pressure of competition in nearly any component of the labour contract and wage–labour nexus.

Market forces tend to permeate production organization with such innovations as the Japanese system of Just In Time production, or more traditionally the flexibility of working time in reaction to the evolution of demand. Similarly, firms look for more rapid employment adjustments, but of course, voluntary labour mobility usually declines along with the scarcity of job opportunities, which has been observed for a decade in Europe. Perhaps one of the most numerous innovations concerns pay systems, which have been transformed in various directions: diffusion of profit sharing; individualization and decentralization of wage bargaining; reduction of seniority wage opportunities; recognition of individual merit and ability; much more than general increases decided through collective bargaining. Finally, even the welfare state is transformed since slow growth reduces the tax basis, whereas a high level of unemployment, frequently of long duration, and the rapid development of early retirement increase social expenditure. Consequently, many reforms have been implemented in order to curb the recurring tendency of welfare systems to run into deficit. In other words, the wage–labour nexus has become dominated by the logic of competition and the objective of a 'lean state', at odds with its central role during the 1960s.

The European single currency is part of this general picture, since it brings other pressures and opportunities to the restructuring of the wage–labour nexus. The fixing once and for all of exchange rates among members removes the 'security valve' that devaluation represented, and conversely appreciation of the national currency. This will bring a major change for the national *régulation* modes that used to solve income distribution conflicts by an accommodating monetary policy (i.e. possibly more inflation and in many instances devaluation). Some industrial relations systems already take into account the objective of competitiveness of national firms without using exchange rate variations. But others do not, and are therefore undergoing some pressure: long-term unemployment, erosion of the extent of legal protection, and welfare benefits. The motto 'let us make labour markets more flexible' is adopted by many governments undertaking more or less ambitious reforms. For instance, the French government in 1995 and the German government in 1997 tentatively changed labour laws and welfare components in order to fight both unemployment and for be ready the euro.

Such reforms are not so easy, as evidenced by the general strike in France in December 1995, or the similar mass protests in Germany. Similarly, the fact that European multinationals now optimize their production over the whole continent has caused a highly emblematic first Euro-strike, when Renault decided to close its Vilvorde factory in Belgium. Finally, since the decision to create the euro, national governments, experts from the EC, and the Advisory Council of the ECB talk more and more frequently of the need for daring and radical reforms of labour laws and the welfare system. There is a strong presumption that the old *régulation* modes cannot enter unchanged into the next century, and the euro is adding one reason for such reforms. This would be the case even if, by an extraordinary conjunction of favourable factors, the wage–labour nexus became increasingly more Europeanized, in tune with the ECB policy.

This last comment raises the important issue of a new institutionalization of the wage–labour nexus, which cannot be summarized as a simple convergence towards pure labour market mechanisms, an ideal which is out of reach and not necessarily optimum for the society as a whole (Boyer 1993b). Furthermore, the euro may resemble the gold standard system, but with a major difference: during the 20th century, wage-earners have won significant welfare benefits, concerning education, training, health care, housing, and retirement. These components definitely remain managed at the national level, but not at all at the European level. Therefore, the present European construction is threatened by a hidden but important risk. Workers may finally decide that the Amsterdam Treaty is a source of reduction in their social and economic rights and that it does not provide any new advantages. Hence, a polarization between an internationalized elite that would reap the benefits of the euro, and various social groups, nationally centred, which would bear the costs of adjustments. This is one major institutional and political deficit of EMU.

This danger has been perceived by EC experts as well as by the European Parliament. The Maastricht Treaty does display some social clauses, precisely to restore such a balance between economic objectives and social concerns. But it is to be noted that these clauses are quite few and only set minimal rights or legislation about equal treatment of men and women, work duration and shift work, as well as information procedures when a European firm closes a plant. Of course, under the aegis of the 'social dialogue', representatives of business associations and workers' unions periodically meet in order to define possible agreements which could become the skeleton of a social legislation at the European level. For the time being, the achievements of this dialogue have been very modest, concerning for instance parental leave, part-time jobs, or information disclosure by European multinationals. The closure of the Renault factory at Vilvorde has highlighted both the need for such cross-border negotiations and legislation, and the considerable difficulties in implementing the embryo of a social Europe. The negotiation of the Amsterdam Treaty has neither fulfilled the wishes of unions, nor the statements of the President of the European Parliament, according to which the new treaty should have displayed an important social component (Gil-Robles 1997).

This is not a real surprise, since the density of cross-border links between unions is quite weak, whereas business associations and sectoral interest groups have far more opportunities to meet and co-ordinate their strategy, especially when the EC is designing new rules or legislation (Schmitter 1997a,b)—not to mention the high frequency of financial transactions which tend to optimize in real time the rate of return of invested capital and therefore exert a strong influence on exchange rates, stock market indexes, and public bond interest rates. By contrast, workers are quite immobile and severely lack the dense co-ordination procedures that would be necessary to defend their common interests at the European level. This asymmetry has another important consequence for the viability of EMU.

A Single Monetary Policy but Contrasted National *Régulation* Modes

Thus, monetary policy becomes European, but labour policies remain national, and quite heterogeneous. Indeed, since World War II the capital–labour accord has had many contrasted configurations, which are far from equivalent (Boyer 1988). The second structural deficit of EMU is precisely that it is difficult to have a common monetary policy in the presence of such different national interests, economic specialization, labour laws, and even business cycle patterns. Of course, this is not a total novelty: since the implementation of the European Monetary System, the Bundesbank has played the role of a Stackelberg leader in the determination of European interest rates. They were set according to the situation and needs of the German economy, and other countries had to follow even if their domestic situation was different. The management of German unification is a good example of such an asymmetry: real interest rates have been raised to finance the German public deficit, at the very moment when other economies needed an expansionary policy. The euro project intends to develop a more balanced European monetary policy. Germany has accepted abandoning the highly symbolic Deutschmark—not without significant political cost at home—provided Europe adopts a German style monetary policy. This means a highly independent ECB with the quasi-exclusive objective of controlling inflation.

If money was neutral, as most neo-classical economists assume, all economic agents, being fully rational, would immediately adjust their behaviour to this new context, and in reality the ECB would not exert any influence on real economic activity, but would only curb inflation. Unfortunately, this is not the way real economies are managed. If, for instance, many unions are in conflict to attract members, or if wage bargaining is fully decentralized to enterprise unions, then casual observation as well as game theory teach that nominal wage rigidity will prevail, since no one will accept *ex ante* a reduction in the relative wage. John Maynard Keynes had already pointed out this configuration in the chapter devoted to the formation of a nominal wage in his book *General Theory of Employment*. The argument can be updated and it delivers a suggestive analysis about the dilemma the ECB is facing.

The Contrasted Institutional Architectures of France and Germany

Monetarists tend to credit the Bundesbank for German achievements in terms of low inflation and, until recently, rather moderate unemployment. They imply that the same policy implemented at the European level would deliver the same macroeconomic achievements. This might be true in a purely theoretical Walrasian world, with an exogenous monetary supply. But these two hypotheses do not fit with the basic features of contemporary economies. On the one hand, many institutional arrangements govern each market organization and deliver different adjustment processes, and the labour market is a good example of such a variety. On the other hand, credit is largely endogenous since its volume results from the behaviour of the banking system and the strategy of borrowers, and therefore the central bank only marginally affects this process by changing a series of interest rates. Consequently, the same monetary policy may deliver totally different results according to the way product, credit, and labour markets function. A comparison between Germany and France is somewhat enlightening.

In Germany, the independence of the central bank and its commitment to price stability are fully embedded in other institutional forms and internalized by other economic actors: workers, unions, firms, business associations, *Länder*, and the federal government itself. Consequently, a strict budgetary discipline is implemented, since the Ministry of Finance cannot ask the Bundesbank to finance any public deficit. Simultaneously, the history of the labour movement has produced a very specific process of wage bargaining, which is co-ordinated at the sectoral level by powerful and unified professional associations. Furthermore, the German growth regime is built on the competitiveness of exports, by quality differentiation and not only price (Streeck 1997). Thus, the monetary regime enforced by the

Bundesbank is structurally compatible with the form of competition, state interventions, international insertion, and even more the wage–labour nexus. A priori, the change brought by the euro is of degree not of nature: the social partners should now look at the ECB and no longer at the Bundesbank and adjust their strategies accordingly.

For France, the picture is quite different. First, there is strong competition among rival unions not to accept any concessions. Consequently, wage formation evolves very slowly, mainly via the disciplinary role of high unemployment, and certainly not via an internalization by the social partners of the costs of poor job creation. Second, until the early 1990s, the government frequently used monetary creation in order to finance public deficits, since the central bank was basically controlled by the Ministry of Finance. Of course, the French inflation rate usually was higher than the German one, but until 1986 it was fairly simple to alter the exchange rate between the franc and the mark in order to compensate for the loss of competitiveness experienced by the French exporting sector. Furthermore, exports were conceived as a complement to sales to the domestic market and the growth regime was mainly led by the dynamism of consumption, itself related to the rapid growth of the real wage (Bowles and Boyer 1995). In this second configuration too, the accommodating French monetary policy was in tune with state interventions and the highly conflictual wage–labour nexus. Therefore, the independence given to the Banque de France in order to comply with the requirements of the Maastricht Treaty brings a real novelty into the *régulation* mode, far more challenging than the shift from the Bundesbank to the ECB.

This difference in national policy styles has important consequences. In Germany, growth rate and unemployment are not directly affected by EMU, and the tools available to the *Länder* and federal government are only marginally affected. In France, by contrast, the very core of state interventions are affected. Given the near *anomie* of industrial relations, a drastic reform of wage formation at the initiative of social partners is hard to imagine. Thus, unemployment has been the cost of keeping the parity between the mark and the franc unchanged. In this respect, the euro is a follow-up of this process, with possible lock-in effects on the future of state intervention and the form of competition. This institutional analysis delivers a surprising result: even if for a decade many macroeconomic indicators tend to be synchronized both in Germany and France, this outcome certainly does not result from a convergence of the respective *régulation* modes. Therefore, the same policy of the ECB will probably have a distinct impact on both sides of the Rhine. Potential political conflicts are in the making—the more difficult to solve, the more vocal have been statements about the complete independence of the ECB. But this result is not specific to the important but problem-ridden German–French relations.

Wage Bargaining and an Independent Central Bank

From a theoretical point of view, the opposition between France and Germany can be generalized by considering two dimensions: first, the degree of central bank independence; and second, the degree of co-ordination of wage bargaining across firms, sectors, skills, and regions. In retrospect, one may compare the relative macroeconomic performances of OECD countries according to the four configurations obtained by combining these two criteria (Hall and Franzese 1998). It emerges that the best results are obtained when an independent central bank is facing social partners able to co-ordinate efficiently their decisions about nominal wage formation. The worst case (i.e. rapid inflation and relatively high unemployment is observed in the opposite case, see Table 2.2). However, the most interesting cases are the following. When central bank independence was associated with very little organization of industrial relations, inflation was nearly the same (4.8 per cent in IV and II in Table 2.2) from 1955 to 1990. This supports the now fashionable idea that central bank independence is good for price stability or at least low inflation. But, the cost in terms of higher unemployment is important, since the absence of wage co-ordination brings increased unemployment (+ 3.3 per cent). Therefore, contrary to the monetarist vision, which assumes that money is neutral in the long run, in this configuration, monetary stability has a significant cost in terms of growth and employment. This non-neutrality is related to the institutional structures governing industrial relations.

TABLE 2.2. The independence of the central bank delivers contrasting macroeconomic outcomes according to the institutions governing the wage–labour nexus (1955–90)

Degree of co-ordination in wage bargaining	Level of central bank independence			
	Low		High	
Low	I		II	
	Misery index	12.2%	Misery index	10.9%
	Inflation	7.5%	Inflation	4.8%
	Unemployment	4.7%	Unemployment	6.1%
High	III		IV	
	Misery index	8.9%	Misery index	7.6%
	Inflation	6.2%	Inflation	4.8%
	Unemployment	2.3%	Unemployment	2.8%

Source: Hall, P. and Franzese, R. J. (1998).

Wage co-ordination seems quite important for reducing unemployment, whatever the statutes of the central bank. If highly decentralized and unsynchronized wage formation could be replaced by a centralized and/or synchronized system, then the gains in unemployment are between 2.4 and 3.4 per cent, and inflation is the same (Table 2.2, IV vs. II) or slightly inferior (Table 2.2, III vs. I). This is further evidence that monetary policy cannot be assessed independently from the prevailing institutional architecture, and that it is not necessarily the unique or the ultimate anti-inflationary tool.

This general conclusion is confirmed by a large amount of research, which has used different tools and data: an analysis of the role of wage formation in the completion of the Single European Market (Marsden 1992); a study of governance modes and their relations with the monetary system and labour market institutions (Soskice and Iversen 1997); an in-depth study of the origins of German macroeconomic success (Streeck 1997); an analysis of the Dutch 'miracle' (Visser and Hemerijck 1997); the investigation of the transformations of Italian institutions under the pressure of the euro (Regini 1997); an historical retrospect of the links between the monetary regime and labour market institutions (Boyer 1993a). Thus, there are grounds for expecting that the single European monetary policy will encounter significant difficulties in the context of very distinct industrial relations systems and especially wage formation.

This point had been completely neglected during the preparation phase of the Maastricht Treaty, but may play a key role in the future of European integration. Of course, if wage systems remain basically unchanged, it is likely that labour-market segmentation, or still worse Balkanization, will be the implicit solution given to the inability to work out innovative labour contracts. In fact, if unions are weak and divided, if industrial organizations are heterogeneous, and if the national legacy in industrial relations has produced strong ideological opposition between firms and workers, then adverse macroeconomic outcomes are quite likely. Unemployment and social exclusion of the low skilled workers will be the particular cost to be paid for such conservatism in industrial relations. The efforts to be deployed in order to offset these adverse consequences will be greater, the more distant domestic labour institutions are from German ones. Will Germany be immune from any structural adjustment? The answer is not that self-evident.

From the Bundesbank to the ECB: A Shift Detrimental to Germany?

If the text of the Amsterdam Treaty is to be followed strictly, the ECB should decide its monetary policy according to average European indexes and primarily the evolution of average inflation. But inflation rates remain rather different. For instance in 2000, inflation in Ireland is forecast to be around 2.8 per cent, but only 1.1 per cent in France, and 1.2 per cent for Germany. This is a significant discrepancy around the average European rate, forecast

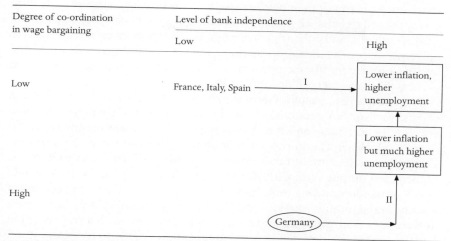

Degree of co-ordination in wage bargaining	Level of bank independence	
	Low	High
Low	France, Italy, Spain ——— I ———→	Lower inflation, higher unemployment
		↑
		Lower inflation but much higher unemployment
		↑
High		II
	(Germany) ——————————→	

I: *Greater independence of the European Central Bank* with respect to the objectives of the national governments.

II: *Greater heterogeneity in wage structure* across Europe than within Germany (before reunification).

FIG. 2.3. The European Central Bank: some undesirable/unexpected consequences (lower inflation, but higher unemployment).

to be around 1.7 per cent. The heterogeneity of wage formation, productivity increases, and forms of competition across nations explains this discrepancy, which is likely to remain even if the common European monetary policy ends up synchronizing all national business cycles, which is currently not the case.

Given this heterogeneity, the ECB ought to adopt a more severe policy than the Bundesbank would have decided, even if the target for European inflation were still the German underlying inflation rate. From a more theoretical point of view, the model proposed by Hall and Franzese (1998) stresses that heterogeneity in wage formation has increased in Germany. Thus, if industrial relations outside Germany are not reformed, the following paradox could emerge from implementation of EMU (Fig. 2.3).

For Germany, the European monetary policy is no more decided according to the situation and interests of Germany. For example, an idiosyncratic shock equivalent to unification should not a priori alter the monetary supply by the ECB as the Bundesbank did after the collapse of the Berlin Wall. Conversely, if the other members of EMU grow faster than Germany, the interest rate should be higher than required to smooth the German business cycles. Thus, after the implementation of the euro, one could logically expect lower German inflation, at the cost of higher unemployment. A surprising result indeed! For other countries with highly decentralized wage bargaining, if lower inflation is to be obtained on a medium-term basis, more unemployment than before the euro is to be expected. Since the euro was supposed to enhance growth and promote job creation (de Silguy 1998), workers, unions, and public opinion might be disappointed by this unexpected outcome. Of course, the European boom initiated in 1997 may hide the higher underlying structural unemployment level, but as soon as a recession occurs, this basic fact will be apparent.

The unexpected result for Germany, shown in Fig. 2.3 and discussed above, originates from an econometric study for the period 1955–90 (Hall and Franzese 1998), and is confirmed by a simulation of a multieconometric model (Fair 1998). When the European economies shift from the current monetary regime to the euro, it turns out that Germany is hurt the most in terms of increased output variability. According to these analyses, the euro would be a Pareto-deteriorating move! Social partners may perceive the origins of such a disappointing outcome and decide to synchronize wage formation in Europe overall. Since the institutional structures for such a co-ordination are missing for the time being, they could simply decide to set wages in accordance with the German wage. This wage would itself be negotiated between IG Metall and the German metal industry employees, both of them taking into account the signals emitted by the ECB, instead of the Bundesbank. This very simple hierarchical device would prevent price stability from being obtained at the cost of higher unemployment in the majority of the eleven members of the EMU (Soskice and Iversen 1997). But this happy end is not entirely likely, because it assumes that all national, sectoral, and local unions in Europe will immediately look at the ECB's signals now, and no longer at those of national authorities, or at the domestic economic situation. For instance, the Irish or Portuguese workers' unions should not exploit bargaining power linked to a national booming economy (the respective GDP forecasted rate of growth being 7 per cent and 3.2 per cent in 2000) but take into account the preservation of the competitiveness of domestic firms, at least in the sector exposed to European competition. Such a rational calculus may take place, but it cannot be taken for granted, nor will it be general, given the strategic game which take place when many unions compete for membership (Boyer 1993a).

Will this conflict be limited to the domain of industrial relations or will it emerge in the political arena?

Emerging Conflicts over ECB Policy

Intact, the legitimacy granted by German public opinion to the Bundesbank will not be capitalized automatically by the new European Central Bank. First, the adhesion of many European countries to the idea that the ECB should be independent is quite recent. It has to prove its positive outcome, by promoting financial stability and possibly rapid growth. This hope will be disappointed if the first steps of the ECB bring more restrictive policies

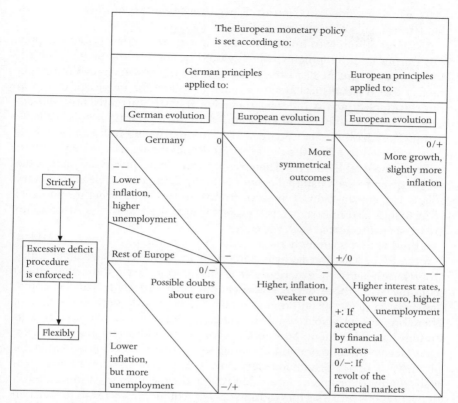

Fig. 2.4. European Central Bank management: conflicting interests of member states.
Notes: +, positive impact; −, negative impact; −−, strongly negative impact; 0, neutral impact. Symbols before diagonal lines indicate impact on Germany; those after, indicate impact on other countries.

than previously. The objectives and the tools of the ECB would become a matter of public concern, since political process may change what has been agreed by the Maastricht and Amsterdam Treaties. Nevertheless, it is not easy to change a treaty which has been signed by fifteen members, which may have conflicting views about the needed revisions, or have changed their objectives in relation to a transformed economic context. Second, even if all member states agreed the text of the Amsterdam Treaty on the statutes of the ECB, the heterogeneity of national *régulation* modes introduces potential conflicts concerning the conduct of monetary policy (Fig. 2.4).

Should the German principles be still applied to German evolution, the ECB being the faithful follower of the Bundesbank?—some observers have pointed out that the ECB is located in Frankfurt. But, of course, other governments and central bankers may complain that this was not the aim of

EMU, which intended, in contrast, Europeanization (i.e. more symmetry in the determinants of monetary policy).

A second option is to implement the same general concept but to apply it to European developments, which would respond to the previous objection. However, this neglects the heterogeneity of short-term evolution and the fact that the statistical system needed to follow the impact of common monetary policy across different members states is currently not well developed. It is certainly less sophisticated than the monitoring tools available to the US Federal Reserve Board. Furthermore, the interest groups, which indirectly used to affect the policy of the Bundesbank, have no equivalent, at the moment, at ECB level. There is, therefore, much uncertainty about the weight given to each national economy in the fixing of European monetary policy. The constitution of interest groups on this issue, whether informal or formal, is also uncertain—the more so since the text of the Amsterdam Treaty seems to forbid such pressures.

A third option, seemingly rather unlikely but not to be excluded, considers that the ECB, whatever its firm statements in favour of price stability, may progressively learn by experience that the EU is in fact a somewhat closed economy with more degrees of freedom than expected. Thus it could, implicitly at least, promote not only stable growth but low inflation. Therefore, new principles would be applied to European developments. This strategy would benefit Southern Europe and industrializing countries. Even German public opinion could agree to such a move, provided it finally delivers better results for Germany. This scenario would be the most likely, the more problematic would become the German situation: sluggish innovation in sunrise sectors (Soskice 1997a) could induce a shift in German industry from largely price-maker to price-taker industries. A strong euro (i.e. overvalued with respect to the dollar), would no longer be rational or desirable, even from a German point of view.

These three options can be combined with two contrasted approaches of the Excessive Deficit Procedure (EDP): either the clause could be implemented strictly, the more easily the more buoyant the growth rate; or the inability of a majority of countries to fulfil the criteria during a severe recession or a long period of stagnation would lead to *de facto* rejection of the EDP.

In each of the scenarios, the costs and the benefits of each policy are quite differently distributed between Germany and the rest of Europe. This is strong evidence that even the implementation of the most basic clauses of the Amsterdam Treaty will bring potential acute political conflict, whatever the independent statute of the ECB. Monetary history suggests that the legitimacy of any currency is closely linked with political sovereignty. Thus, the long-term viability of the euro cannot be warranted without a clear and stable political alliance at the European level. Again, the political deficit of EMU is pointed out. But the national policy arena is also severely challenged by EMU.

Economic Policy between Europeanization and Subsidiarity

How will responsibility for economic policy be shared between European and national levels? Before capital liberalization and EMU, each nation state had significant autonomy in using monetary, tax, and public spending tools in order to achieve the macroeconomic results that would satisfy a coalition of interest groups and/or a majority of citizens. This clear division of responsibility is removed and a much more sophisticated configuration is implicit in the Amsterdam Treaty. From a purely technical point of view, is this configuration coherent and viable in the medium to long term?

Back to Tinbergen's Framework

Today, analysts tend to use only neo-classical models in order to assess the consequences of EMU. In this kind of model, markets are assumed to be self-equilibrating, but public authorities and especially the central bank, may create some perturbations by altering money supply—quite unexpectedly with respect to the rational expectations of the private agents who have mastered perfectly the functioning of this idealized Walrasian economy. In such a framework, it is clear that only governments introduce Pareto-deteriorating shocks. Therefore, the central bank should be independent from any political power and should be submitted to the implementation of strict principles, such as price stability or alternatively a given target monetary supply. The Amsterdam Treaty seems to be inspired by this kind of vision.

Unfortunately, such a framework hides more problems than it helps in understanding the formation of European/national economic policies. Thus, it is interesting to go back to a more conventional framework, which was at the core of Keynesian or more generally interventionist conceptions of the role of governments. Basically, markets such as those for credit or labour are not self-equilibrating, due to uncertainty, asymmetric information and power, imperfect competition, and so on. In such a case, governments may have a positive impact on the welfare of society by promoting the return to full employment or alternatively fighting inflation and reducing external deficit.

How should a rational economic policy be decided? Macroeconomic modelling theory has proposed and implemented a useful framework (Tinbergen 1991). In essence, macroeconomic activity is largely endogenous, because consumption, investment, exports, and imports are related to wages, profits, effective demand, relative prices (i.e. variables set by private agents). But generally, involuntary unemployment is observed or an inflationary boom may endanger financial and even social stability. The government may correct these changes since it controls some instruments such as taxation rates, public spending, wage norms for the public sector, interest rates, and exchange rates. By adequate movement of these instruments, a better macroeconomic equilibrium can be reached (Box 1).

At a very abstract level, it has to be assumed that the major macroeconomic mechanisms can be captured by modelling and estimating the related equations. Then, the government may try to decide its economic policy according to target variables concerning growth, inflation, unemployment, or external trade equilibrium. But, of course, under pressure from various social and economic groups, the government may be induced to pursue more objectives than available instruments make possible. In this case, no single objective will be maximized, but a composite of them will be optimized. Indeed, the weight given to each objective might be the solution to a political game played by various groups in order to obtain the support of public policy. If wage-earners are part of the political game of government formation, unemployment and real wages are taken into account by the government, whereas the business community asks for low taxes and high profits, and rentiers' (large institutional investors) high interest rates and low inflation (Palombarini 1997, 1999). In comparison with neo-classical macroeconomic theory, this framework is not without merit. First, it leaves open the question whether the government is stabilizing or destabilizing the economy. Second, it considers a large spectrum of relevant macroeconomic variables and intervention tools, and not just monetary policy. Third, such a formalization builds a bridge between macroeconomic dynamics and economic policy formation, certainly an important theme for any assessment of the euro.

Objectives and Tools of National Economic Policies: 1954–98

Concepts of national economic policy have changed considerably over time, and the emergence of the idea of a common European currency is part of this general process. Therefore, a short historical background is useful in assessing the novelty of the current European configuration.

During the Keynesian era, most governments, including conservative ones, had adopted almost the same four major targets for their macroeconomic policy: promote growth, limit external trade disequilibrium, keep inflation under control, and operate near full employment. Only the weight given to each objective used to vary according to the colour of the political coalition: more emphasis on full employment for social democrats, more importance granted to price stability for more right-wing governments. Furthermore, the diffusion of Keynesian macroeconomics had made popular the following assignment of public intervention tools to the different macroeconomic objectives. Both monetary supply and public spending contributed to the level of output and price, whereas taxes could be used as an incentive to moderate wage demands, and therefore limit unemployment. Finally, the exchange rate was set by public intervention, with

Box 1. An established but still useful method for analysing economic policy

Let us represent by X the vector of endogenous macroeconomic variables, Z the vector of policy instruments and if the relations are assumed to be linear, then an economy can be, as a simplification, represented as

$$X = AX \quad X + B \times Z$$
$$(n, 1)\,(n, n)\,(n, 1)(n, m)(m, 1)$$

which can be solved as

$$X = [I - A]^{-1} \times B \times Z = C \times Z$$
$$(n, 1) \qquad\qquad\qquad (n, m)(m, 1)$$

which summarizes the impact of economic policy tools on macroeconomic variables. Therefore, governments may choose target variables for a subset of m endogenous variables, and set accordingly the economic policy instruments

$$\begin{matrix}(1, m)\\(m+1, n)\end{matrix} \begin{pmatrix} OBJ_2 \\ OBJ_2 \end{pmatrix} = \begin{pmatrix} C_1 & C_2 \\ C_3 & C_4 \end{pmatrix} \times Z; \text{ or to simplify: } OBJ_1 = [C_1 C_2] \times Z$$
$$\qquad\qquad (n, 1) \qquad (n, m) \quad {(m, 1)} \qquad\qquad (m, 1)\ (m, m)\,(m, 1)$$

Therefore, if the matrix C is of rank m, any objective OBJ* can be fulfilled by an adequate Z*, provided it belongs to admissible value for Z* (positive interest rate for instance)

$$Z^* = [C_1\,C_2]^{-1} \times OBJ^* \qquad \text{with } Z^* \in \mathscr{L}$$

In the general case, there may exist more objectives than instruments and the 'optimal' policy associated to a given weight of objectives is set according to

$$\begin{cases} \text{Max} \quad \alpha \quad \times \quad OBJ \quad P > m \\ \qquad\quad (1, p) \qquad\quad (p, 1) \\ OBJ \quad = \quad C \quad \times \quad Z \\ \qquad\qquad\quad (p, m) \quad (m, 1) \\ \quad Z \in \mathscr{L} \\ (m, 1) \end{cases}$$

Key: A and B are two matrices representing the structural form of the macro-model linking endogenous and exogenous variables. C is a matrix that represents the model under its reduced form. OBJ is a vector representing the various objectives of the government.

Source: freely adapted from Tinbergen (1991).

Box 2. The various phases of economic policy in european nation states (1954–2001)

---

1. The Keynesian era (1954–72)

$$\begin{pmatrix} Q \\ X-M \\ P \\ U \end{pmatrix} = \begin{pmatrix} \mathscr{C}_1 \end{pmatrix} \times \begin{pmatrix} M \\ e \\ G \\ T \end{pmatrix}$$

Output — Q
External trade — $X-M$
Price — P
Unemployment — U

M Money supply
e Exchange rate
G Public spending
T Taxes

Objectives with constraints $(G-T)/Q \leq \alpha$

2. An income policy variant with limitation of public deficit spending

$$\begin{pmatrix} Q \\ X-M \\ P \\ U \end{pmatrix} = \begin{pmatrix} \mathscr{C}_2 \end{pmatrix} \times \begin{pmatrix} M \\ e \\ G \\ W \end{pmatrix} \quad \text{(\textit{more} output if \textit{more} public spending)}$$

3. The monetarist/conservative alliance (1979–1985)

$$\begin{pmatrix} Q \\ X-M \\ P \end{pmatrix} = \begin{pmatrix} \mathscr{C}_3 \end{pmatrix} \times \begin{pmatrix} G \\ e \\ M \end{pmatrix} \quad \text{(\textit{more} output if \textit{less} public spending)}$$

4. The free capital mobility and the Schumpeterian move (1986–)

$$\begin{pmatrix} Q \\ P \\ X-M \end{pmatrix} = \begin{pmatrix} \mathscr{C}_4 \end{pmatrix} \times \begin{pmatrix} RD \\ i \\ T-G \end{pmatrix} \quad \text{(innovation as the engine of growth)}$$

---

little influence from private capital, unless during acute external financial crises. Therefore, governments took pride in achieving a 'fine-tuning' of macroeconomic activity and usually obtained political support from the public for this achievement. As the subsequent part of the story tells, this self-attributed economic merit by politicians was partly or mainly an illusion (Box 2)!

After 1967, inflationary pressures became difficult to contain and public deficit tended to surge and therefore limit the ability to continue typical Keynesian full-employment policies. If one of the conventional instruments came to be missing, it had to be replaced by another. For instance, various income policies: either strong and well-organized social partners agreed on wage and price restraint in order to limit inflation and still more enhance employment; or labour markets were decentralized and uncoordinated, and a tax-based income policy was tentatively introduced, for instance, by taxing any wage or price increase above an upper limit. In fact, countries able to implement such a corporatist social pact usually enjoyed less unemployment and less inflation than others (Dore, Boyer, and Mars 1994). But this was certainly not the end of the story.

After 1979, a new monetarist and conservative alliance came to the fore in both the USA and UK, and this model of economic policy has spread across the world, quite independently from the colour of the government. First, unemployment is no longer a government concern because it is assumed to be voluntary and a response to a structural rise in the so-called 'natural rate of employment'. During this period, social deregulation has taken place in many countries and tended to destroy the very legitimacy of any incomes policy. Thus, wage formation is no longer an objective of public authority concern. Given the regime of managed flexible exchange rates, the budgetary policy loses a large part of its efficiency. The Keynesian multiplier is supposed to decrease towards zero. For supply-side economics, any public spending is made at the cost of private consumption or investment. Thus, due to crowding-out effects, more public spending means even lower output and employment. Again, the structure of macroeconomic adjustments has changed. So did political alliances and consequently the concept and implementation of a national economic policy.

Since the mid 1980s, a different and new concept has emerged. With financial liberalization, the multiplicity of new financial instruments, and the 'globalization' of some markets, the exchange rate is no longer a variable which can be significantly affected by the national central bank. The interest rate becomes an instrument which can be used to curb the inflation rate according to the so-called Taylor rule, according to which any incipient inflation should be checked by raising the real interest rate. This same action reduces inflation expectations; it thus has a positive influence on the exchange rate. This leaves the problem of how to monitor the level of activity. The new tool for public intervention has become innovation policy, via subsidies or tax reductions for research and development expenditures. Basically, this neo-Schumpeterian orthodoxy has been implemented by many governments. Finally, the public deficit is assumed to influence, at least partially, the external trade position of each country. The IMF frequently uses this argument in its structural adjustment plans for developing countries. It is important to note that the management of domestic effective demand is rarely taken into account today, especially in Europe. In the USA, the policy mix is much more balanced and could be a reference for the ECB, at least for some scenarios.

Thus, the euro arrives after this long-term trajectory, and is partly explained by the quest for new intervention tools. If intra-European exchange rates are governed by the expectations of international financial markets, the instability thus created becomes an obstacle to economic integration. The euro might be a solution but then, what should be the division of tasks between European authorities and national governments?

An Unprecedented Configuration for European and National Policies

The situation created by the Amsterdam Treaty is radical. It is neither absolute autonomy of independent national states, nor is it a typically federalist configuration (Dehove 1997; 1998). Responsibility for economic policy is now shared at two levels and nested, in the sense that neither the supranational rules nor the subsidiarity principle exert a dominant role (Box 3).

Clearly, monetary policy is the full responsibility of the ECB, in charge of maintaining price stability in Europe. But the credibility of the euro and especially its exchange rate with respect to the dollar is significantly affected by the conduct of national budgetary policies. Given the fixed exchange rate system which is irrevocably installed by the euro between the eleven members, the Mundell–Fleming model implies that budgetary policy becomes the only efficient instrument left to national governments to control the domestic level of activity (Wyplosz 1997). Therefore, each nation state may have an incentive to free-ride on the collective benefit produced by the wise budgetary policy taken by other nation states (Laskar 1993; Martin 1995).

Box 3. The new architecture for European/national economic policies: some countries are able to resist unemployment, others are not

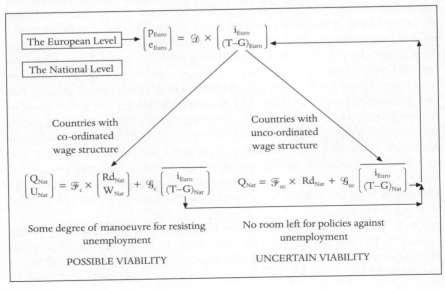

$$\text{The European Level} \longrightarrow \begin{bmatrix} P_{Euro} \\ e_{Euro} \end{bmatrix} = \mathcal{D} \times \begin{bmatrix} i_{Euro} \\ (T-G)_{Euro} \end{bmatrix}$$

The National Level

Countries with co-ordinated wage structure

Countries with unco-ordinated wage structure

$$\begin{bmatrix} Q_{Nat} \\ U_{Nat} \end{bmatrix} = \mathcal{F}_c \times \begin{bmatrix} Rd_{Nat} \\ W_{Nat} \end{bmatrix} + \mathcal{G}_c \begin{bmatrix} i_{Euro} \\ (T-G)_{Nat} \end{bmatrix}$$

$$Q_{Nat} = \mathcal{F}_{uc} \times Rd_{Nat} + \mathcal{G}_{uc} \begin{bmatrix} i_{Euro} \\ (T-G)_{Nat} \end{bmatrix}$$

Some degree of manoeuvre for resisting unemployment

POSSIBLE VIABILITY

No room left for policies against unemployment

UNCERTAIN VIABILITY

Thus, the Amsterdam Treaty has extended the rule put forward by the Maastricht Treaty, and sets a 3 per cent limit to the maximum public deficit as a fraction of GDP, in order to convince the financial markets that the credibility of the euro cannot be challenged by the misconduct of any national budgetary authority.

This clause in the treaty is highly controversial. For many economists it is a symbolic and redundant rule, since the ECB is forbidden to buy any national public bond, or to bail out any bankrupt domestic bank (Wyplosz 1997). Still worse, in the case of severe recession, this clause removes an instrument from national authorities, as they are responsible for resisting unemployment and promoting high growth. Furthermore, from a purely institutional point of view, this clause violates the subsidiarity principle, which is essential in the process of European integration. A common counter-argument states that governments should use the 1998 European recovery to build a budgetary surplus which will be useful during a future recession in order to alleviate unemployment, without hitting the 3 per cent threshold for public deficit (EC 1998a,b). But national governments, under the pressures of their con-stituents, seem to have different objectives, perhaps because the electoral schedule brings an intrinsic short-termism to decisions on economic policy. In any case, this conflict of interpretation and responsibility will now undoubtedly trigger many conflicts. This dilemma will be exacerbated by the heterogeneity of national *régulation* modes and especially industrial relations systems.

On the one hand, the economies that enjoy wage co-ordination still have a tool to affect the level of unemployment (see Crouch, Chapter 8): the social partners will adapt their strategy to the euro and still have an influence on the level of economic activity, even if budgetary policy were nearly neutralized by the 3 per cent limit. Eventually, the bargaining between business associ-ations and workers' unions may concern public welfare management, with the objective of reducing the level of public deficit (e.g. by internalizing the costs of unemployment). Recently admitted member states, such as Finland, have evolved accordingly and negotiated contra-cyclical devices concerning unemployment benefits, pension funds, and nominal wage formation (InfEuro 1998). Under this condition, the medium-to long-term viability of the euro is roughly warranted, provided of course, there are no major national unexpected shocks.

On the other hand, where wage formation is unco-ordinated, the perspective is more gloomy. Frequently, the public deficit is high because the poor configuration of industrial relations has been converted into welfare spend-ing (e.g. early retirement funding) or structural public deficit. Thus the bud-getary tool is nearly neutralized, unless governments launch an ambitious plan for rationalizing and reforming the whole structure of public spending and taxation. But they often face strong social and political opposition, as was observed in France in December 1995. However, this move towards a lean state does not solve short-term adjustment problems, but is a means for promoting higher growth and innovation. In this respect, the incentives for research and development have exactly the same long-term horizon as industrial relations' reform, and are unable to have a short-term and significant impact on employment. In this case, the subsidiarity principle boils down to the crude absence of fiscal solidarity across European countries. EMU exacerbates underlying structural problems but prevents a socially acceptable solution, given the overarching principle of the need for euro credibility.

To sum up, the dividing line between the Europeanization of monetary policy and the subsidiarity of budgetary policy brings a structural disequilibrium and potential political conflict, and exacerbates the heterogeneity of national industrial relations and *régulation* modes. This discrepancy is not restricted to economic policy, since it is much more severe in the arena of domestic policy formation in general.

The Long-term Legitimacy of the Euro within the National Policy Arena

Should any government join EMU? Within each domestic society, will anybody gain from implementation of the euro? Will politicians obtain permanent support for the current phase of European integration? Is the Amsterdam Treaty resilient to a large variety of world conjunctures, specific sectoral crises, and domestic political opposition to a part of the measures and processes set into motion by EMU? To all these questions, European officials have the same and fairly optimistic answer: the euro will bring financial stability; it will reduce uncertainty, thus enhance growth and employment, in such a way that every economic agent and citizen will eventually gain. This follows a somewhat conventional vision of institution-building: politicians propose institutional arrangements that increase the social welfare of society (Posner 1981), and individuals accept these proposals. Only irrational activists or backward-looking politicians could oppose such improvements.

But this view is far from satisfactory, since many Pareto-improving innovations can be blocked in their diffusion by the prevalence of existing conventions and institutions (Boyer and Orléan 1992). Indeed, the major economic institutions require political intervention and often the permanent enforcement of law (Streeck 1996; Sabel 1997). This view explains far better the historical record (North 1990), as well as the variety of national institutional arrangements (Hollingsworth and Boyer 1997). The euro is not an exception, since it was designed and created, neither by financial markets nor by economists, but by heads of government, in order to overcome the political disequilibrium created by the destruction of the Berlin Wall and the new dimension of Europe (Milesi 1998). But then assessment of the economic consequences of the euro is much more complex than a simple exercise in monetary theory. It becomes a debatable topic, which can be given different answers in various countries.

Until now, the European project has been mobilizing the political elite in order to convince reluctant economic or social groups to accept reforms, which would otherwise have been blocked. Such a phenomenon has been seen not only in Italy, where a European tax has been levied in order to comply with the Maastricht criteria, but also in Spain and Portugal, countries which have come to identify democratization and modernization with adhesion to the EU. Since January 1999 the issue has been transformed: how will public opinion accept the good and less palatable consequences of the conduct of budgetary policy, competition enforcement, and the implementation of a new series of norms and rules?

But there is a more structural analysis of the viability of the EMU: in the long run, will the groups benefiting from it be more numerous and politically active than the groups which will be hurt by the endogenous trends at work within each domestic society? Some French public polls give some hints: the unequal consequences across the different groups and members of society are clearly perceived (Table 2.3).

TABLE 2.3. France: The euro is perceived to have different consequences for various social groups

	Few problems	Transitory difficulties only	Long-lasting problems	No opinion
Large firms	**62**	32	4	2
Younger people	**60**	31	7	2
Small- and medium-sized enterprises	37	**53**	6	4
Retailers	22	**65**	11	2
Savers	20	**51**	21	8
People with low incomes	7	**49**	**41**	3
Older people	1	8	**90**	1

Source: SOFRES (1997), 110.
What are the likely consequences of the euro for the following groups? (%)

On the one hand, large firms and certain younger people are considered to be able to adapt quite easily to this new configuration. All over Europe, business associations and large enterprises are the most active supporters of the euro—including those in the UK. Their strategy is already directed towards the entire continent, and monetary integration allows their choice of location to be easier and less risky. For young people, the impact of EMU is less clear. In many countries, they are the most unemployed age group, and it may be argued that one of the hidden evils of a united Europe is to have privileged mid career workers and early retirees penalizing the entry of a new generation into the job market. However, perhaps EMU will trigger ambitious labour reforms, which would allow the reversal of this adverse selection against young people, but the jury is still out.

On the other hand, low income groups and older people are expected to experience lasting problems in coping with the new European order. The difficulties might be more transitory for small- and medium-size enterprises, retailers, and small savers. Basically, most of these rely either on an extended welfare system, which has tentatively been reformed to prepare the economy for the euro, or on the domestic/local markets which may decline relatively as European integration promotes a new division of labour across borders. Those least able to deal with modern technology, foreign languages, or managerial tools will probably experience a decline of their relative income. This downgrading has been taking place for two decades in the USA, but it would be a relatively new phenomenon for European countries, where collective agreements, legislation, and a quasi-universal welfare system has contained the widening of social inequality—although the UK has already explored such a path (Atkinson 1998).

Thus, EMU will contribute to shifting the borderline between winners and losers. In democratic societies, citizens express themselves on various occasions, including elections to the European Parliament. But turnout is especially low for these elections compared with local and national ones. This means that even the consequences of Europeanization are dealt with mainly within the domestic political arena. More generally, internationalization and globalization are still matter of domestic politics (Keohane and Milner 1996).

The Political Viability of European Integration at Stake

In a sense, both processes of globalization and Europeanization display some similarities: the more internationalized actors try to redefine the national rules of the game, using the leverage provided by their access to other territories (Boyer 1997). Of course, this group can try to influence the design of the rules of the game for the international system itself. But this second process is far more difficult than the first, due to the diversity of interests and the lack of a unified supranational state. *Mutatis mutandis*, the deepening of European integration has introduced equivalent tensions, but the project of a federal European state is less distant than the unification of the world under a single hegemony. Today, the European political process is subject to two contradictory forces.

The economic and social actors who have access to the European Community benefit from extra markets, knowledge about relevant legislation and subsidies, and cross-border networks. Thus, they are generally better off than the agents whose horizon is limited to local or regional transactions. Some of these Europeanized actors can even participate in the process of rule formation at the level of Brussels, Strasbourg, or Frankfurt. Of course, this power has to be shared with other members of the European elite and the perception of own interest are therefore transformed by this very process of interaction at the European level. Thus, there is the potential formation of a European elite and by extension polity (Schmitter 1997c), even if it is not devoid of conflicts and tensions. For instance, about 70 per cent of current national legislation is no more than the translation and implementation of rules and treaties decided at the European level. But these Europeanized actors are few in proportion to the total population.

For a vast majority of citizens, European affairs are exclusively or mainly a matter of domestic polity. First, because their contacts with foreign actors are rather episodic and superficial. Second, because their main access to political power is via national politicians who are held responsible for decisions taken both at the national and European level. Of course, since the Brussels authorities are generally far from the national politicians, this sometimes allows transferring responsibility for adverse consequences of Europeanization to the so-called 'Brussels Bureaucrats'. Third, and more basically, the most significant advances in European integration and especially EMU, have been decided after intergovernmental conferences, where heads of governments have signed international treaties on the model of those of Maastricht or Amsterdam. From a democratic point of view, the main voice of the average citizen is still expressed within the national political arena. Thus, an emerging risk: that nationalist movements and parties will take the lead in organizing protests against the adverse effects of European integration on either selected social groups or the majority.

In the future, these two groups with conflicting interests and visions could enter into frontal, if not violent, opposition about the trajectory to be followed by European integration: to forge as quickly as possible a true European polity where each citizen could have a say about such radical transformations as EMU, common European diplomacy, defence and security; or to reject any further Europeanization in the name of the preservation of democracy and transparency, and the defence of national identity. In some extreme cases, the destruction of previous European advances, such as the euro, could even take place. The first solution would be highly preferable; but it takes decades to build new institutions, and European political innovations might be far slower than the emergence of the major structural problems triggered by EMU. The second solution builds on already existing political institutions at national level, but seems to forget that European economies have become so interdependent that the affirmation of national autonomy would have significant economic costs. Nevertheless, it is easier to destroy institutions than to build them, and populist arguments are generally more appealing than rational plans calling for the forging of a Euro-polity.

But this is a crude dichotomy, and is only a starting point for a more satisfactory, but of course, complex framework. First elaborated in order to understand the origin of the 1992 Italian political crisis (Palombarini 1997), it can be extended to a stimulating analysis of the dynamics generated by EMU. Under which conditions will the euro be viable in the different domestic political arenas? Only if the economic evolution that the euro sets into motion affects the various social groups in such a way that the support for the deepening of European integration grows through time and delivers a continuous democratic support to the governments, which have proposed and implemented the current phase of Europeanization. But this process has become quite complex as it concerns monetary integration, financial deregulation, single market extension, and the limit over national public deficits (Fig. 2.5).

Basically, the very implementation of the euro shifts the boundaries between social groups or even redefines them. The large international firms have, of course, a basic interest in all four structural changes. This is not the case for medium-size and domestic firms, which might be hurt by the deepening of the Single Market. This is according to an opposition, which can be perceived in all countries, and appears in polls and surveys (see Table 2.3). Also, welfare dependents, most civil servants, farmers, and low skilled workers are unlikely to benefit from the new concept of economic policy and state intervention, which is implicit to EMU strategy. Depending on the initial size of these groups, economic specialization, the specificity of interest aggregation via political party formation, the nature of the constitutional and political order, the same European policy may have quite different impacts on the legitimacy and durability of pro-euro governments. Another important variable has to be added: individuals do not react only to the consequences of the euro on their material life and status, but may have general feelings about the desirability of European integration, on purely political or ideological grounds. If the launching of the euro initiates a long economic boom, its acceptance will be easier and will give more time to solve emerging problems. If, however, European growth in sluggish and uncertain, the fate of the euro could be completely changed.

But many other scenarios are opened from these interactions between economy and polity. The challenge of the euro may actually trigger a move toward more solidarity at the national level. Thus, the losers could be compensated by the winners and a new social pact and cohesion could emerge within each national state. Or, in contrast, the inertia of the past

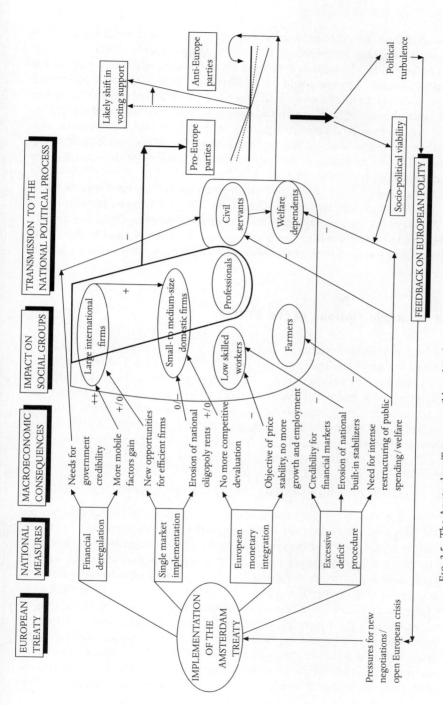

Fig. 2.5. The Amsterdam Treaty: possible political consequences in the medium to long term.

Note. +, positive impact; −, negative impact; 0, neutral impact Diagonal lines indicate ambiguity between two possible impacts.

institutional architecture may deliver unemployment and social exclusion as adjusting variables to the euro. If socially excluded individuals or groups tend to be politically excluded as well, by not voting and being part of the political process, Europe could well follow the American track. Widening inequalities would not be so challenging for the stability of the pro-European elite. But alternatively, given the ideological traditions of some countries, these groups may feed extremist parties, with drastic anti-European results. In other words, as soon as the interplay of political, economic, and social forces is taken into account, the legitimacy and viability of the euro is a key issue for the next decade.

The future is largely open, and this hint concerns the very core of EMU (i.e. the objective and the role of the ECB). The precision of the clauses of the Amsterdam Treaty may give the impression that everything has already been decided and therefore the trajectory of the euro is already fixed—on the model of a rocket to the moon launched by NASA. This feeling is largely misleading.

The Strategic Options of the ECB

Alternative policies might be decided without altering the text of any European treaty, for three main reasons: the various clauses authorize contrasted interpretations of the need of economic policy co-ordination; the consequences of severe and unexpected national crises; and of course, the opportunity to strengthen economic policy co-ordination if a fraction of member states agrees to do so (Jacquet 1998; Muet 1998). Again, a brief historical retrospect is useful in order to understand the factors that shape the changes in monetary principles and regimes.

The Mundell–Flemming Impossibility Theorem Revisited

The so-called Mundell–Flemming impossibility theorem is a good starting point. This core analytical framework about the macroeconomics of an open economy states that it is impossible to have simultaneously complete capital mobility, a fixed exchange rate, and an autonomous monetary policy. Its interest is to demonstrate the possibility of a plurality of national monetary and international financial regimes. Indeed, most of the theoretical possibilities have been realized since World War II (Fig. 2.6). The launching of the euro defines the fourth phase of a rich and interesting story.

From the end the war until 1971, the international regime was based on strong public control over international capital mobility, a legacy of the dramatic financial crises of the inter-war period. Within the Bretton Woods system, each national government had to declare a fixed external parity to the

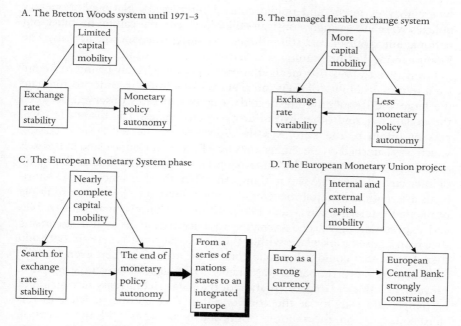

Fig. 2.6. Stages of European monetary integration: the Mundell–Flemming impossibility theorum perspective.

International Monetary Fund (IMF) and stick to it unless a cumulative trade deficit, or more rarely capital flight, forced a devaluation, which was, in theory, operated under the control of the IMF. In this context, the monetary policy enjoyed considerable autonomy at the national level, and this was captured by the Keynesian IS-LM model. Interest rates, along with tax and public spending, were the key variables in determining the level of activity by the joint action of the central bank and the ministry of finance which were frequently closely and directly linked to government strategy, and largely discretionary (Fig. 2.6A).

From 1971 to 1978, this configuration underwent some structural transformations which have been preventing such a fine-tuning by economic policy at the national level from continuing (Fig. 2.6B). First, the creation of the Eurodollar accelerated international capital mobility and put pressure on the system of fixed exchange rates. Since inflation was quite high and heterogeneous across countries, the Bretton Woods system could not be sustained. The deconnection of the dollar with respect to gold set in motion a system of flexible but managed exchange rates. Increasingly, exchange rates were set according to the expectations of inflation by the financial markets and the domestic interest rate set by the central bank (i.e. a mixed system where market forces and public control interacted). National monetary policies were increasingly constrained by international capital mobility, but national authorities could still influence the level of economic activity. The Keynesian ideal of fine-tuning was decaying but not dead!

From 1978 to 1998 European countries were desperately trying to organize a minimal stability of their internal exchange rates in order to mitigate the large and frequently unexpected variations of rates observed between the dollar, yen, and other extra-European currencies. The distant but still present origin of the euro was the European Monetary System (EMS), which was launched on December 1978 by a European Council held in Brussels (de Silguy 1998: 43–70). The underlying factor pushing towards the fixing of internal exchange rate was nothing other than the dramatic surge of short-term international capital movements, which tended to be a large multiple of normal external trade (Palan 1998). Therefore, purely financial variables and expectations governed exchange rate formation. It is not surprising that many crises took place within the EMS, the most severe in 1992 and then 1993. How could full public control be imposed when even the alliance of major central banks was unable to go against private speculative movements? But the implementation of the Maastricht Treaty has again put exchange rate stability at the core of national economic policies. In this third configuration, the majority of European countries, with the exception of Germany, had lost any autonomy in their monetary policy (Fig. 2.6C). This is precisely the origin of European Monetary Union: set irreversibly internal exchange rates and recover some degree of freedom for a common European monetary policy.

Now a totally new configuration is scheduled. The only continuity is about private capital mobility which continues to govern the evolution of exchange rates at the world level. In a sense, the completion of financial liberalization under the euro will have a major impact on the single market and bring an optimization of the rate of return all over Europe, once the risk of exchange rate variations have been totally removed. Building the credibility of the euro will probably be the first objective of the ECB. If this is understood as preserving the exchange rate between the euro and the dollar, then the Mundell–Flemming theorem implies that the autonomy of the European monetary policy will be severely restricted. Of course, one might think that keeping a very low inflation rate is an insurance against a weak euro, but conceptually the two objectives are distinct and imply different interventions. Despite low inflation, financial markets might prefer to transfer their assets to Wall Street, which would provide higher interest rates and long-term stability. For instance in 1998, the Japanese economy was experiencing a near deflation, but the interest rate was so low that short-term capital was flooding into US markets. Consequently, the yen slid against the dollar. Paradoxically, if this scenario turned out to be correct, EMU would extend to the European level the deadlock previously experienced at the national level (compare Fig. 2.6C and D).

Thus, some interesting lessons are to be learnt from this historical retrospect. First, there is no perfect monetary regime which would last for ever. On the contrary, the very success of a given international/national regime feeds destabilizing forces that call for the emergence of another configuration. Second, the euro is to be understood as an attempt to alleviate the contradiction between monetary policy autonomy, full international capital mobility, and the preservation of the single market. Third, the ECB will face the following dilemma. Should it stick to the objective of price stability whatever the consequences for the euro/dollar exchange rate? Or will it be induced first to assess the euro as a strong currency, which would later benefit the fight against inflation? Or could international capital mobility be institutionally reduced, thus opening new perspectives to the ECB?

Three Options with Contrasting Outcomes

The present situation can be extrapolated in different directions, which in the long run may make a lot of difference to European integration. It is interesting to present them from the more likely to the quite unlikely (Fig. 2.7).

Most analysts agree that price stability will be the main objective of the first decisions of the ECB, because it is essential for financial markets and

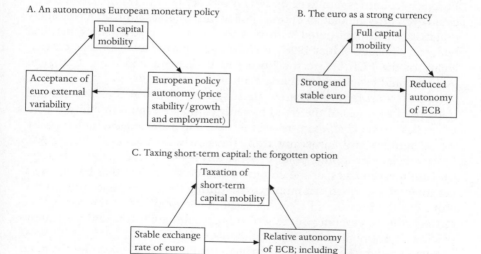

FIG. 2.7. The future of the European Central Bank and the euro: Three options and outcomes.

for those countries that used to enjoy a strong currency, such as Germany. Initially, it was assessed that this anti-inflationary objective would deliver, as a side effect, a smooth evolution of the euro with respect to the dollar. Nevertheless, a more careful theoretical and applied research now tends to conclude that in contrast, the volatility of the external rate of exchange will be increased. In the absence of any risk about internal exchange rates, with the same objectives of the central bank before and after the euro, monetary policy is likely to be less accommodating as soon as price uncertainty is dominant with respect to demand uncertainty (Cohen 1998). Thus, willingly or unwillingly, the ECB would converge towards nearly the same policy as the Federal Reserve System, not so much by ideological conversion to a more pragmatic view of the monetary policy (Aglietta and de Boissieu 1998), but because the ECB would take into account the continental size of the European economy after January 1999, or progressively learn to do so (Fig. 2.7A).

This first strategy has itself a pro-growth variant. Instead of looking exclusively at the inflation rate, the ECB could try to get the best trade-off between growth and stability. After all, a majority of European countries have complied with the 3 per cent criteria for public deficit in 1998, precisely because economic recovery has alleviated the pressures on public finance (along probably with some creative accounting). More generally, a pro-growth monetary policy could deliver Pareto-superior results (Fitoussi 1998). Again, the Mundell–Flemming model suggests that an adverse shock common to all European countries should be dealt by monetary policy (Wyplosz 1997). One could even imagine that an optimal policy mix emerges from an increasingly pragmatic ECB confronted with powerful Euro-11 co-ordinating national budgetary policies (Muet 1998). Political pressure in favour of the accountability of the ECB before the European Parliament and other European bodies would propitiate such a variant of the main scenario.

But, of course, an alternative strategy may focus on the strength and stability of the euro. If the trend towards complete capital mobility is considered as irreversible, then the will to maintain a stable euro/dollar parity would remove any autonomy from the newly created ECB (Fig. 2.7B). From a strictly economic point of view, this is not a very rational strategy, because it reproduces, at the continental level, the policy that has been so detrimental to growth and employment during the convergence toward the euro. But the pressure of some national public opinions or the perception of the actors intervening in the global financial markets make this strategy possible, if not highly desirable.

Furthermore, the notion of a strong currency is not self-evident. There are several possibilities. First, it could mean an overvalued euro with respect to the dollar and the yen: the deflationary pressure imported would be paid for by a loss of market share and a further de-industrialization (Munchau 1998).

Second, and more realistically, a strong currency allows a lot of freedom in the conduct of the monetary policy, directed towards typical domestic objectives: given the credibility built during past episodes, the central bank may have a strategic effect and be relatively immune from confidence crises when, for instance, a short-term poor macroeconomic index is released. The Bundesbank had this privilege and this explains why the reaction of financial markets differed for the same decision taken by the Banque de France. Despite all the precautions taken by the Amsterdam Treaty, it will not be easy to convert this credibility from the Deutschmark to the euro. Contemporary financial markets scrutinize any structural weakness and act accordingly. Public economic policies have to cope with this drastic requirement and it is not an easy task (Lordon 1997).

Third, a strong euro may mean that it becomes a reserve currency challenging the long-lasting dollar hegemony. This definition is in no way equivalent to the previous one since, for instance, the Swiss franc is clearly a strong currency without aspiring to be a reserve currency. Even the Deutschmark has not developed as a real challenge to the dollar. The share of Deutschmarks in total world official reserves has been nearly constant over the last two decades (14.9 per cent in 1980, 14.1 per cent in 1996), and the decline of the dollar has been very modest, from 68.6 to 62.7 per cent during the same period (Peet 1998: 23). In 1996, the reserves in ECUs represented only 1.7 per cent, whereas the rise of the yen has been relatively modest, from 4.4 to 7 per cent. Clearly, Europe could gain a lot from a strong euro, but the road is still long before being independent from the US dollar.

Fourth, if European countries could pay their debts in their own currency, then the euro would become strong. Basically, this is the privilege of the US economy, and of course, it would help to reduce the current interest charges on public debts if countries could repay with their own currency and still enjoy low interest rates. This implies that Europe would have a powerful financial centre, which would compete with Wall Street in attracting savings and mobile capital from all over the world. In this respect, the way the current Japanese major financial and creeping economic crisis will be solved will have a long-lasting impact on the evolution the euro and, more generally, financial intermediation at global level.

The depth of the Asian financial crises reminds the financial community itself that speculating may in some cases stabilize markets and be good for individuals who get rich—but quite dangerous for the systemic stability of the global financial system, when the game is played on highly sophisticated and abstract future indexes. This message was usually voiced by Keynesians (Minsky 1982) and critical analysts (Aglietta 1995) and the proposal of James Tobin to tax short-term capital was then received as unrealislize by most governments and, of course, financiers. It is therefore highly remarkable that one of the most visible speculators has written a book in order to denounce the danger of unleashed international financial speculation on the very stability of the whole system (Soros 1997). Thus, the probability of a third scenario has increased since Summer 1997: the implementation of a Tobin tax on short-term capital (or alternatively institutional barriers to speculative capital) would give a nice issue to the Mundell–Flemming impossibility theorem. A more or less stable exchange rate of the euro could be made compatible with a relative autonomy of the ECB monetary policy. In this case, the merits of the euro would be evident (Fig. 2.7C).

However binding might seem the monetary clauses of the Amsterdam Treaty, a lot of options are open. The road actually taken will depend on the circumstances. Will the European boom be as durable as the American one? Will the Japanese major financial and creeping economic crisis be solved in 1999? Will speculation on Wall Street end in a soft or a hard landing? How quickly will a political arena be constructed around the ECB? The same wealth of futures can be contemplated for the other aspects of the European Union.

A Single Treaty: A Multiplicity of Conflicting Political Programmes

The challenge of international treaties is to try to be as precise as possible but simultaneously to compromise over important issues, where underlying representations and national interests may differ significantly. A careful reading of the European treaties brings considerable optimism about the flexibility which can be managed through a text, so difficult to agree on. The diversity among the eleven members of EMU is so great, that it would be surprising not to observe quite soon conflicts of interpretation and the forging of a jurisprudence in order to live with the Amsterdam Treaty, without negotiating a new charter. But of course, the extension to new members may call for such a drastic revision of the institutions if the EU. Some clear tensions may already be perceived under various headings.

The Links between Monetary, Budgetary, and Structural Policies

Many observers have pointed out a basic ambiguity in the launching of the euro. After all, this was a surprise nobody would had expected in early 1997. But the agreement for an independent European monetary authority, along with disciplinary rules for national budgetary policies, is located at the crossing of two strategies and visions of the world

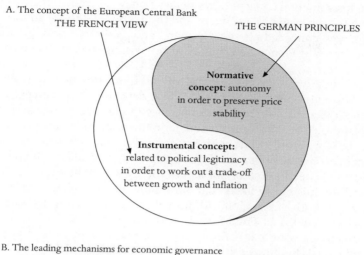

A. The concept of the European Central Bank

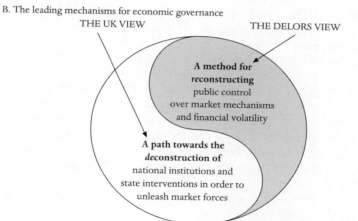

B. The leading mechanisms for economic governance

FIG. 2.8. The Amsterdam Treaty: conflicting outcomes of its implied dynamics.

For the French, it is a step to build a political union which would constitute the European Union as a clear economic actor, with a full capacity to govern macro-economic adjustments. For the Germans, the objective is to remove monetary management from any political pressure and to induce the Europeans to under-take structural reforms, i.e. to substitute many bold microeconomic actions to a macroeconomic regulation, without any relevance, in the absence of any asymmetric and exceptional shock.   (Bourlanges 1998: 143)

This opposition is permeating all aspects of ECB management (Fig. 2.8A). Traditionally, French governments, whatever their colour and orientation, have an instrumental concept of monetary policy. Of course, the Banque de France has been made independent and the ECB is still more autonomous, but this was conceded to the Germans and other partners in order to convince them of French determination concerning the entire euro project. The final objective is to work out a better trade-off between growth and inflation, under the strong impulse of intergovernmental co-ordination. The German vision is quite opposed. The independence of the central bank is an integral part of a normative concept of a good economic system. No discretion should be left to government for influencing monetary policy, which should be submitted to transparent and firm rules. Furthermore, each domain of economic policy should be independent, at odds with French voluntarism on a need for co-ordination of the ECB and the Euro-11 Council.

Therefore, it is highly likely that during the initial implementation phase of the euro, both sides of the Rhine will have conflicting feelings about the policies decided in Frankfurt. But of course this is now no longer a German–French issue but a European one, which makes the matter even more difficult. The Northern countries tend to follow German principles, because they have a long experience of adjusting their policies in accordance with the decisions of the Bundesbank. But the Southern countries may be receptive to the French position according to which the euro should be submitted to a common political will. The irony is that after all, Europeans might be interested in adopting a different concept of monetary policy: the US one (Thygesen 1992). There, legitimacy is reached via the publicity of the deliberations of the Fed and a check and balance between the federal government, Congress, and the central bank. A rough comparison suggests that this accountability benefits the overall performance of the American economy, probably because the objectives are set in conformity with a large variety of interests.

The issue of the ideal governance mode under the euro is widely controversial (Fig. 2.8B). For the British, the Single Market (and if they eventually join it, the EMU), is conceived as a device to destroy or considerably erode all the institutional arrangements which have been so detrimental to British and European performance during the 1970s and 1980s. Therefore, the basic aim would be to create a free-trade zone with competitive products, labour, and credit markets. The idea that Brussels could impose new and complex rules of the game or constraints appears as a heresy going against the victory of 'market' against 'bureaucracy'. According to this position, political integration is not required; it would be even be dangerous since it could recreate, at the continental level, the regulations that have been finally terminated or eroded in the UK, a move which is assumed to have reversed its long-run decline.

For Jacques Delors, the former President of the EC, along with a majority of social democrats, the agenda is strictly the opposite. The internationalization of economic activity has eroded the capacity of control and monitoring by national public authorities. But a new form of control can be reinstituted at the now relevant level (i.e. the European). Also, for social democrats free markets are neither efficient nor conform with minimum social justice. They therefore have to be monitored by adequate regulations—which should be decided at the European level if strong externalities spill over across national borders, but at the national or regional level, if it is not the case. The subsidiarity principle intends to give a clear criterion for the agenda and non-agenda of Brussels, at odds with the *laissez-faire* vision, which postulates that economic performance will be better the more that the system is decentralized.

This ambiguity is no less challenging than opposition about the statutes of the central bank. For the British, the European construction is a means for implementing free trade on the continent, ultimately to be part of the larger world movement in favour of deregulation, in alliance with North America. For social democrats, by contrast, European integration means well-organized competition and the constitution of a strong regional zone, which could become increasingly independent from the dollar, American technology, and even culture. When the French and British prime ministers meet the German chancellor, the potential sources of misunderstanding are numerous, but conversely diverse and a priori paradoxical compromises can be struck, inspired by quite opposed long-term objectives. For instance, an alliance of the British and Germans on the issue of structural policies may coexist with an alliance between French and Germans about EMU. Until now, this kind of ambiguity has been fairly fruitful for European integration, but there is no guarantee that this happy outcome will continue with the euro (Bourlanges 1998).

Deepening of European Integration Versus Admission of New Members

There are many other sources for potential conflict, both within the Amsterdam Treaty itself and still more concerning its compatibility with the extension of memberships from fifteen to twenty-five countries. Again, visions, objectives, interests, and strategies clash in at least two groups (Fig. 2.9).

Is the EU a matter of economic efficiency or politics? This ambiguity has long been at the core of European integration, and this paradox has already been pointed out in in this chapter. Nevertheless, the euro further highlights this issue. Economic history suggests that no money can exist without clear political backing. But two contrasting conclusions can be derived from this. The defenders of national sovereignty argue, quite rightly, that the current

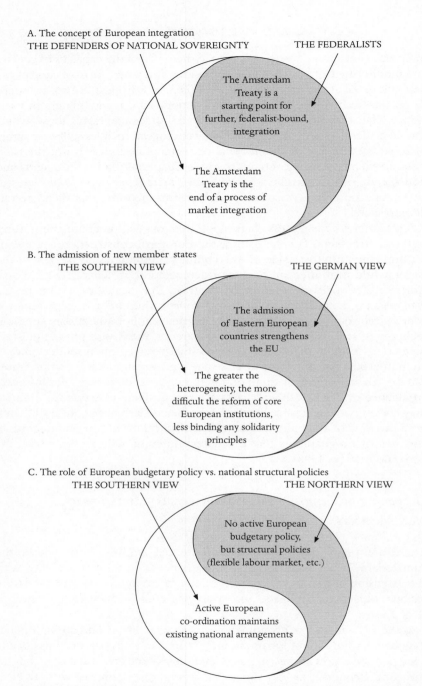

A. The concept of European integration
THE DEFENDERS OF NATIONAL SOVEREIGNTY   THE FEDERALISTS

The Amsterdam
Treaty is a
starting point for
further, federalist-bound,
integration

The Amsterdam
Treaty is the
end of a process of
market integration

B. The admission of new member states
THE SOUTHERN VIEW   THE GERMAN VIEW

The admission
of Eastern European
countries strengthens
the EU

The greater the
heterogeneity, the more
difficult the reform of core
European institutions,
less binding any solidarity
principles

C. The role of European budgetary policy vs. national structural policies
THE SOUTHERN VIEW   THE NORTHERN VIEW

No active European
budgetary policy,
but structural policies
(flexible labour market, etc.)

Active European
co-ordination maintains
existing national arrangements

FIG. 2.9. The Amsterdam Treaty: additional potential conflicts. The federalist, German, and Northern perspectives.

status of the euro is not viable because no supranational state governs it, and that conversely a national state without its own currency is a contradiction in terms. Federalists do not disagree with the first statement, but they think that the political gap has to be overcome precisely by creating a European state, which should be the ultimate warrant of the viability of the euro (Fig. 2.9A). There is, of course, still another position, already mentioned, which insists on the radical novelty of EMU and the implicit political construction of the Amsterdam Treaty—which is neither an embryo for a European national state, nor a step towards a federalist state (Théret 1997; Dehove 1997). In this context, the treaty could well represent the zenith of European integration, since it will be quite difficult to go further and create a European polity.

Should the EU first reform its institutions and then admit new members or the other way around? This is intrinsically a rather difficult question which challenges the very significance of European integration. But again, two positions are present and difficult to reconcile (Fig. 2.9B). On the one hand, the Germans consider that the inclusion of former European 'socialist' countries is a high priority both for geopolitical reasons and the traditional role played by Germany with respect to Poland, Hungary, and other Central European countries. If the political project is clear enough, the economic aspect is more difficult to deal with, given the considerable heterogeneity of economic institutions and specialization of many of these countries, and their difficulty to comply with present European norms and requirements. Furthermore, the rebuttal by major Western economies to extend their contribution to the European budget makes quite problematic the survival of the present interventions for agriculture and regional structural funds. The dilemma between polity and economy is especially acute. On the other hand, Southern European countries fear being marginalized by the opening to the East. First, typical mass production may go to Poland or Hungary instead of Portugal and Spain. Second, the structural funds available for them would be drastically reduced. Third, the centre of gravity of Europe would shift towards the East, with many economic and political consequences. Still other governments, not directly concerned, may think that the greater the heterogeneity of economic and political institutions across members, the more unlikely is the success of any reform of the core European procedures, given the unanimity principle which is applied in the vast majority of decisions. A logical analysis suggests that the process of integration should be differentiated by competence and/or participant members (CEPR 1995). But this 'Europe à la carte' challenges the ideal of a single market and common currency, and would probably make inextricable a decision process already very slow and cumbersome.

Are structural policies a substitute for or a complement to the coordination of budgetary policies? Again, a North–South dividing line appears

(Fig. 2.9C). Northern countries (Germany has already been mentioned) consider that no active European budgetary co-ordination is necessary. The viability of the euro depends on active structural policies on labour market institutions, financing the welfare state, tax system, education and training systems, public sector management, and so on. EMU would define the only macroeconomic mechanism at work in Europe, all other topics being decentralized to the more micro level. In the language of disequilibrium theory, European unemployment would mainly be classical (i.e. caused by an insufficient supply linked to a too low profitability). Southern countries (including France) have a different vision. Most of the difficult adjustment processes during the 1990s can be attributed, not so much to an intrinsic rigidity of European institutions, but to the strains brought by restrictive macroeconomic policies. Thus, employment would largely be Keynesian (i.e. caused by insufficient demand), itself generated by the monetary policy of high real interest rates and budgetary austerity. Co-ordinating national economic policies would make much easier the adjustment to world trends in competitiveness and innovation. Again, a synthetic position has been proposed by a group of economists: why not reduce the social and fiscal taxes levied on low skilled labour in order to act both on the supply and demand side (Drèze *et al.* 1994)? Such a policy seems to have been implemented in various European countries, with a different mix of supply and demand components.

Alas, such a compromise is not always available for other topics and issues. The ambiguity of the Amsterdam Treaty is both a trump and a hindrance to the further deepening of the political institutions which is required for long-term viability of the euro. Therefore, contrary to a common belief, the Amsterdam Treaty is not the end of European history.

The Euro: the Starting Point for Unintended Structural Adjustments

The surprisingly tranquil and smooth transition from the second to the third stage of EMU has given a false feeling of security (only shaltered by the unexpected decline of the dollar during the first half of 1999). Can this success be extrapolated to actual implementation and the first steps and difficulties experienced then? Is there any firm prediction of the final outcome of the euro, or do experts disagree strongly? For some, Europe will end as a variant of *laissez-faire* economy, after a *de facto* victory of the British vision, particularly in terms of industrial relations. The euro could contribute significantly to the evolution towards this scenario, because it strengthens competition among institutional regimes, tax systems, and of course, firms and individuals. For others, Europe is bound to be politically integrated into a federal state, just to fulfil the requisites for a viable common currency. Opponents may comment ironically on this modern Hegelian vision (the EMU is rational therefore it will exist!), but the Europeanists reply quite rightly that since its beginning the European project has been made by the very same strategy, that the euro pushes at the extreme.

Political debates and academic controversies are built on dual oppositions, as if black and white were the only colours available—or more seriously as if the principle of 'third excluded' was true. If the pro-euro group is wrong, then the anti-euro one is right, and conversely. The central message of this chapter is that this position is erroneous and misleading and no more than a caricature of a highly complex process. Nevertheless, the conventional debate has the merit of defining a clear starting point for the more convincing scenarios.

A European Dream: Keynesianism at the Continental Level

For the Europeanists, EMU is an incentive to improve co-ordination among economic agents and nations; ultimately it is the first step towards a fully integrated Europe. Basically, all economic units and political bodies will be constrained to take into account the new structural conditions created by EMU and to innovate in order to build the other economic and political institutions which are required for its long-term viability. Therefore, whatever the initial ideological orientations of its advisory council is, the European Central Bank will finally adopt a Federal Reserve System style: clear political accountability and search for an optimal mix between price stability and growth. Similarly, national governments will perceive the externalities associated with domestic budget management and implement procedures to optimize the global policy mix between monetary and budgetary tools.

Given the optimistic expectations generated by this smooth handling of economic policy, firms experience strong incentives to innovate in terms of both products and processes (Boyer and Didier 1998): thus the Single Market would finally deliver the long-term benefits which have been expected since 1985. Social partners themselves learn that wage co-ordination is better than a myopic strategy and total decentralization. Therefore, either each national bargaining process takes into account the wage evolution set by the German social partners, who themselves respond to the signals of the ECB, or explicit European wage negotiations take place at the sectoral level or within multinationals. In both cases, job creation is preserved and is not directly affected by ECB policy. Thus, the final quasi-neutrality of money would not be the outcome of a 'state of nature' but the result of a highly sophisticated institutional architecture of checks and balances between various economic and political actors (business, unions, national governments, European Central Bank, European Parliament, European Commission).

In a sense, this is a rejuvenation of Keynesianism at the European level, which, incidentally, would preserve most national legacies in institutional frameworks. A still more optimistic vision would conclude that, in the long run, this scenario envisages a fully fledged federalism. A minimal taxation and public spending policy should exist at the continental level, in order to optimize the policy mix and organize cross-border fiscal solidarity. This would enhance the political legitimacy of the entire European project, the common currency being a part of a broader coherent configuration.

A European Nightmare: Free Markets and the Balkanization of Societies

For the anti-euro group, EMU is a disintegrating device of post-war national institutions and the inception of a Europe governed by free-market forces and ideologies, with absolute loss of collective control over economic activity and the end of the pursuit of social justice. These arguments are the exact opposite of to those above. European monetary policy is condemned to be more monetarist than the Bundesbank, because the clauses of the Amsterdam Treaty are binding and the financial community expects this. The only discussion concerns the intermediate objectives followed by the ECB: an index of aggregate monetary supply or direct European inflation rate (Aglietta and de Boissieu 1998). But well before January 1999, the debate was set: the ECB will adopt the same intermediate objective as the Bundesbank (i.e. a money supply target), even if it is not necessarily the most efficient (The Economist 1998b). Growth and unemployment indexes are not even mentioned under the phrase 'the monetary policy is not responsible for the European unemployment problem, nor should the central bank take into account job creation as an objective'.

On the domestic side, national governments and parliaments will be possessive of their prerogatives in taxation and public spending, the more so since budgetary procedures are somewhat idiosyncratic. Thus, the free-riding of each national authority is quite rational, only limited by the 3 per cent EDP clause. When a recession occurs, no manoeuvre will be left to fight unemployment. Then, the tax levied on excessive public deficit will be unpopular in the domestic political arena. Some national governments may even challenge the orientations of the ECB, if they perceive, rightly or wrongly, that its restrictive or inadequate policy has exacerbated domestic problems, nearly impossible to solve within the constraints of the Amsterdam Treaty. In this gloomy macroeconomic context, the Single Market triggers more defensive competition than creative innovation: firms de-localize their activities from one country to another, in a permanent search for a more permissive institutional regime. High wage regions lose jobs, while firms put strong pressure on regional/national governments to obtain the maximum subsidy for job creation and the minimal taxation of profit and capital gains. Consequently, the tax base of the most welfare-oriented countries is eroded, and advanced labour legislation is challenged by new industrializing regions and tends to penalize low skilled workers. Industrial relations evolve towards a complete Balkanization of wage bargaining: unions are unable to organize across borders even within the same sector or the same multinational, and domestic firms exploit their bargaining power in the context of a large pool of unemployed workers, including those who are medium or highly skilled.

Some analysts have forecast a *de facto* convergence of most national industrial relations systems towards a British configuration (Crouch 1994). This system is far from ideal since it allows the coexistence of a large pool of unemployed people, along with wage increases due to the scarcity of highly skilled workers. Further, rising wage inequality does not necessarily solve the unemployment issue. The fact that welfare benefits are closely linked to a limited regional/domestic space or are company-specific, hinders labour mobility—contrary to what would be expected, given the considerable heterogeneity of national unemployment rates. Clearly, due to the inability to forge new co-ordination mechanisms or European institutions, a market logic would govern most economic adjustments and even influence the formation of economic policy, by reducing state intervention and promoting a privatization of most welfare components and collective services. One could even imagine competitive wage reductions or, alternatively, productivity wars (Flassbeck 1998), which would give a typical Hobbesian flavour to this scenario. But of course, it can be challenged by proving that such defensive strategies are less likely with the euro than without (Artus 1998). The victory of the free market and supply-side economics would mean an Americanization of continental Europe, a gloomy scenario for the anti-euro group, but probably a desirable one for highly skilled professionals and European multinationals.

These two scenarios are built on the analysis of the same European treaty, a fact which by itself implies that no evident determinism is at work and that a much more complex analytical framework has to be worked out.

European Integration, Transformed Political Arena, and Changing Institutional Forms

The above developments suggest a three-level analysis, which in turn may generate a spectrum of scenarios (Boyer 1999). Basically, the initial and structural change comes from EMU (i.e. a new European innovation which, by definition, will alter the way national *régulation* modes operate in a very significant way). But the domestic political arena is itself transformed: the monetary policy which used to be decided at national level, with more or less democratic controls, has irreversibly shifted to the ECB. Simultaneously, with the other clauses of the Amsterdam's Treaty, decisions which were part of national sovereignty (e.g. the control of migration and borders) now become an issue only dealt with at the European level. Therefore, the domestic political arena is shrunk by two mechanisms. On the one hand, national legislation becomes the locus of implementation of European rules and directives, which restrict the autonomy of national interest groups. Some of them may protest and the conflict might be more acute than those already observed for fishing or migrating birds issues! On the other hand, the common monetary policy and the enforcement of a competition policy at the European level, will necessarily alter the nature of national institutionalized compromises and still more the whole architecture of institutional forms, at least for many countries. The economic strains experienced by the domestic agents will be converted into political demands, mainly addressed to national governments and in some cases European authorities.

Thus, this three-level interdependency sets into motion a rich dynamic. It is hard to make any forecast, since the problem is similar to the famous one found in astronomy, when three planets interact and may evolve according to a whole spectrum of complex dynamics, from a smooth trajectory to a chaotic evolution, as the mathematical theory of chaos shows. Since strategic behaviour is common in political economy and innovations can always take place—contrary to astronomy where such a phenomenon cannot exist—the final dynamics of the euro will be still more complex than previously analysed. This three-level analysis allows us to propose a taxonomy for various scenarios, including the Europeanists' dream and the Hobbesian nightmare.

Both Keynesians and federalists think that European co-ordination or institution-building should be proposed in order to minimize the transformations to be made in national *régulation* modes, even if they differ about the transfer of political sovereignty to European bodies. For Keynesians, modest co-ordination procedures could solve the issue of national heterogeneity as well as the externalities associated to the public budget. This is not easy to implement: how to comply with the recommendations from the Euro-11 Council given the specific timing and procedures of each national budget (Dehove 1998)? For the federalists, the subsidiarity principle should be used to minimize the responsibilities transferred to Brussels, in theory preserving the maximum autonomy of local political authorities. This scenario minimizes change at national level, but maximizes innovations at the European level.

The *laissez-faire* scenario assumes, in contrast, that European institutional construction has come to an end with the Amsterdam Treaty. Therefore, it is up to national institutions, firms' strategies, and individual behaviour to adapt to the new era. But the social costs associated with such a restructuring will strain national solidarity, transferring a fraction of the cost to the welfare state system. The domestic political agenda cannot stay unchanged—and it would be surprising if such a Hobbesian trajectory did not produce new political demands and accordingly social and economic regulations.

Thus, both scenarios adopt quite extreme hypotheses, do not take into account the positive and negative feedbacks between polity and economy, and drastically simplify a complex dynamics to two 'attractors' (i.e. a necessary convergence towards a single configuration, of course different). But jointly, they express most of the forces and dynamics which would be present in almost any scenario. How to elaborate richer and more diverse scenarios?

Some Strategic Parameters Governing the Future of EMU

The European Central Bank has decided its intermediate objective (i.e. a monetary aggregate target), but what will really be its final objective? The Mundell–Flemming model again helps to frame some strategies (Fig. 2.10).

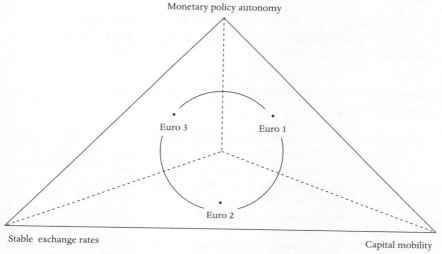

FIG. 2.10. Three strategies for the future of European Monetary Union.

- The most likely strategy seems to be Euro 1, which accepts full international capital mobility but focuses its action towards purely or mainly internal objectives, whatever the consequences for the variability of the exchange rate. Some subvariants may alter the weight given respectively to price stability, growth, and in some extreme cases a modest concern for euro/dollar parity. Actually, the general statement about the desirability of the euro as a strong currency calls for a second scenario.
- Strategy Euro 2 aims at stabilizing the exchange rate or more generally building the euro as a competitor of the dollar for world financial intermediation. Given the extreme mobility of financial capital, this would mean that the ECB would neutralize its governance role in terms of domestic monetary and credit policy. No doubt most European actors, except modern rentiers and financiers, would object to such a strategy and would try to build active lobbies in Frankfurt in order to influence the decisions of the ECB.
- For completeness sake, a third option is opened and may be relevant in some rather extreme configurations. This strategy, Euro 3, could take place after a major international financial crisis, which would have shown how unstable might be a world financial system governed by short-term speculation. If, for instance, the three members of the triad agreed to create a new international system with fixed but adjustable exchange rates, then each central bank, and of course the ECB, could obtain both a drastic reduction in exchange rate uncertainty and substantial control over domestic monetary policy. This would benefit the legitimacy of the euro, which would have been an intermediate step in the reconstruction of the new financial system.

No determinism can be invoked, since in a different world, European and national configurations, each of these strategies has a chance of being implemented and accepted.

Innovations in European Institutions in Response to Emerging Problems

European institutions and procedures will have to evolve in order to cope with the likely indirect fallout of the euro, as well as emerging political problems. Relations between the 'ins' and the 'outs' might prove problematic. For instance, small- or medium-size countries at the margin of the EU may have an interest in competitive devaluation and not respect EMS rules which the ECB would like to impose on them. It has to be remembered that, after all, Italy, Spain, and the UK benefited from the devaluation of their currencies in 1992–3 following the breakdown of the EMS. Devaluation, especially in the context of slow and low nominal wage indexing, may have a short- to medium-term positive impact on growth and employment. Under some circumstances a run on the euro could well take place.

Alternatively, the very success of the euro may create positive externalities: lower interest rates, less uncertainty about the costs of selling to European markets, and greater national influence on new institution-building at the European level. Therefore, one could observe a run towards the euro, as outsiders observe that members are better off, and that multinationals prefer to open new plants and branches within the euro zone. Remember the warning by Toyota to the British government if did not join the euro, and conversely the opening of a new Toyota plant in France, despite far more constraining labour laws. The euro will have definite consequences for European geography, and probably give rise to a new division of labour among member states (Krugman 1992).

Combining the orientations of common monetary policy with induced innovations concerning other economic and political European institutions delivers many scenarios, more or less coherent and promising (in theory, no less than $3 \times 6 = 18$ configurations). But the story is not complete since it does not take into account the political and economic process of adjustment within each member state: some societies are able (or know how) to cope with the euro, others do not.

Conclusion: A Largely Open Future—Many Surprises May Occur

Many conflicting visions can be mobilized to capture some of the consequences of the euro. The Europeanists would argue that the founding fathers always intentionally created structural disequilibria in order to obtain the required common institutions. Historians would insist on the long-term trends governing contemporary Europe, whereas some social scientists would borrow from technological innovation analysis the concept of path dependence. Still others, inspired by Schumpeter and Popper, would insist on the radical unpredictability of this unprecedented innovation. The vast majority of analyses quite rightly use already existing theoretical tools to forecast the consequences of the euro. Each theory teaches about one aspect or another of this process. But unfortunately, many authors, by specialization, tend to take the detail for the whole picture, since they imagine that such a multidimensional innovation can be captured by formalizing the one or two features with which their pet theory can deal. By contrast, this chapter has described the spill-over from one aspect of the euro to another, with a clear concern for the structural compatibility of the euro with existing national political and economic institutions. The theoretical interpretation borrows both from the recent advances of *régulation* theory (Boyer and Saillard 1995) in terms of hierarchy among institutional firms and from comparative institutional analysis (Aoki 1996), which stresses the complementarity of economic institutions.

The rational expectations school has popularized the idea that economic agents can anticipate accurately the consequences of any change in economic policy. Otherwise, the economic system is assumed to be stationary and thus all economic agents arrive at perfect knowledge of its functioning and become as learned in economics as theoreticians are. When this framework is applied to EMU, the issue is only about the time required by individual agents to compute or learn the rational response to this new environment. These models describe macroeconomic adjustments over several periods, but they are not really dynamic in the sense of the endogenous transformations of a system which take place under the flow of permanent innovations. In fact, nobody knows if there is a viable configuration for the implementation of the Amsterdam Treaty. Therefore, this chapter has proposed a dynamic approach, which takes fully into account the disequilibria and conflicts that are generated by EMU. History matters and is more than the arrow of time taken into account by econometric models estimated over previous time series.

For a substantial majority of the economics profession, at least until the last decade, the market has been considered as the canonical and almost unique form of adjustment mechanism. They are therefore only able to describe the interactions that occur within a fully decentralized economy. By definition, almost any other organization, especially public bodies, brings inefficiency into the system. However, the conditions under which markets can deliver Pareto-optimality have been shown to be very restrictive (Boyer 1996). However, firms, associations, communities, and even states may solve co-ordination problems and provide benefits that the market is unable to perform or deliver (Hollingsworth and Boyer 1997). Consequently, this chapter takes full account of the fact that the euro will not operate in a pure market economy but within nationally embedded capitalisms: the outcomes are likely to be at odds with those forecast by neo-classical models. But, of course, this makes the whole analysis difficult and some cases cumbersome by comparison with the elegance and the limited relevance of most theoretical texts about the euro.

Business Cycle Synchronization does not mean Structural Convergence

Since May 1998, almost all observers have to take the euro seriously, even if most were surprised by the fact that no less than eleven countries could comply with the convergence criteria. Looking carefully at national business cycles has nevertheless highlighted some basic questions (Peet 1998). One could always exert pressure on a spring so that it is reduced to a small size, but as soon as the pressure ceases, expands dramatically! *Mutatis mutandis*, the same story could be told about the convergence of the eleven members of EMU. Of course, all governments wanted to be part of the first wave and to avoid the political cost of inability to comply. Therefore, these governments have taken short-term decisions and sometimes structural reforms in order to be ready.

But what will happen next? Will inflation rates be more heterogeneous than in 1997 and early 1998? Will not the underlying diversity in *régulation* modes imply a permanent lack of synchronization of national business cycles? Synchronized or not, the eleven members do not enjoy the same social, political, and economic *régulation*. Therefore, the same monetary policy (or alternatively competition enforcement or labour law) will not have the same impact. From a purely technical point of view, the channels of monetary policy differ quite significantly across Europe. For instance, in the UK, an increase in interest rates has a much more important impact on real economic activity, due to the structure and the organization of the mortgage financial markets, whereas a similar influence is not present in Germany or France (Dornbusch, Favero, and Giavazzi 1998). This heterogeneity could persist over several decades and pose acute political problems.

This structural and institutional analysis brings a series of interesting results concerning some paradoxes of European integration. It may explain why implementation of the euro is so frequently associated with a plea for labour market flexibility. Furthermore, it brings some complexity into the debate. Last but not least, this chapter provides some hints about what should be at the top of the agenda for the next European negotiations, in order to adapt institutions and procedures.

The Seven Paradoxes Revisited

Conventional neo-classical theory is unable to explain some basic facts about European integration. Now, a better integration of political and economic factors allows some interpretation of the paradoxes that emerge when a monocausal analysis is applied to EMU.

1. Why do most governments and the European Commission present EMU as a purely economic project aiming at transaction cost reduction and exchange rate uncertainty removal? Mainly because European integration has been realized by intergovernmentalism and not by a clear agreement on the constitution of a supranational state. Also, structural reforms, which would have been opposed in the domestic political arena, have been presented as constraints imposed by EMU. This strategy cannot last for ever.

2. Why did the Werner plan fail in the 1970s, whereas EMU was actually launched at the end of the 1990s, in the context of free-market ideologies and a huge distrust of the ability of governments to have any positive influence on macroeconomic activity? Such a daring 'constructivism' is at odds with contemporary beliefs. It is precisely because the full deregulation of finance had so severely restricted the autonomy of European nation states,

that this proposal became timely. Still more, the apparent neutrality of monetary management makes more necessary a complete reform of post-war economic institutions. For some governments it is a method for making free-market economics more acceptable to a reluctant public opinion.

3. Why did European officials present such a bright picture of the consequences of EMU? In the absence of a European polity, this was the only method to build support and prevent any political conflict. If the welfare of any economy and individuals is increased, it would not be difficult to work out political compromises in order to share the benefits of EMU! Furthermore, a degree of functionalism has always been present in the European integration process and this kind of optimism has often been helpful and crucial.

4. Why are social and economic elites in favour of EMU, while modest social groups are generally against? Even when intensive pro-European propaganda has been pursued by governments, most citizens perceive that EMU will have some costs for lower social groups. Why? First, the last two decades have seen an erosion of solidarity within most European societies. Second, the absence of a European welfare state is clearly perceived. This asymmetry in European construction provides a premium to nationalist and/or nostalgic movements which defend previous forms of solidarity, via domestic welfare systems.

5. Why is Southern Europe so enthusiastic about the euro, despite the considerable adaptation costs, whereas Northern Europe is somewhat reluctant, even though its basic institutions are almost in tune with EMU? For the first group, monetary integration means economic modernization and political democratization. Polity comes first, economy second. For the second group, these achievements have been obtained for a long time. Thus, EMU is basically considered as a domestic issue, around which political oppositions are redeployed.

6. Will not the voluntarism deployed in the implementation of EMU have adverse political effects such as splitting the European countries between 'ins' and 'outs'? Within each domestic society, will not the euro exacerbate political and social divisions, giving again a premium to nationalistic ideologies? The benign neglect of the political foundations of EMU certainly jeopardizes the economic viability of European integration. Pure economic forces could well disintegrate European social space, in the absence of a clear principle of solidarity, brought by intergovernmental political agreement.

7. Conventional wisdom teaches that politicians should govern and markets should allocate scarce resources. Events during the last decade suggest the opposite division of labour: the financial community assesses each day the relevance and sustainability of governments' projects, and conversely, governments are proud of their rational and sound management of economic resources. Basically, modern rentiers (pension funds, large

institutional investors, mutual funds) exert their hegemony by promoting financial stability and high rates of returns on invested capital, and they discipline accordingly industrial firms as well as governments. In many countries, wage-earners seem to be out of the political game, even if they represent a majority of the population.

The merit of an institutional and structural analysis is to give some general interpretation of such diverse facts, starting from the same premises. Of course, the explanations are far from complete, but there is necessary trade-off between the precision of a theory and the extension of its explanatory power.

Another conclusion of this chapter is to challenge the frequent and superficial opposition between pro- and anti-euro. For the former, all economic and political actors will learn to take into account the functional constraints inherent in EMU and will decide collectively to design and implement a completely coherent system. For the latter, EMU is no less than a free-market ideology in disguise, obtaining horrific results in terms of growth, employment, inequalities, and even citizens' rights. Both visions oversimplify a complex interaction process between forging a new European political arena, the transformation of national institutions, and the feedback of both these into the national political arena.

These interactions are so rich that a pure combinatory approach delivers more than hundred more or less coherent scenarios, unequally appealing and sustainable in the long run—not to mention the induced radical innovation in domestic and European institutions which will quite likely take place in response to strong political conflicts, contradictions between economic and political rationales, and possibly severe structural crises.

Preparing the Next Reform of European Institutions

A final conclusion is that the current configuration is not necessarily stable, and therefore every one needs to think seriously about the next phase of European negotiations. There are at least nine analytically distinct but actually closely interrelated issues with respect to the final architecture of Europe.

1. Since the European Central Bank will never be fully legitimized and credible without clear accountability, it is essential to consider the embeddedness of European monetary policy in national and European political arenas.

2. The excessive deficit procedure is not a real co-ordinating procedure among national budgetary policies. It is therefore essential that a better policy-mix should be aimed at, by creating more or less challenging co-ordinating procedures, not to speak of a minimal fiscal federalism.

3. European institutions and decision-taking procedures have become obsolete and inefficient. They cannot be reformed and rejuvenated without a clear recognition of the political project implicit in EMU and accordingly the development of a fully fledged political arena.

4. It would be daring to assume that the national institutional architecture inherited from the Golden Age could persist unchanged into the 21st century. EMU makes more urgent, reforms which should be undertaken under the pressures of the production paradigm shift and the new configuration of the international division of labour. But this does not mean an inevitable return to a mythical state of pure and perfect competition. A spectrum of alternatives already exists, and new ones will created under the pressures created by the euro.

5. The admission of new member states should be carefully assessed and designed. On the one hand, it is an opportunity to redesign completely obsolete European institutions, but on the other, it brings back such an heterogeneity that any common ambitious policy will be difficult to achieve in one or two decades (i.e. the time required to forge a minimal compatibility with the core of European integration).

6. The euro as a world currency may create as many problems for the international system that it solves at the continental level. The American, Japanese, and European monetary policies cannot try to be autonomous simultaneously, without creating major structural instability.

7. The Asian financial crises show that a little speculation is good for financial market stability, but too much may destroy them and provoke major recession. The fate of the Japanese major financial and creeping economic crisis will strongly interfere with the final status of the euro and the willingness of the EU to accept complete financial mobility.

8. European authorities should be ready to make proposals in order to redesign a complete international system in which public authorities will monitor the rules of the game, for finance, trade, foreign investment, intellectual property rights, and innovation.

9. In order to foster a lively political debate across Europe, but also in order to cope with contemporary sources of competitiveness, the subsidiarity principle should really be put to work to prevent an ultra-nationalist backlash, always possible as soon as the success of integration falters. Paradoxically, subsidiarity might well be one solution to the long-term viability of the euro.

3

The Political Economy of European Union Financial Integration: The Battle of the Systems

JONATHAN STORY

The subtitle 'battle of the systems' refers to competition in market and political arenas between national financial institutions which are embedded in very different national contexts. This chapter presents, in schematic form, key elements of national financial systems from France, Germany, and the UK/USA. I argue that the German and French financial systems are key components in national embedded mercantilisms: their different institutional configurations have evolved with a purpose of fostering national, social cohesion, while reducing national vulnerability to world politics and markets through running trade surpluses and accumulating corporate and central bank reserves. In particular, a central feature of their financial systems has been to protect national corporate property as far as possible from bankruptcies and from foreign takeover. The UK/USA, by contrast, have pursued internationalist policies, predicated on flexible labour markets, open markets for products and corporate assets, and liberal trade policies where, as John Stuart Mill argued, the objective of international trade is imports, not exports, as countries trade because they are different. In the first, corporate financing derives from retained earnings and bank borrowing, supplemented by share issues with restricted circulation; in the second, corporate financing is notoriously more dependent on share issues and on secondary market trades. The paradox of European Monetary Union (EMU) is that France and Germany, two countries with embedded mercantilisms, are the principal protagonists of a measure that can only accelerate the victory of shareholder capitalism on the European continent.

Different Types of Financial System

How a financial system has come to be designed influences the character of the capital allocation process, national economic performance, and international economic and financial relationships. This is done through the process of control over corporations and organizations. In Europe, and besides the now moribund Soviet mono-bank, there are three alternative financial–industrial control structures, which have been on offer as models for imitation this century: the state-led financial system, found in France; the German bank-based system; and the Anglo-American shareholder system.

All financial systems are active intermediaries between political and social structures and relationships, and corporations or organizations operating in some form of market arrangement. In the four types of financial regime, the role of public officials range from *laissez-faire* to active participation in a political market for resources of all types. At one extreme, public officials enjoy autonomy, set the macroeconomic policy, competition policy, and international trade parameters under which enterprises operate, and essentially all other industrial outcomes are left to markets. These outcomes are considered legitimate precisely because impersonal forces are at work. Quite simply, the argument runs, corporate restructuring is called for because the consumers decree it, and the shareholders have heeded their cry. At the other extreme, public officials become fully fledged participants in the market process. Their involvement on behalf of 'the government' may include full or partial ownership of corporations, public stakes in financial institutions with major influence on investment or lending decisions, influence on credit allocation through the process of bank regulation and supervision, or some combination of these channels. The nature of the corporate control structure and bank–industry linkages may have a significant bearing on the willingness and ability of public officials to affect industrial outcomes. In the last analysis, the financial system provides the arteries of the state's resource flows. Politics and markets are inseparable.

The State-led Financial Market System

France is the reference-point for the state-led financial market system (Zysman 1983: 99–169) as providing some 'third way' between US capitalism and the Soviet system. As with Germany, the years prior to 1945 cast a long shadow over post-war financial arrangements. The defeat of 1940 was blamed by both Vichy and the Resistance on the failings of France's pre-war 'stalemate society' (Hoffman 1963) where the influence of the two hundred families who elected delegates to the Regency Council of the Bank of France, created by Napoleon in 1800 (Bonin 1989; Goodman 1992) had become a symbolic 'wall of money' standing in the way of national reconstruction. The Council was abolished by the leftist government of 1936. Marshall Pétain's Vichy regime in 1940 then launched its own national revolution, creating professional associations to organize and modernize the economy under state direction (Burrin 1995; Sternhell 1978). It was guided in part by Catholic social doctrine, which condemned both free-market liberalism and the class struggle of Marxist doctrine. The regime sidelined 'apatride bank capitalism', associated with the older Protestant and Jewish banks, and provided the opportunity to restrict competition in favour of the large, Catholic banks.[1]

The state–corporatist mechanisms, rooted in legislation of 1941 and 1945, were designed to overcome the hesitancy of bourgeois France to invest in the nation's industrial regeneration. Central to the inflationary growth policies pursued under the aegis of the Ministry of Finance in the four decades following the end of the war was the idea that state influence alone could transform short-term savings into long-term investments. Equity markets were sidelined on quasi-Marxist grounds that the interests of a narrow class of shareholders were not compatible with those of the nation as a whole, in a vibrant economy based on high levels of employment, the near equal of Germany. This overdraft economy (Loriaux 1991) was constantly modified by shifts in public policy and by the economic and social forces which its successes generated.

The Ministry of Finance became the dominant focus for savers and borrowers as it regulated the capital market directly. Deposit-taking institutions with surplus funds placed them in the capital markets, and were taken up by public sector institutions which lent them to specific industries, such as housing, agriculture, nuclear energy, or regional investments. Both lending and borrowing institutions fell under the tutelage of the Ministry of Finance, which formally drew up investment priorities through elaborate consultations with trade associations recorded in 'The Plan', through negotiations with the Ministry of Industry or in response to requests filtered through the political parties. Public officials in the Ministry of Finance enjoyed prestige conveyed by their position in the state hierarchy, and because of the value of their contacts across the extensive state sector to those seeking access to it.

France's financial system had never been free of political controversy. As resources of personnel and time in the Finance Ministry were scarce, such a state-centred administrative mechanism at the heart of the financial system promoted a queue. Organizations with close contacts and claims on the loyalties of public officials, such as state-controlled economic enterprises or large private firms, got served first. Small- and medium-size firms were squeezed aside, so their representatives joined one or another of the political armies contending for privileged access to the state's resources through elections. The regular cycle of local, regional, or national elections thus also

---

[1] The Catholic banker Henri Ardant went so far as to express his hope for a united Europe under German leadership: After the war, he stated, Germany should act 'to eliminate the tariff barriers within the great economic space and move as soon as possible to a single European currency' (quoted in Burrin 1995: 271).

became contests between competing producer coalitions for a silver key to public finance.

Reforms had been introduced in 1966 to ease the budgetary burden of financing of the state-influenced corporate sector, and to create French universal banks on the 'German model'. But it was in the early 1970s that the system ran into serious difficulties as inflation rates rose, followed by world oil prices. In 1972, the left-wing parties under Mitterrand's leadership signed the Common Programme of the Left. This programme proposed extensive state ownership as well as control over the financial system, and launched France into two decades of partisan and electoral struggle where control of banks, insurance companies, and capital markets were among the major stakes.

The French state-led financial system promoted inflationary growth, compensated by regular devaluations. The rising cost for the Ministry of assuaging demands for subsidized credit was measured in the 1970s by the sharp rise in external debt, and the widening trade deficits with Germany. The whole edifice ground to a near halt, when in 1981 the new Mitterand administration extended the public sector just as the external debt exploded, and domestic savings shrank. France's financial market reforms of 1984–8 along US lines were introduced in order to promote Paris as an international centre, and above all to lower the cost of government financing. In particular, the financial market reforms would facilitate foreign private or public investment in French paper: it would allow the Bundesbank to buy French Treasury paper, much as the Bundesbank reinvested the dollars in its abundant reserves in the US Treasury bond market.

In a state-led financial system, financial resources are not alone in flowing through the hands of public officials. Patronage flows too, in the form of appointments to the management and boards of state enterprises or to large private enterprises in receipt of various state benefits. Public officials enter into competition among themselves, through their own organizations and to a lesser extent through their proclamations of party political fealty. Their legitimacy derives from a claim to act in the public interest, expressed in the extension of rights for employees within the public domain. Institutions whose resources they deploy directly or indirectly expand their stakes in business enterprises, extending further the field open to public patronage in the pursuit of private promotion. Corporate cross-shareholdings centre around state financial institutions. Indeed, a cynic could argue that such a state-led system has a vested interest in nationalizing private enterprise in order to expand the reach of public officials, and then of privatizing the assets in exchange for comfortable positions in the management or on the boards of companies. Ownership of these corporations is less significant than the fact that they remain on the career circuit, and that they stay within the bounds of what is in effect a political market for economic control. Such a political market extends throughout the multiple levels of government, as local mayors become businessmen and bankers for their local communities through resources obtained through the political process. Ultimately, the state can lose its status as acting in the public interest, and merges into the surrounding maze of non-transparent political markets.

The fear and then the reality of financial dependence informed the prolonged political struggle in France between the vision of bank–industry relations, introduced by Finance Minister Debré in 1966 with his *chef de cabinet*, Haberer, and Mitterand's commitment to an extensive nationalized sector. Debré's bank reforms enabled two investment banks to form federations of companies, accounting in the aggregate for 48 per cent of industrial value added and 60 per cent of exports (Bellon 1980: 74). Their nationalization would bring the greater part of industrial and commercial property directly or indirectly under state control. This prospect after 1972 hitched economic policy to the electoral timetable, discouraged private sector investment, and delayed reform of the financial system. The 1982 nationalizations then mobilized the conservative parties in favour of sweeping privatizations, which the socialist government initiated by stealth through allowing state enterprises to issue non-voting preference shares on the capital market. The 1986–8 conservative government's vigorous sale of state enterprises was interrupted by the October 1987 stock market crash and by Mitterand's second presidential victory (Bauer 1988: 49–60; Dumez and Jeunemaitre 1994: 83–104). His defence of the status quo on ownership effectively starved state-owned companies of capital, and prompted successive socialist governments to promote cross-shareholding, jointly owned subsidiaries, or the sale or issue of state shares on the markets. With the return of the conservatives in the April 1993 elections, privatization was resumed but cross-shareholdings were maintained.

The driving motive behind the creation of cross-shareholding groups was to prevent nationally owned industries being 'dissolved in Europe' (Pastré 1992). This view was widely held. The limits to France's commitment to the European Union's internal market became evident when the Chirac government in 1986 imposed limits on foreign ownership of denationalized corporations. Re-elected in 1988, Mitterrand invited the legislature to protect French corporations against 'roving, predatory money which grabs everything without effort' (*Financial Times* 2 November 1989). The idea of national majority ownership in large corporate groupings took a number of forms. First was the old Gaullist concept of 'participation', whereby employees would own shares and acquire an indirect stake in management. The idea appeared in a variety of guises, such as the 1993 law offering shares to employees at a 20 per cent discount. Second was the modified socialist strategy of 1983–6 to constitute industrial poles centred around nationalized banks. As former Prime Minister Mauroy explained, the formula would enable nationalized firms 'to conquer foreign markets' (*L'Année Politique* 1987: 125). Third was the 'hard core' concept of the 1986–8 conservative government, whereby the law reserved 25 per cent of privatized firms' capital to major bank or corporate shareholders, selected by the state. The socialist governments of 1988–93, trapped by Mitterrand's refusal to privatize state corporations and by the banks' shortage of own capital, to sought to harness the major state insurers to the same purpose. The EU's second banking directive, finally adopted in December 1989, opened the door to EU-wide banking for US or Japanese banks licensed in a member state, while the tripartite social security system acted as a restraint on the growth of funded pensions products in an open capital market. That left the state insurers as the bastions of national ownership (Story and Walter 1997: 261–2), in France as in Germany. The largest cross-shareholding pole in French capitalism was created in 1994, with the privatization of UAP (Union Assurace de Paris) by, for and with the support of the state. But in 1997, AGF (Assurances Générales de France) sold out to the giant, Allianz, which lay with its sister reinsurer Munich Reinsurance, at the heart of Germany's national cross-shareholding structure.

The contradiction at the heart of French policy was thus to seek to embrace Germany in the EU and in the North Atlantic alliance, while promoting a national capitalism strong enough to compete on a footing of equality with Germany's. The novelty in the EU's internal market programme, and even more so in the ambition to create a single currency, was the French elites' determination to use the EU as the vehicle for cracking open the German financial system for corporate governance, while keeping as much control and ownership over their own. But cracking open the German financial system also required the support of the 'Anglo-Saxons'—support that clearly was conditional. And it meant opening up further the domestic market for corporate assets. The burden of this struggle between France and Germany for leadership in Europe, while preserving national cohesion for some at home, was borne internally by the widening numbers of 'outsiders' among its own citizenry as unemployment rose inexorably.

The Bank-based System

The bank-based system of corporate control is associated with Germany, where the rules of the game have traditionally enabled banks to take deposits, extend loans to firms, and issue securities on capital markets in a tight relationship to clients. The foundations were laid at the time of the Franco-Prussian war by German industrialists, eager to convert depositors' short-term savings into long-term corporate lending by banks. Germany's dramatic history as a unified state from 1870 to 1945 casts a long shadow over financial markets in the Federal Republic. Association between Jewishness and finance capital first erupted in the 1873 Berlin financial crash, following hectic speculation fuelled by the five billion franc indemnity paid by France to Prussia for the war of 1870. Catastrophic losses were incurred. As Fritz Stern has written, after 1873 Germans of right and left never lost a powerful sense of anti-capitalism (Stern 1990: 240–2). German economic policy turned to protection against foreign competition, and to state promotion of cartels. In the 1920s, war reparations, inflation, and reconstruction kept German banking fragile, and interest rates high. National Socialism derived much of its ferocity from the promise to deliver Germany from the tyranny of 'cosmopolitan' finance, symbolized in Berlin as Germany's financial metropolis. As Dr Kopper, the speaker for the board of Deutsche Bank, said in 1994, both Communism and National Socialism saw the interest rate as a source of exploitation—'The systems collapse and the prejudices survive' (Handelsblatt 15 June 1994).

Capital markets, located especially in Berlin, grew up alongside, so that much of German corporate external financing prior to 1914 came through equities, whose shareholders received sizeable dividends. At the end of the war, and again after 1945, loans outstanding to corporations were converted into bank equities at knock-down prices. Bank and insurance laws from the 1930s were designed in part to stabilize the system, while capital markets were decentralized from Berlin to the Länder. This decentralized structure of the financial system was strengthened after the war by the growth of the savings and communal banks, which lent to local businesses and then from 1969 on, to governments. They account for over four-fifths of banking activity, and provide commercial bank, consultancy, and market support for Germany's small- and medium-size businesses (Deeg 1998: 93–101). Given the strong reliance of these companies, as well as Germany's large limited liability companies, on borrowing as the prime source of external financing alongside internally generated funds, the German system flourished best when interest rates were low. Low interest rates were best assured in post-war Germany when the trade sector showed a solid surplus. In short, there was a very close association indeed in Germany between the macroeconomic management of the currency and the microeconomic management of firms.

Between 1970 and 1993, Germany's accumulated trade surplus amounted to over DM1,420 billion (OECD 1994a). Western Europe absorbed 70 per cent of total exports, and was the overwhelming source of the cumulative surplus. The heart of Germany's strong position is quality engineering, notably in machinery and transport. The Federal Monopoly Commission reckoned that a hundred of Germany's largest companies accounted for one half of total exports (German Monopolies Commission 1987: 15) with eighty-eight of the largest companies run as joint stock companies and the three large banks and Allianz, as major shareholders—a stakeholding source of the surplus which was a main target of the 'liberal camp'—all those states confronted with the challenge of absorbing

Germany's exports—in the negotiations on the European financial area in the years 1973–92.

'Bank power' was a recurrent theme in the politics of the Federal Republic, much like the 'German model' was in French politics. And as in the French debate, the 'bank power' arguments in Germany provided a very partial view of German corporate financing. The 'bank power' debate was essentially about the role of the 'big three'—Deutsche, Dresdner and Commerz. Significant equity stakes in non-financial companies were said to be held by banks and by investment companies run by banks, who act as both commercial and investment bankers to their clients. In effect, the major German banks' functions altered considerably from the 1970s on, as their securities' activities expanded, and corporations became flush with cash. By the early 1990s, Germany's ten largest banks had reduced the number of their participations over 10 per cent from a cumulative value of 1.3 per cent of all capital of non-banks in 1976, to 0.5 per cent in 1993.[2] The large banks held only 11 per cent of supervisory board seats (Bundesverband der Deutschen Banken 1990).

The major banks muddied the waters by maintaining that, with equity as well as debt exposures to their clients, banks exerted a vital monitoring role in the management of corporations, including active supervisory board participation and guidance with the benefit of non-public (inside) information. Yet in recession, supervisory boards were charged with incompetence. In the case of AEG in 1982, of Metallgesellschaft in the winter of 1993, and of the Schneider construction group in April 1994, the impending disaster had not been monitored; the banks were seen as ready to lend to large groups, regardless or unaware of the risk; supervisory boards were accused of operating as closed shops (*Financial Times* 7 July 1982; *Manager Magazine* August 1993; *Die Zeit* 22 April 1994). In the last resort, bankers were co-guardians of a stable, property-holding democracy which has co-opted labour unions through their representatives' acquired positions on works councils and on corporate supervisory boards.

The big banks' key role towards the corporations was as managers of proxy votes at the annual general meetings of Germany's AGs (*Aktiengesellschaften*). One study on proxy votes in annual general meetings of thirty-two of the fifty largest AGs showed that 72.7 per cent were wielded by the private banks (Gottschalk 1988: 294ff). Banks, in other words, are part of a nexus of banks, insurance companies, and industrial corporations (Ziegler, Bender, and Biehler 1985: 91–111; Esser 1990: 17–32; Jenkinson and Meyer 1992: 1–10) which own each others 'shares and share each others' supervisory board seats. At the heart of this nexus lie Allianz and Munich

---

[2] The banks' 'glasnost' came in the form of public communications from the Bundesverband der Deutschen Banken on 25 July 1987, 29 March 1989, and 29 Oct. 1993.

Reinsurance, the two Munich insurance and reinsurance giants. As Wolgang Schieren, the head of Germany's leading insurance firm, admitted, 'Allianz is today a holding company, whose objective is to hold participations' (*Die Zeit* 12 September 1991).

Protecting Germany's listed corporations from takeover constitutes the heart of the commercial banks' case in the permanent debate about 'bank power' (Auschuss für Wirtschaft des Deutschen Bundestages, May 1990: 9). Their legitimacy derives from their vital protective function against foreign marauders. The argument was most clearly laid out by Alfred Herrhausen, speaker for the board of the Deutsche Bank (a few days before his assassination), in an address to the '*Prominenz*' of German politics and business in October 1989. It would be inadvisable, he declared, for legislation to oblige banks to sell their stakes:

I can anticipate excited protests if banks sell our stakes in important German firms to foreigners on the grounds of the continuing and in principle welcome trend to the internationalization and globalization of the economy. (*Die Welt* 27 October 1989)

Banks, he said, could abandon their voting and proxy powers. But who would replace them?

I do not have to illustrate to you what would happen if, on the basis of a clear decline in attendance, annual general meetings were to become dominated by active minorities. We have repeated experience of such active minorities. God help us, if our economy should become their plaything.

In other words, German capitalism was legitimate only within a national community.

Walter Seipp, Speaker of the Commerz Bank, put the point more bluntly:

If today you restrict or forbid stakeholding for German banks, the Federal Republic will become a sports arena for foreign banks, then you have Jimmy Goldsmith and other people here, and they will demonstrate to you how to buy, sell and strip industrial stakes in a market economy on the American model. (Ausschuss für Wirtschaft des Deutschen Bundestages. Offentlichen Anhörung, May 1990. Protokoll Nr. 74: 130–1)

In the German context, this argument was impregnable. It flattered the fears of trade unions, the concerns of politicians, and the vehement hostility to an open market in corporate assets. It was rooted in German labour, social, and corporate law. It described government and business practice to stall foreign takeover bids. It appealed to national pride in the manufacturing strength that underpinned the Deutschmark. It equated open share markets with the split banking systems of 'the Anglo-Saxons'.

The major advantage claimed for the financial system of corporate governance in Germany is that it has provided stable long-term finance for German firms—large, medium, and small. Private limited companies in particular expanded in number from 70,000 in 1970 to over 370,000 by the early 1990s. These family-owned firms form the bedrock of German business, being highly specialized on world export markets, often as tied in subcontractors to the large corporations, and financed largely through retained earnings or borrowing from banks when the occasion requires. They are notably averse to public listing on the German stock exchange, for fear of diluting their owners' control over the business. In particular, they are embedded in local policy networks, where local banks play a key mediating role between local politicians, firms, trade unions and trade associations. Their battle field resides in competition on product markets, as the national economy remains open to foreign suppliers. But the system has two serious disadvantages: one affecting all those firms dependent on bank borrowing, and the other relating to the propensity of insiders to the senior management of large corporations to collude.

Firms dependent on external bank borrowing benefited by cheap finance when interest rates were low. These macroeconomic conditions were secured when the Bundesbank could manage domestic monetary policy, relatively autonomously of international financial flows, as was the case from 1975 to 1979. But in 1981, the Bundesbank decided to increase interest rates. Firms with high debt exposures fell like ninepins, 12,000 in 1982 alone. In the 1980s, interest rates came down slowly again, while the Bundesbank sought to promote equity markets in order to reduce the vulnerability of firms to bank borrowing. Then came German unity, the surge in interest rates to contain related inflationary pressures, and a further spate of bankruptcies. Worse, the French government's decision to keep the franc's parity with the mark meant that French interest rates were pulled up to German levels. In France, 70,000 firms declared bankruptcy in 1993 alone. UK firms endured a similar punishment on account of the government's insistence on hitching sterling to the tight exchange rate mechanism (ERM) of those years.

To function well, the insider elites of corporations (the managers) must duplicate the market disciplinary functions performed by impersonal capital markets in the UK and the USA. As mentioned, this task is all the more difficult to achieve as German firms' dependence grows on more volatile, and less predictable world markets. Because they have to satisfy the demands of their stakeholder constituency of workers, suppliers, clients, and the local community, there is an incentive for firms to invite shareholders to patience and to reduce dependence on banks through strategies aimed at conquering market shares. There is a marked propensity for senior managers to defend the status quo, and to lay the blame for failures not at on the financial system of corporate governance, but on personalities (Harvard Business School 1996: 9–495–055).

The financial system as a whole must be prepared to deal with the consequences of large trade surpluses, which flow from joint corporate interest in market shares. Domestic inflationary pressures have to be kept down through rapid recycling of funds earned from exports. This entails the building up of portfolio investments in other markets around the world. Revaluations of the currency from exports and investment income abroad may be delayed by further external portfolio investments, as well as by corporate direct investments abroad as domestic production costs continue to rise relative to other locations around the world.

The central paradox of such a cross-shareholding system for large corporations, with close ties in to medium and small subcontractors, is that it seeks to limit foreign ownership and market access, while requiring open markets for corporate assets in other countries alongside open access for exports including heavy reliance on export finance. Not least, corporations become detached from banks as their external sources of funds on world markets grow, while regulatory segmentation within the financial system breaks down as financial institutions compete across boundaries for new clients. Germany's embedded mercantilism, in other words, began to unravel within on account of its external successes, while its external successes were envied in France as an expression of Germany's rise to hegemonic power in Europe.

The Equity-market System

In this essentially Anglo-American approach, bank functions are split by legislative action between commercial banking and financial market institutions. The former may provide short-term financing for firms, but the major source of external financing for firms is the capital market. Although both the USA and UK adopted their own specific responses to the Depression of the 1930s, both followed similar lines of development, despite the 'socialist' rhetoric of post-war Britain and the 'capitalist' megaphone of the USA. The theoretical basis of government policy for both had been provided for more than two hundred years by the concept of 'laissez-faire', the doctrine opposing government intervention in the economy except when necessary for the maintenance of law and order. Companies are owned by proprietor shareholders, who are considered as the principal beneficiaries of an enterprise. This attitude started to change during the latter part of the 19th century, when small business, farm, and labour movements began asking the government to interfere on their behalf. Further modifications came with the experience of World War I, and then following the Wall Street Crash when the Senate in 1933 adopted the Glass–Steagall Act, which separated US commercial and investment banking, and was intended to break up the House of Morgan, which operated as a 'universal bank' for US corporations and took the blame for the Depression. As a result, commercial banks were placed at a disadvantage in dealings with non-bank financial institutions. This became a serious handicap in view of the growth in the US bond markets, which benefited securities houses.

In the capital markets, shares of corporations are held by the public, either directly or through institutional vehicles like funds managed by insurance companies, mutual funds, and pension funds, and are actively traded. Corporate restructuring, involving the shrinking of the firms assets or their shifting to alternative uses or locations (Ergas 1986) is triggered by exploitation of a control premium between the existing market capitalization of a firm and that which an unaffiliated acquirer (whether an industrial company or an active financial investor) perceives and acts upon by initiating a takeover effort designed to unlock shareholder value through management changes. There is a high level of transparency and reliance on public information provided by auditors, with systemic surveillance by equity investors and research analysts. Concerns about unwanted takeover efforts prompt management to act in the interests of shareholders, many of whom tend to view their shares as put options (options to sell). The control structure of this essentially outsider-based system is mainly confined to arm's length financing, including takeovers and internal corporate restructuring, although investment banks may be active in giving strategic and financial advice and sometimes taking equity positions in (and occasionally control of) firms for their own accord.

This model, to operate to maximum effect, assumes that the more powerful stakeholders in the firm (shareholders, managers, and customers) regard this process as legitimate. Its central claim to that legitimacy resides in an assertion that, everything else being equal, it is the most efficient to maximizing wealth. Its supporters also argue that free markets are the most compatible of all systems with democracy as a system of limited government. If, for instance, financial markets are free to allocate savings to the most efficient rather than the most politically influential users of capital, then the returns for the savers will be higher than if some of them use their vote to extract rents from less remunerative, but politically determined investments. Labour market legislation in particular has to be supportive, so that labour forces may be shrunk or shifted in task or location with the minimum of friction. The model also assumes that the government will not prove a light touch for corporate lobbies seeking to avoid restructuring or takeover through access to the public purse, as a less demanding source of funds. Government's major task is to provide the regulatory and legal structure within which open capital markets may function, and to supply a safety net for the unemployed, the infirm, or the old. Not least, this Anglo-American approach assumes that the two kings of the corporate roost are shareholders and customers: if other types of financial systems in world markets have different priorities, benefiting other interests, they will eventually be forced to adapt or to lose market share to rivals focusing firmly on consumer and shareholder interests.

Major reforms were implemented in the US securities markets in 1975, followed a decade later by the 'Big Bang' in the London markets, ending the separation of brokers and jobbers, and opening the markets to full participation by US or Japanese investment banks and European universal banks. In the UK, equity ownership became much more widely diffused. Labour market legislation was liberalized. Corporate profits improved, and non-residential investment took off. London became the European Union's prime city of capital, and the 'third leg' in the triad of world financial centres, together with New York and Tokyo (Hamilton 1986; Goldfinger 1986). As London lacked the economic base of Japan or the USA, its hinterland could only be supplied through integration with the EU. The major alliance was forged with Germany. Deutsche Bank moved its Eurocurrency operations from Luxembourg to London in 1984, and then acquired the UK merchant bank, Morgan Grenfell. The move signified Deutsche Bank's recognition of 'the pre-eminence of the London market in the domain of corporate finance and money management' (*Financial Times* 28 November 1984). Other British-based investment banks were later bought up by German, Dutch, and French universals.

The London markets were notably different from those in Paris and Frankfurt. They were wholesale markets, servicing businesses from all over the world: they were not domestic markets, primarily funding national corporations. British companies therefore looked often with envy at the financial services provided their counterparts in Germany. Whereas German corporations distributed rather modest proportions of earnings as dividends, British corporations paid out high proportions, obliging them to earn high rates of return in order to retain the loyalty of investors on whom they remained dependent for future capital. Their managers did not have the retained earnings to invest in the human capital of their workforce, or to invest in risky developments of products and processes. Their attention was permanently fixed on their corporations' share price, for fear that a reduced dividend could have serious consequences in terms of a lower share price and a predatory takeover.

Yet German or French financial institutions used the London markets where they could lend on their surpluses, borrow for their customers, or speculate on the booming markets for foreign exchange, equities, or futures and options. Simultaneously, they, or their governments, sought to protect their national markets from the 'cosmopolitan' influence of London. As the Bundesbank stated with uncharacteristic forthrightness, Germany's universal banks must not be forced 'by virtue of the EU regulations to switch over to a system of functional operation in the financial services sector, such as predominates in the Anglo-Saxon countries' (*Bundesbank Yearly Report* 1989).

Mitterrand's hostility to 'predatory, roving' finance was interpreted into the reformed French insurance law of December 1989, enabling state insurers to have up to 25 per cent of capital held by private investors. Under the French presidency, the second bank directive allowed bank–insurance tie-ups, opening the way in EU legislation to recognize national financial conglomerates (Story and Walter 1997: 261–2). As the policy's defenders claimed, such cross-shareholdings created 'a powerful and organized financial "heart" of corporate ownership' (*Le Monde* 8 October 1991).

Anglo-American capital markets, then, were incompatible with the inherited institutions and national political cultures of Germany and France. In different ways, shareholder capitalism was held at bay in favour of managerial prerogatives, which were formally justified in terms of their contribution to national welfare. Yet the advantage of the Anglo-American financial market system of corporate governance is that it places competition between corporations before competition between states. Shareholders reward or punish corporations, and are indifferent to whether the reward or punishment is meted out to workers and managers in one country or another. As its opponents, ranging from German business to the French communist party, have repeatedly pointed out, it is 'anational', or in the language of an earlier generation of Europeans, it is 'apatride'.

The Paradox of EMU

The paradox of EMU is that France and Germany, two countries with embedded mercantilisms, are the principal protagonists of a measure which can only accelerate the victory of shareholder capitalism for large- as for medium-size corporations. This requires some explanation, because had the preservation of national ownership of large corporations been an overriding priority in Bonn and Paris, a more moderate alternative to monetary union would have been negotiated that allowed capital markets to remain separate, and shareholders to stay mainly national. Such a measure was in effect proposed by Finance Minister Balladur in early 1988 along the lines of a common currency, whereby the EU unit of account would have been used in the settlement of intracentral bank accounts to sustain a commonly managed confederal exchange rate regime—much along the lines of the original design negotiated in March 1979 by Chancellor Schmidt and President Giscard d'Estaing.

The background to Balladur's proposal was provided by the Paris financial market reforms, and the adoption in January 1987 by Prime Minister Chirac of the 'hard franc' policy, following an eleventh and acrimonious parity realignment of the franc in the ERM. The French government was convinced that the fundamentals of the French economy were now sound, and that the problem lay not in France but in German mercantilist practices. Rather than have the Bundesbank accumulate dollars as the counterpart to German external surpluses, the French Ministry of Finance sought to have the Bundesbank hold European Currency Units (ECUs), and use them to subscribe to French Treasury bonds (*Le Monde* 27 September 1987)—as the Bundesbank had done since the 1960s with regard to US Treasury bonds. The French government, in other words, was requesting that the German government treat it on an equal footing with the USA. The use of the ECU as a central bank unit of account would also avoid the convergence demands that the Germans had appended to the single currency discussions of the early 1970s. A recycling of German trade surpluses through German ECU investments in French Treasury bonds would permit a relaxation of macroeconomic policies, and a rapid easing of pressures on the European labour markets. This was the intent behind the creation in January 1988 of the Economic and Financial Policy Council, within the bounds of the 1963 Franco-German Treaty.

Finance Minister Balladur expressed the French position in a memorandum of February 1988 to the EU Finance Ministers, proposing a 'common currency', and a European central bank. 'The ERM', he wrote, effectively exempted 'any countries whose policies were too restrictive from the necessary adjustment' (Gros and Thygesen 1992: 312). The proposal entailed the progressive construction of a 'European Reserve Fund', with the task of keeping EU currencies stable. This Fund would have foreign exchange reserves placed at its disposal by the central banks. In the longer term, it would prepare the way for completion of the monetary union (Aeschimann and Roché 1996: 88).

Kohl recognized that French dissatisfaction with the ERM would have to be accommodated (Balkhausen 1992: 71), but the Ministry of Finance and Bundesbank were reserved. The German Cabinet hammered out a common position, presented in a February 1988 resolution:

The longer-term goal is economic and monetary union in Europe, in which an independent European central bank, committed to maintaining price stability, will be able to lend effective support to a common economic and monetary policy. (*Financial Times* 23 June 1988)

Foreign Minister Genscher summarized the German government's position (Genscher 1989: 13–20): free capital movement, priority accorded to price stability, political independence of a European central bank, no inflationary financing of government deficits, and a federal structure, in the manner of the institutions of the Federal Republic or the USA. In effect, the German government countered with a maximalist proposal, even more maximalist that the 1970 Werner Report, which had suggested a federal currency and a

European central bank, accompanied by a centralized EU economic policy body, with extensive counter-cyclical fiscal powers (EC 1970). The German government could reasonably expect that the French government would not accept such an offer.

The French government thus faced a dilemma: negotiations on the liberalization of capital movements were proceeding in the context of the EU's internal market programme, and the German government was in effect asking France either to accept continuation of the ERM under conditions of free short-term capital movements within the EU, and with the rest of the world. This spelt further regular realignments of exchange rates, with the Bundesbank operating as *de facto* central bank for the EU, and making policy for other member states together with the US Federal Reserve as manager of the world's key currency. Or the German government was suggesting EU monetary union on German terms.

At the European Council of Hanover on 27 June, the EU political leaders agreed to incorporate the central bankers into talks on monetary matters. Jacques Delors, President of the Commission, presided over their committee, which was joined by three monetary experts. Delors presented the report in spring 1989. It represented a victory for the German position, not least in that the report made clear that the 'transition' to a single currency represented a marathon with a receding winning post.[3] The European Central Bank (ECB) was to be independent; there were to be binding rules on government spending; the report incorporated the earlier Werner Report's proposal of a three-stage transition; and the narrow ERM band was presented as providing a 'glidepath' to monetary union. The bland text, replete with barely concealed differences, was vaguer with regard to timing. Stage one in July 1990 entailed liberalization of capital movements; stage two, to start at an unspecified date, was to witness new institutions (with unspecified powers), precise but not binding rules relating to the size of budget deficits, and a reduction in margins of currency fluctuation; the third stage, also starting at an unspecified date, would lead to 'irrevocably fixed' parities, the replacement of national currencies by a single currency, and would only be embarked upon once all the instruments of the internal market were in place (an efficient competition policy, regulation of takeover bids and corporate control, a set of common fiscal policy goals, and close monetary policy co-ordination).

In summer 1989, France took over the rotating-term EU presidency for the second half of the year, as Germany accelerated towards unity. At the EU Strasburg summit of 8–9 December summit, the EU heads of state and government stated support for the German people to 'refind unity through

[3] 'The Delors Committee', wrote Helmut Schmidt 'did not satisfactorily state why it turned down a partial solution, whereby the ECU would serve as a parallel currency alongside national currencies and gradually squeeze them out. This refusal closes a pragmatic way, which the bond markets are already taking' ('Am Sankt-Nimmerleins-Tag?' *Die Zeit* 7 Sept. 1990).

free self-determination', and Bonn concurred in Paris' request that a new intergovernmental conference be held prior to the German elections in 1990, with a view to incorporating monetary union into the Treaties.[4]

German unity was completed on 3 October 1990, followed by the victory of Chancellor Kohl's coalition in the December general election, the first all-German general election since 1932. Meanwhile, at the European Council in Rome, 27–28 October 1990, Kohl and the German Minister of Finance won acceptance of the Bundesbank's conditions. These had been circulated in an unofficial paper, 'Compromise Proposal for the Second Stage of EMU' among other central banks. They were presented as *'non-negotiable'* (emphasis added) demands (*Frankfurter Allgemeine Zeitung* 26 September 1990): political union; price stability, completion of the internal market; political independence of the ECB and member banks, and an ECB monopoly on all necessary instruments. Prior to union, price levels had to converge on a stable and low norm. There was to be no inflationary financing of government deficits, and there were to be binding rules on government spending.

This German position was incompatible with French demands for a 'common currency'. Mitterrand therefore overrode his Finance Minister and decided to concede, as the price to pay for France gaining a voice in an independent ECB (Aeschimann and Riché 1996: 91). But he continued to maintain, after Kohl had agreed to surrender the mark by January 1999, that the economic governance of a united Europe would have to be predicated on the Council of Ministers, and answerable to the European Parliament. Mitterrand forceably reiterated the French government's position at the time of the September 1992 referendum on the Maastricht Treaty:

Those who decide economic policy, of which monetary policy is only one instrument, are the politicians elected by universal suffrage, the heads of state and government who make up the European Council.   (*Le Monde* 5 September 1992)

At the Brussels summit of December 1994, the EU governments welcomed Delors White Book on growth, competitiveness, and employment, which proposed a growth policy for the EU through the development of EU-wide infrastructure projects, combined with an industrial policy predicated on competition in the market place and reform of labour market institutions. President Chirac returned to the theme, indicating thereby that the French concept of 'economic governance' of the EU was not to be circumvented.[5]

---

[4] 'Les Douze acceptent que le peuple allemand retrouve son identité' (*Le Monde*, 10–11 Dec. 1989). No date was named for completion of monetary union, reflecting Kohl's reticence and Thatcher's opposition.

[5] 'L'Europe selon Chirac' (*Le Monde* 25 March 1996). 'A la Banque centrale européenne, que nous avons voulu forte et indépendante, il reviendra de garantir la solidité future de la monnaie européenne. Mais c'est au Conseil des Ministres, institution réprésentative des états, qu'il appartiendra de définir les orientations de la politique economique de l'Union, à l'unanimité chaque fois que c'est l'essentiel.'

The outcome of negotiations on monetary union was thus stacked heavily in favour of Germany having its way with regard to conditions. Both sides used the future as a place to locate their present disagreements: the German delegation had negotiated a marathon of an obstacle course, with only a distant prospect of more than a few member states reaching the finishing line on 1 January 1999. But at the last moment, Mitterrand won Kohl's commitment to override the battle of the experts as to whether the timetable or the conditions should take precedence. By agreeing to an 'irrevocable' commitment to the timetable, Kohl in effect signed the Deutschmark's death warrant.

This negotiating victory for France only compounded the price to be paid for a European Central Bank, modelled on German lines. Continental labour markets were resistant to falls in wages as a means to absorb the unemployed, and therefore provided a prime target for Keynesian demand management. The German government suspected with reason that any French government would lobby for continental-wide fiscal reflation and therefore pushed, in the course of 1995–6, for further EU agreements to restrict budgetary outlays. The alternative Keynesian device would be for the ECB to keep interest rates as low as possible in order to encourage investment and consumption. That option was implemented in January 1999, when eleven member countries introduced the euro on the fixed rates to national currencies agreed in April of the previous year. Low interest rates across the Euro-11 ensured a resumption of moderate growth within the year.

In the meantime, the wholesale capital markets of all member states signing on to join the ECB in 1999 would convert out of national currencies to Euros, creating a capital market potentially the equivalent of that in the USA. Financial integration and EMU thus represented a revolutionary programme which promised to denationalize market structures, and blow open national bond markets/cross-shareholdings, impact labour markets, and transform national politics. It would create one Europe-wide market for bonds and equities denominated in euros, but it would not end differential treatment of investors. Nonetheless, all financial institutions would be competing without the previous discrimination provided by trade in national currencies. The European financial market place would be composed of vigorously competing centres, which would have to provide a broad range of services or disappear into niche positions. Under a single currency and with an independent central bank, German, French, or Italian bonds would be rated and priced as if they were New York or California bonds in the US municipal markets. This would place significant constraints on public financing throughout the Euro-11.

Highly liquid markets and contestable financial markets would provide corporations throughout the EU with a new range of opportunities for external financing, but those opportunities would likely go hand in hand with greater scrutiny of management and workforce performances. Shake-outs, downsizing, management accountability, and shareholder value along Anglo-American lines would thus continue to permeate Europe. Intensified competition spelt dissolution of national cross-shareholdings, and an end to quasi-permanent credits given generously to corporations, on a relationship basis, which fail to earn adequate returns for performance-oriented share-holders. In turn, the pressures for greater accountability spells further moves in France and Germany to Anglo-American accounting, intensified political debates on corporate governance, growing pressures to develop Europe-wide interest groups and political parties to martial demands and convert them into policy through the European policy process, and increasingly tough bargaining in the Council of Ministers.

This would not represent a triumph of market forces. Rather, it would be the probable consequence of a political decision. Were European political and business leaders quite so revolutionary? There was no indication to suggest that they were. Germany was not a proponent of 'Big Bangs' in delicate policy areas and preferred to do things consensually. France was ambitious, but existing arrangements and commitments weighed heavily. The UK was the best-prepared as far as the capital market was concerned, but lacked political support to join the Euro-11. Meanwhile, France sought to Europeanize Germany, whose political leadership in turn had to oblige business leaders and the general public who abhorred financial instability and the prospects of inflationary European policies beyond their control.

The prospect of repetitive cycles stretching into an indefinite future provided the central motivation to cash in the political capital invested in the EU's most ambitious project to date. Indeed, monetary union is seen as a catalyst for future initiatives toward political union. By contrast, the Bundesbank has argued that for monetary union to succeed, it has to be sustained by a polity capable of absorbing the inevitable and perhaps extreme tensions associated with such a revolutionary step. Only the existing states now have the legitimacy that enable them to answer to the central political question: By what right do you rule? The EU institutions can only legislate or implement what the states agree to. It was therefore reasonable to argue that a less ambitious path to a more integrated Europe, one that resorted to the tried and tested EU negotiating technique of using the future as a place to locate present disagreements, could have proven more capable of reconciling the diverse practices of Europe's interdependent states with the necessary constraints of cooperation on monetary and exchange rate policy, than a Big Leap to one currency and one capital market. But that way would only have been possible if financial systems of corporate governance in Germany and France were not embedded mercantilisms, in other words if they were capable voluntarily of moving the Anglo-American way on their own or in the context of the internal market legislation.

This they were not prepared to either do, or to admit to doing. Mergers in the financial or in the non-bank sector in the Euro-11 in the early months of the euro's existence indicated clearly that the old national reflexes, to exclude foreigners taking over prized national assets, were as lively as ever. How come, then, that corporate behaviour remained national, while the Euro-11 had taken a giant step into a federal currency? One answer would hold that EU legislation regarding capital markets has to catch up with monetary policy, and end the barriers to cross-border trade inherent to the various practices of national preference. Another holds that it was national calculations which drove the EU towards a single currency, and national calculations which continued to prevail in the market for corporate assets after the euro's introduction.

In other words, the rationale for monetary union from the 1980s onward was the prospect of German unity, and thereby of Germany's emergence as Europe's prime power, dictating monetary and exchange rate policy to other, lesser states. Both French and German political leaderships agreed that abolition of the Deutschmark was essential to further consolidation of the European peace since 1945. The catalyst for the Big Leap to Europe's Big Bang was German unity: France feared that German unity provided Germany with the temptation not to liberalize but to consolidate its national practices as Europe's hegemon. Kohl was more than aware of what that French reading of events meant for future relations. So both governments decided to make the Big Leap into a federal currency, and away from the haunting past of 1870, 1914, and 1940. That meant monetary union, but monetary union also spelt a single capital market, ending national capitalisms.

The states were prepared for monetary union, but they were less prepared to acquiesce in surrendering national corporate ownership and control. Consolidation of a single capital market lay ahead. In the meantime, the paradox of a Euro-capital market is that it provides the means and the incentives for corporations and financial institutions to consolidate on a national basis. Such behaviour would be consistent with the history of Europe's competing national mercantilisms; it would not be consistent with the European states' espousal of a federal currency.

4

Who Wins and Who Loses in the City of London from the Establishment of European Monetary Union

LEILA TALANI

The purpose of the following chapter is to analyse the impact that the establishment of EMU will have on the City's markets and institutions, both in the case of Britain deciding to remain outside EMU[1] and in the case of its entry.

In the light of the insights coming from this examination, it will then be possible to assess the City of London's overall position towards EMU on the basis of the opinions expressed by leading representatives of the City in interviews with the author of this essay and in other occasions, with the aim to explain the British government's attitude towards EMU on the dawning of January 1, 1999 and to predict its likely future position.

In the next section, therefore, the impact of EMU on each individual market of the City of London, and, relatedly, on the institutions acting in them, will be studied and conclusions drawn on the advantages and disadvantages for London as a leading financial centre of the establishment of a European single currency area.

The Impact of EMU on the City of London's Markets and Services

London Money Markets

London short-term money markets, constitute, together with the Foreign Exchange and with the bullion market, also called the London gold market, the bulk of the prosperous City's wholesale markets (Shaw 1981), that is,

---

[1] Indeed, on October 27, 1997, The new Labour Chancellor of the Exchequer ruled out the possibility for the UK to join EMU in the first run, but this, of course, does not mean that the British government cannot decide to enter the new European monetary area in the future.

markets trading in big amounts, of six figures or more. The institutions active in the money markets are the hundreds[2] of banks of the City of London and they operate mainly through deposits, apart from the Certificates of Deposit market.

The traditional London money market is represented by the market in Treasury and commercial bills, that is, promissory notes by the government and commercial firms, guaranteed by the so-called Accepting Houses[3] and discounted by the traditional and closed club of Discount Houses.

These houses act as the *trait d'union* between the Central Bank, which operates in the discount market as lender of last resort, and the commercial banks through securing their short-term balances and investing their resources in bills and other short-term securities. In turn, the Bank of England uses the discount market to influence the liquidity of the banking system. It purchases bills from the houses to increase cash, or sells them to mop up liquidity, while changes in the rates at which these operations are carried out signal the willingness of the central bank to modify the banking system interest rate patterns.[4]

In parallel with the traditional sterling money market, a secondary sterling market, consisting of inter-bank, unsecured[5] deposits has developed from the '60s onwards. Equally unsecured is the local authorities' market, through which short-terms loans are made available to British local authorities and their surpluses are mopped up (ibid). The development of the Certificate of Deposit instrument has allowed for the establishment of a CD market in the London money markets which include also a Euro-commercial paper market.

However, the most prosperous and important of the short-term London money markets by far, is represented by the London Eurocurrency market. The Eurocurrency market was established in London as a result of the rigidities in the United States' banking system that allowed international and national interest rate differentials to persist. The most important of these rigidities was the so-called 'Regulation Q', which limited the rate of interest that US banks could pay on deposits. In addition, beginning in 1965 the United States

---

[2] There are over 565 foreign banks in London, more than in any other city in the world, to which there must be added British banks.

[3] Traditionally, the Acceptance houses were represented by the restricted club of the merchant banks, but in 1981 the range of banks whose acceptances are 'eligible' was greatly widened including also many foreign groups.

[4] With the Thatcher government, the traditional practice to fix a binding key interest rate for the banking system, the old Bank rate and its successor Minimum Lending Rate, were ended for good, but the informal rates fixed for discount market operations by the Bank of England are equally binding.

[5] This meaning that there is no lender-of last resort acting in this market.

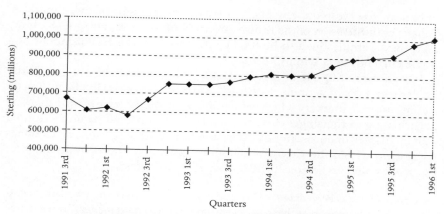

FIG. 4.1. Total other currency deposits in UK banks (1991–6).
Source: Bank of England Quarterly Bulletin. Various issues.

imposed a series of measures designed to restrict capital outflows and to improve the balance of payments position, thus forcing the borrowers to the Eurodollar market rather than the domestic dollar market.[6] At the same time, however, these restrictions were not crucial for the development of the Eurocurrency market in London, since it continued its rapid growth even after the US controls were removed in January 1974. The extremely friendly environment that the British authorities were able to create represented the main reason for the success of London as the host of the euro-deposits. This was obtained by avoiding subjecting banks acting in the Eurocurrency market to official reserve requirements or deposit insurance costs and thus ensuring lower costs and enhancing competitiveness.

London's Eurocurrencies market is still thriving by far distancing sterling deposits, which, in the first quarter of 1996 were £688,800 million, as compared to the £1,021,080 million of foreign currency deposits.

Thus, deep, well-developed, money markets, both sterling and foreign currency ones, are a key feature of the UK financial system, making a major contribution to, and being partly the result of, London's position as a leading financial centre. A market-oriented environment, notably the absence of

---

[6] The foreign Direct Investment Regulation prevented US multinationals from financing overseas operations with funds borrowed in the United States while the Voluntary Foreign Credit Restraint Program restricted US bank foreign lending and the Interest Equalisation Tax discouraged foreign borrowers from raising funds in the United States through securities issues.

minimum reserve requirements, is a particular strength of these markets. Whatever the decision of the British government towards joining EMU, however, they were destined to be highly influenced by the establishment of a single currency area within Europe.

Indeed, were the UK to join EMU, the fixing of exchange rates and the implementation of a single monetary policy in Europe will affect directly sterling money markets which, alongside with the other national markets participating in the single currency, would be substituted by an integrated money market in euros. In this event, the loss of sterling money markets is considered within the City of London a competitive threat by itself since, as the City Research Project (BBA *et al.* 1996: 3) notes:

Foreign Banks have been drawn to London in part to undertake money market activities in an offshore market that was free from reserve requirements and restrictive regulation. But the open nature of the UK banking system has also meant that foreign banks have substantial sterling deposits and loans. Thus the efficiency of the domestic sterling money market is important to London's position as a centre for overseas banks.

Moreover, at the time of the establishment of EMU, some other issues emerged as sensitive ones whose solution in one sense or another was likely to exert a great influence on the City's position towards EMU. A very important question related to whether banks would be allowed to access liquidity only through repo-operations[7] with their own Central Bank with some rationing of liquidity within all national Central Banks, or whether remote access would be permitted. Clearly, remote access without rationing of liquidity could allow one national Central Bank to develop as a leading centre for open market operations and there would consequently be a strong likelihood that the market activity in euros would concentrate in this centre, although national markets would obviously need to remain. The City of London seemed fairly confident that, if open market operations allowed remote access and did not ration liquidity, in the event of UK's participation, then London would become the natural access to ECB liquidity via the Bank of England. Therefore the main centre for money market dealing in euros (BBA *et al.* 1996). However, this optimistic scenario could be put into question by the gathering in another European financial centre (the most likely being Frankfurt) of a 'critical mass of banks' to establish the European money market (ibid).

---

[7] Repo arrangements consist of institutions selling stock to primary dealers against arrangements to repurchase. These arrangements are active in the London gilt-edged market since 1996.

Moreover, the City's position as a participant could be very adversely affected, if onerous reserve requirements were imposed by the ECB at zero interest rates or at interest rates lower than market rates. In this respect, it is important to emphasise that London is a leading international, not only European, financial centre and thus its competitive position towards New York or Tokyo would be greatly undermined by the imposition of similar restrictions. Moreover, onerous reserve requirements could spur the development of offshore European money markets, as the EU banks minimize the amount of deposits subject to punitive charges. These off-shore markets, if the UK were inside the EMU area, would necessarily be set outside the City of London and possibly in one of its international rival financial centres. This, of course, made a very strong case *against* Britain's participation in EMU altogether. Indeed, if the UK did not participate in EMU, sterling and other London based-money markets would clearly continue in existence. On the other hand, an ECB regime with requirements set higher than those in the UK, which meant *any* requirement since in the UK there is *none*, could help the competitive position of London markets. Alternatively, it could let London become the centre for euro-euro deposit trading, as it would become a natural location for excess liquidity seeking to escape the onerous, or even not so onerous, ECB regime. Moreover, the City's position as an *international* money market centre, namely, its dominant position in the already established Eurocurrency and Eurocommercial paper markets, would not undergo any threat.

The other major issue concerning the London's money markets was the question of terms of access to TARGET[8] for banks in non-participant countries and the outcome of the debate over the provision of intra-day liquidity. The TARGET project provides connections within the EU-wide Real Time Gross Settlement (RTGS) systems, which allow high value payments in euro to be made in real time across-borders within the EU, rather than just in individual countries in the single currency area. TARGET comprises one RTGS system in each EMU member state and an inter-linking mechanism to connect them. Member states not in EMU will be entitled to connect to TARGET, but the terms and conditions for access to intra-day liquidity remained undecided up to the very last moments before the establishment of EMU.

The main point at issue in the EMI debate was whether non-EMU Central Banks should have access to euro intraday liquidity on the same terms

---

[8] The acronym TARGET stands for Trans European Automated Real-time Gross-settlement Express Transfer, a pan-European system interlinking EU Real Time Gross Settlement (RTGS) systems, that is systems in which payments instructions are transmitted on a transaction-by-transaction basis within direct members of a system and are settled individually across Central Banks accounts in real time.

as Central Banks within the euro area. In the opinion of both the City of London (BBA *et al.* 1996) and the Bank of England (1996) such access had to be available, since intraday liquidity helps ensure a fully efficient payments system. Moreover, restrictions to access to TARGET could not be justified in terms of the need to avoid monetary policy spill-overs. Indeed, the availability of intraday liquidity is largely irrelevant for monetary policy, and it is difficult to believe that an occasional spill-over to overnight accommodation would have significant implications for the operation of EMU area monetary policy.[9] The latter could in any case be deterred by the rates of interest charged for overnight borrowing. Accordingly, restrictions on intraday liquidity could not be justified by monetary policy considerations, and would have to be viewed as discriminatory in the context of the Single Market legislation. However, how effective such measures would be in practice in inhibiting market development, including the establishment of an euro-euro market in the UK will depended on the costs and efficiency of TARGET in comparison with the range of alternative methods of making cross-border payments that will continue to be available. In particular, banks use correspondent banking, the ECU clearing system, and direct access to other payments systems to make cross-border payments. Correspondent banking is the most widely used mechanism and it consists of the banks using as their agents banks in other countries with access to the local payments system. This mechanism would continue to be available in stage 3 but, while it is relatively efficient and cost-effective, it leaves a bank exposed to settlement risk *vis-à-vis* its correspondents. The ECU clearing, which is a mechanism run by the ECU Banking Association for settling transactions denominated in the basket ECU, was expected to develop into a euro clearing system, with end-of-the-day net credit and debit balances settling across TARGET. As with all such end-of-day net systems, it does not eliminate settlement risk between direct members, or provide intraday finality of funds. Finally, direct access to other countries' payments systems (RTGS or others) would also be available to banks with subsidiaries or branches in other countries, and through remote access from a bank in one country to another country's payments system.[10] Thus, even if the countries participating to EMU sought to restrict non-members' access to TARGET, this by no means would result necessarily in a competitive disadvantage for the 'outs'.

---

[9] By the end of 1997, the terms of non EMU member states participation to TARGET had not still been solved. See Bank of England (1997), pp. 14–16.

[10] By the end of 1997 it was clear that that a Euro RTGS system parallel to sterling one would start function from January 1, 1999, the so-called: CHAPS Euro. This provided its member banks with a UK facility to make wholesale euro payments from the beginning of 1999; and they, in turn, will be able to provide a full euro wholesale payments service to their customers. See Bank of England (1997), p. 14.

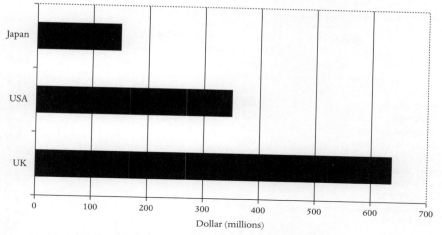

FIG. 4.2. Foreign Exchange turnover (April 1998).
Source: *Invisibles Facts and Figures* (1999), London: British Invisibles.

In conclusion, among the costs of participation for the London's money market it was necessary to also include those relating to the need to adjust to new monetary policy operations directed by the ECB. This would clearly require changes to established UK practices, including the adoption of repo-operations as a monetary policy instrument. More important, it would require the likely abolition of the Discount House system and of the discount market which, under EMU, would not be allowed to rely on the Bank of England's role as lender of last resort.[11]

The London Foreign Exchange

The London Foreign Exchange market is the largest in the world. Its daily turnover was of $637 billion in April 1998, accounting for 32 per cent of global turnover, more than New York and Tokyo combined. In 1995, the majority of its activity was linked to the US dollar. Its dominant role in global trade focused, in particular, on the $/£, $/DM and $/Yen trades with the $/DM business predominating in the spot market, while in the forward market trades in the three currencies pairs were of the same magnitude. The market was a wholesale one dominated by banks, accounting for over 70 per cent of trading. Its truly international nature was made clear by the fact that non-UK-owned banks were responsible for almost 80 per cent of market turnover,

[11] For the other changes see BBA *et al.* 1996.

TABLE 4.1. Relative shares of total turnover in London by currencies traded (1995)

	%		
	Spot	Forward	Total
£/US$	3.1	8.3	11.5
US$/DM	11.8	9.7	21.5
US$/Yen	5.7	11.3	17.0
US$/Swiss Franc	1.7	3.7	5.5
US$/French Franc	0.9	4.5	5.5
US$/Canadian$	0.5	1.9	2.4
US$/Australian$	0.4	1.2	1.6
US$/lira	0.4	2.9	3.4
US$/Peseta	0.2	1.8	2.1
US$/Other EMS	0.8	5.1	5.9
US$/Other	1.2	2.9	4.2
£/DM	2.8	0.4	3.2
£/Other	0.4	1.0	1.3
DM/Yen	1.9	0.3	2.2
DM/other EMS	4.8	0.9	5.7
ECU denominated	1.1	3.0	4.1
Other Cross Currencies	2.3	0.8	3.1

Source: Bank of England Quarterly Bulletin, November 1995.

while sterling was involved in less than 20 per cent of all transactions (BBA *et al.* 1996: 31).

Given its evident global character, if the UK remained outside the EMU area, the competitive threats for London as a centre for foreign exchange trading activity were judged to be fairly low. On the contrary, it was anticipated that the City would still remain a major location for trading in euros. The loss of revenues consequent on the disappearance of former currencies would clearly be directly proportionate to the number of currencies participating in EMU, as well as dependent on the turnover of trading in euros. However, it would certainly be lower if sterling did not take part in the single currency area, since trading in sterling would not disappear.

On the other hand, if the UK was in the single currency, the disappearance of trading between former national currencies in the EMU area would account for less than 20 per cent of turnover on the London market, a lower proportion than that estimated for the other European Foreign Exchange. Again, this loss could be overcome by trading in euros (Levitt 1996a).

Overall, the London Foreign Exchange would remain neutral to EMU whether sterling entered or not. The only likely implications were legal ones, namely the need for agreement on relevant market conventions and of legal preservation of contracts continuity in conversion from previous currencies to euros.

Lastly, as far as the infrastructure was concerned, the fact that most of the foreign exchange trades were settled on a bilateral basis meant that there would not be the same need for centralised infrastructural preparation that would be required in the wholesale money markets.

The Capital Market

As a premise, it is worth clarifying that the Capital market comprises those markets buying and selling securities. The London Capital market, where securities are listed and traded and where market-makers and brokering agencies operate, is the London Stock Exchange. This was called from 1987 onwards, when it linked with the London Eurobond Houses, the International Stock Exchange, where both primary[12] and secondary[13] markets in securities take place. The Exchange is a Recognised Investment Exchange (RIE) under the terms of the Financial Services Act of 1986.

Since the Big Bang, firms which opt to be market makers in specified securities agree to display their prices by means of the Stock Exchange Automated Quotation system (SEAQ) and this makes them accessible on screens to other traders. Other smaller firms have not become market makers, and continue acting as mere brokering agencies, buying and selling securities in transactions with market makers on behalf of their clients.[14] Securities, in turn, may be broadly divided into two categories: shares, which may be both equity and preference ones, and bonds.[15]

Bond Markets

Whereas shares may only be issued by commercial undertakings, bonds, which are mainly fixed-interest rate securities, are issued by commercial undertakings

[12] Is the new-issue market, that is, the market for the issue and placing of new shares, bonds etc etc.

[13] A place for the buying and selling of existing stocks, shares, and bonds.

[14] For more information on the changes in the City after the Big Bang, see Reid (1988).

[15] An equity, or ordinary share, represents a share in the ownership of a company: the equity shareholders jointly own the company and have the right to vote at general meetings. They are entitled to dividends, but only after all other creditors have been paid, and if the company makes a loss, their shares fall. Preference shares do not confer voting rights and entitle to dividends only up to a fixed maximum, but the claims of preference shareholders take precedence over those of equity shareholders. Bonds are fixed interest securities which entitle to regular payments of interests and to the eventual repayment of the initial sum lent. Their claims have the precedence on both equity and preference shareholders. They may be issued both by private companies and by governments and others public bodies. See Artis (1996).

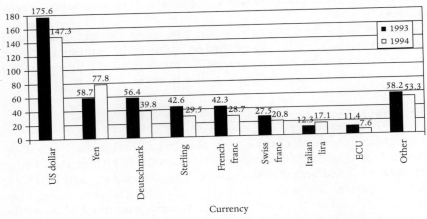

FIG. 4.3. Currency composition of international bond issues, (1993–4).
Source: Bank of England Quarterly Bulletin, Angust 1995.

and also by governments, local authorities, and other public bodies including international organizations. Thus it is possible to identify in London both a commercial bonds market and a government bonds one. The first one is constituted by a national bond market and by the completely international Eurobond market.

The Eurobond business is centred in London. The turnover[16] of Eurobond trading in 1993 was £2866bn. The estimated net revenue in 1991 was £327mn (BBA *et al.* 1996: 9). The market share of international bonds in 1994 was 60 per cent for primary market (British Invisibles 1996a) (being total international bond issues in 1994 equal to 420.2$bn[17]) and 75 per cent for secondary market (British Invisibles 1996a). As regards trading in governments' bonds, already before the establishment of EMU a number of governments, including the British one, issued securities denominated in foreign currencies or in ECU placed in the international capital markets. However, the great majority of business remained largely organized on a national basis because of the application of the local presence requirements to national government bond market (Artis 1996).

The British government's bond market is called the gilt-edged market and its primary and secondary trading is concentrated in the City of London,

[16] Figures for turnover may be higher than those for the outstanding debt since bonds, before the deadline, may be traded over and over again.

[17] Figures include euro and foreign issues and publicised placements. Issues which repackage existing bond issues are not included. See Bank of England (1995).

although exact details of market share are unavailable (BBA *et al.* 1996: 7). The transition to a single currency was held to have an immediate impact on the City-based government and corporate debt markets, including the Euro-markets, even if the UK did not participate.

Regarding the corporate bond market, if the UK participated from the outset, UK corporations would have the option, but not the obligation to issue bonds denominated in euros in the transition phase from 1 January, 1999 until 1 January, 2002. However, after the latter date, all new issues would have to be in euro. This raised two major issues. The first one concerned the resolution of legal problems relating to continuity of contracts.[18] The other one related to the possibility, if not need, for companies to redenominate in euros existing debt even before start of phase 3, with all that it implies in terms of costs and of the decision over the legal framework in which to effect these operations.

However, corporations could of course continue to issue debt in other non-EMU area currencies, and also via the euro-bond market. This would allow for the development and establishment of an Euro-euro bond market, that is, an off-shore market in bonds denominated in euros. The latter, were the UK inside EMU, would obviously be outside London, thus certainly undermining London's share of primary and secondary international bonds trading.

Finally, as pointed out by the Report of the EMU City working group, 'competitive pressures on relationships with both issuers and investors could well increase over time as the markets become more integrated (BBA *et al.* 1996: 12).' If the UK did not participate in EMU, then UK corporations could still issue euro-denominated debt, either as foreign bonds within an EMU-area state, or as Euro-bonds in the euro Euro-bond market which, with the UK outside EMU, would certainly be located in London. This meant that, even if the UK did not enter, the London capital markets would need to be able to provide for trading, settling, payments, custody and clearing facilities for the euro-denominated bond markets. Thus a great deal of preparation had to be carried out if London wanted to maintain its dominant position.

---

[18] Indeed, within the City of London it was feared that disadvantaged issuers or investors would try to avoid their obligations under bonds to be re-paid after the start of the transition which were issued in ECU's or other national currencies subsumed by the euro (BBA *et al.* 1996: 4).

However the First Regulation on the introduction of the euro, now in force in all the member states including the UK, ensures that there will be continuity of contracts. Thus, financial contracts denominated in the national currencies of participating Member States will remain unchanged as a result of the introduction of the euro, except for the change in denomination and hence amount at the conversion rate. Bank of England (1997), p. 85.

Moreover, some discriminatory action might be taken against the City's markets, either as a trading location or as a base for cross-border activity. In fact, according to the City, even if the Second Banking and the Investment Services Directive prohibited discrimination, in practice they allowed for some loopholes in the Single Market legislation for financial services. A member state might frame rules in a manner which is not overtly discriminatory but in practice obstructs the business of institutions from outside the member state, by, for example, imposing restrictions on institutions lacking a physical presence in the member state concerned. Moreover, the directives allowed restrictions to be imposed where this is necessary for the implementation of domestic monetary policy or for the 'general good.'[19]

For these reasons, the City of London asked the European Commission to be more active in identifying and addressing failures to implement EU Directives on the Single Market. It also required any member state contemplating issuing new regulations on the grounds of the 'general good' or monetary policy to communicate them to the Commission and to other member states.

As far as the British government's bond market was concerned, if the UK participated in EMU from the outset, new gilt issues after 1 January, 1999 would be denominated in euros, as would new central government debt issues in all EMU-area states. However, as the credit risk posed by each central government issuer would still differ, pricing of all such debt would also show differences. Regardless of EMU, primary market activity would remain national oriented, at least as long as restriction on cross-border primary dealing were not withdrawn, while secondary market activity would remain concentrated in London.

This scenario would be unchanged even if the UK did not enter EMU, but a potential threat would arise if EMU-area states lifted the local presence requirements for the primary market for central government bonds only for each other, and not for non-participants. UK-based firms would then miss an opportunity to compete for this business. Some concerns were also expressed over the possibility for the City to maintain its share in non-sterling business, including that of the new market in euros. Some observers forecast benefits arising within a unified market where instruments are all denominated in euros, in terms of increased volumes, lower spreads and the elimination of arbitrage opportunities and niche markets. Others, however, claimed that the implementation of the Maastricht criteria would reduce the need for central government bond issues and thus constrain growth in the market. The exact impact seemed hard to predict, but the City was keen to point out how the extent to which the EMU-area central

---

[19] These issues are discussed in greater depth in a paper by LIBA (1996).

government bond market would be unified can be overestimated. Indeed, credit facilities would still exist between member states leading to differences in yields and to the identification of a national central government bond acting as the new euro money market benchmark.

The Market in Shares

The City's Big Bang day, 27 October, 1986 completely changed the environment in which share trading took place in the London Stock Exchange. It allowed deep restructuring[20] and recapitalization of the market-making firms due to the elimination of the single capacity system, and replaced the traditional jobbers and brokers. It also allowed for a considerable reduction in costs, because of the elimination of the fixed commission system.[21]

Within a year from the Big Bang, trade in UK shares had doubled and by September 1987, customer business in domestic British equities was running at over £1.1bn a day, against £0.6bn in 1986, with £0.8bn of further deals taking place among market makers. Moreover, in the first year after the reforms, despite the elimination of the fixed commissions, total commission income, far from falling for competitive pressures, increased to £1.16bn from 0.74bn in 1985–86, thanks to the big expansion in volumes traded and the greater activity by higher-paying private investors.[22] Under the new electronic system, the market makers insert into the SEAQ screen network the bid-offer prices at which they stand ready to deal. Firm prices are provided for only for the leading companies shares, the so-called 'alpha'[23] and 'beta'[24] shares. Indicative quotations are given for the smaller 'gammas', even if on request firm prices must be provided for by the minimum two market makers in these shares. Also for the less important 'deltas' firm quotations are given on enquiry. Each share has a screen page from which it is possible to derive the so-called 'touch', the narrowest gap between available buying and selling prices.

---

[20] Indeed, on the eve of the City's Big Bang and in its immediate aftermath a great deal of mergers and take overs went on in the City of London, as the big British Clearing and Merchant banks, as well as interested foreign investment firms, saw the opportunity to enter the renewed London capital market. For a detailed account of the restructuring of the City of London during the City's revolution see Reid (1988).

[21] Nowadays, a substantial proportion of larger deals is now transacted with market-makers 'net', that is without any commission charge, being firms gains represented by the difference between their buying and selling prices. See Artis (1996).

[22] See Reid (1988).

[23] The 'alphas' are the shares of over 130 of the leading companies most widely dealt in; there have to be ten or more market makers in 'alphas'.

[24] For 'betas' there must be at least four market makers.

TABLE 4.2. Funds raised by share offerings in the UK (1989–94) (£ million)

	Ordinary shares (equities)				Preference shares
	Gross issues		Redemptions	Net issues	
	Total	Rights issues			
1989	6,187	2,949	2,636	3,551	1,062
1990	4,402	3,114	908	3,494	728
1991	11,140	9,129	135	11,005	1,137
1992	6,426	3,227	29	6,393	624
1993	16,536	10,891	—	16,534	1,529
1994	14,865	4,926	20	13,739	402

Source: Financial Statistics, various issues.

Also the business in international, or foreign, shares,[25] soared after October 1986, to reach a market share of foreign equities turnover of 65 per cent in 1991. At the end of March 1993 London dealers were quoting firm prices for over 400 European equities and annual turnover had risen to over £150 billion (Artis 1996). This exceptional success of the London international equity market[26], prompted defensive measures in many other European Stock Exchanges. As a result, in recent years the London share of foreign equity turnover has been decreasing (see Figs 4.4 and 4.5).

The impact of EMU on London share markets would be gradual, rather than immediate, but it was likely to pose competitive pressures even if the UK did not join the single currency. If the British government decided to enter, the London market could benefit from the ending of currency restrictions on the investment of institutional investors in the EMU area. At the same time the advent of the single currency might reduce the number of individual stock exchanges in which the investors sought listing, thus intensifying competition with the City.

It was also clear that the decision to enter would prompt an early demand for euro equity dealing and listing facilities, at least in the wholesale business. This urged the adoption of the appropriate measures to adapt the settlement and payments systems, and to allow the London Stock Exchange to trade and list, on request, equities denominated in euros from the beginning of phase 2 (1 January, 1999). UK's participation also poses a number of legal questions relating, for example, to the modality and timing

[25] Shares of companies from foreign countries, mainly European, listed in London by specialised market-makers.

[26] The market-making system for foreign shares is very similar to the one for UK ones, with the participation of both British and international specialized market makers quoting foreign shares on an arm of the Stock Exchange's system, the SEAQ international.

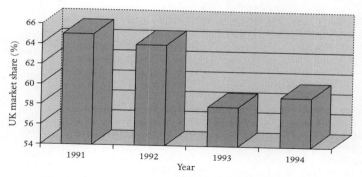

FIG. 4.4. UK share of foreign equities turnover (1991–4).
Source: British Invisibles (1996), *Invisibles Focts and Figures*, London: BI.

Market-share of foreign equities turnover, 1994

	UK	USA	Japan	France	Germany
Foreign equities turnover	59%	34%	under 1%	under 1%	2%

Source: British Invisibles, (1996), Invisibles facts and figures, London: BI.

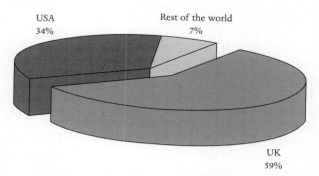

FIG. 4.5. Foreign equity turnover (1994).
Source: British Invisibles (1996), *Invisible Facts and Figures*, London: BI.

TABLE 4.3. The London international financial futures

Financial instruments	Volume Jan-Dec 1994	% of total contracts
3 months Euromark future	29,312,222	19.71
3 months Euromark option	2,943,936	1.98
Bund future	37,335,437	25.1
Bund option	8,574,137	5.77
German BOBL* future	73,043	0.05
3 months ECU future	622,457	0.42
3 months short sterling future	16,603,152	11.16
3 months short sterling option	4,057,878	2.73
long gilt future	19,048,097	12.81
long gilt option	2,357,348	1.59
3 months Eurolira future	3,456,437	2.32
BTP future	11,823,741	7.95
BTP option	8,574,137	0.69
FT-SE 100 Index future	4,227,490	2.84
FT-SE 100 Index option	4,786,656	3.22
FT-SE Mid 250 Index future	40,674	0.03
3 months Euroswiss future	1,698,736	1.14
3 months Euroswiss option	19,245	0.01
3 months Eurodollar future	91,738	0.06
3 months Eurodollar option	12,400	0.01
Japanese JGB future	610,925	0.41
Total of financial contracts	148,726,421	100.00
Total of all contracts	148,726,421	100.00

Medium Term Notional Bond.
Source: British Banking Association, Association for Payment Clearing Services, London Investment Banking Association (1996), *Preparing for EMU: the implication of European Monetary Union for the banking and financial markets in the United Kingdom. Report of the EMU City Working Group*, London: BBA, APACS, LIBA.

of the redenomination of shares, including the decision over rounding conventions to prevent later litigation.[27]

In the event that the UK did not participate in EMU, equity markets would continue in sterling. However, it was possible that issuers from within the EMU area would wish to trade in euros on the Stock Exchange Automated Quotations System (SEAQ) International. As a result, the possible business opportunities posed by offering euro quotations and listing facilities, and related settlement systems, would also need to be ready in order to cope with competitive pressure arising from the consolidation of the other European Exchanges. The City had already begun to see a decline in the UK share of international equity trading and the establishment of the single

[27] For other legal issues see BBA *et al.* 1996: 19.

currency, irrespective of British participation, might heighten the competitive challenge. However, if the preparations were carried out in due time, and the UK markets had adequate access to euroliquidity payment mechanisms, and if the EMU countries did not adopt discriminatory measures, then the City could be reasonably confident that even outside EMU, the UK could live with competition.

The Derivative Markets

This is the market in financial futures and traded options which allows investors and financial groups to hedge against the adverse effect of market swings. In the United Kingdom this trading is carried out in the London International Financial Futures Exchange (LIFFE), established in the City in 1982.

A financial future is a contract to buy or sell a specified quantity of a given financial asset, like a government bond, on a date ahead at a set price. A traded option, instead, gives the purchaser the right, but not the obligation, to buy (call option) or to sell (put option) a specified amount of a given financial asset at a set price within a specific period of time. For this right, the purchaser pays a premium to the seller of the option (Artis 1996: 185).

In the LIFFE futures and options contracts on short–term bank deposits and long-term government bonds are traded in a number of currencies. In 1994 the contract on the German government bond future, the *Bund* future was the most traded by far, with 25 per cent of all contracts traded. Attempts by LIFFE to establish futures and options contracts in foreign exchange were unsuccessful.

LIFFE, is the largest such exchange in Europe with a total volume of business of 148,726,421 contracts in 1994. Already in 1994 it accounted for 17 per cent of market share, in steady growth from previous years. It must be noted that the City of London has a strong market also in Over-The-Counter (OTC)[28] derivatives. The Bank for International Settlements inaugural OTC market survey showed that London is the top booking location for contracts, with a 30 per cent market share, at a considerable distance from the other financial centres (BBA *et al.* 1996: 21).

The considerable UK share of the OTC and exchange traded derivatives markets underlines the contribution of these markets to the City's continuing prosperity. The City estimated 1991 net revenues from OTC interest rate contracts traded in the UK to have been £284 million and from exchange traded instruments on LIFFE £363.4 million in the same year (BBA *et al.* 1996: 27).

---

[28] These are all the operations in financial derivatives which are carried out outside the organised Exchange. See Picchi, F. (1991).

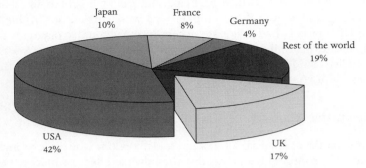

FIG. 4.6. Market-share in exchange traded financial derivatives (1994).
Source: British Invisibles (1996), *Invisibles Facts and Figures* (1996), London: BI.

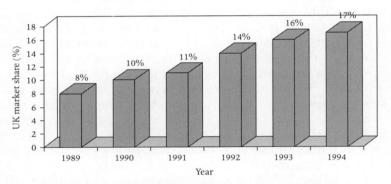

FIG. 4.7. UK share of exchange traded financial derivatives market (1989–94).
Source: British Invisibles (1996) *Invisibles Facts and Figures*, London: BI.

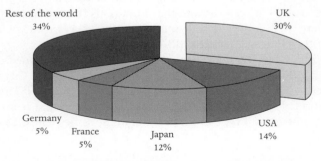

FIG. 4.8. OTC derivatives market shares (1995).
Source: British Invisibles (1996), Invisibles Facts and Figures (1996), London: BI.

TABLE 4.4. Overall EMU impact activity on turnover in financial futures and options-principal exchanges

Rank	Exchange	1994 turnover (mn contracts)	% potential EMU impact*
1	Chicago Mercantile Exchange	156.31	10.65%
2	LIFFE	148.73	92.27%
3	Chicago Board of Trade	139.48	0%
4	Marche' a Terme international de France	93.1	91.65%
5	Deutsche Terminborse	49.32	41.84%

* Percentage of volume of trade in any potential EMU currency interest rate or bond instrument in relation to the total volume of financial contracts.
Source: British Banking Association, Association for Payment Clearing Services, London Investment Banking Association (1996), *Preparing for EMU: the implication of European Monetary Union for the banking and financial markets in the United Kingdom. Report of the EMU City Working Group*, London: BBA, APACS, LIBA.

If the UK participated in EMU then all exchange-listed contracts related to sterling interest rates, along with other EMU area interest rate contracts and the ECU contract, would cease to exist and be replaced by a euro-rate contract. It was held by the City highly likely that this development would take place from the beginning of stage 3. Indeed, the adoption of a common monetary policy within a fixed exchange rate area would lead to the convergence of money markets. However, there would still be some scope for divergence of national interest rates linked to credibility of the irreversibility of the transition for all currencies.

Exchange-traded contracts derived from national government bond prices of EMU participants could continue to be traded during the transition phase due to the credit risk between member states. However, in general, there would be a concentration of business on the euro-denominated benchmark instruments. Also over 90 per cent of trading volume in interest rate and bond products was, in 1994, composed by assets in currencies which could potentially be replaced by euro, it would be of critical importance for LIFFE to win high market share in the new market arena.

If the UK did not take part in EMU, then sterling and gilt contracts would continue to be traded. Thus, the proportion of trading volume that would be replaced by euro-denominated contracts would be around 70 per cent. Therefore, also in the event of non-participation, the City of London had to be able to offer euro-denominated exchange-listed contracts if it wants to retain its dominant position in derivative trading.

Thus, regardless of British participation in EMU, the main competitive issue for the City of London in derivative markets was represented by its capacity to attract the highest percentage of business in euro-rate futures and options and the euro-denominated benchmark EMU-area government bond futures and options. Related OTC products would develop in parallel.

To this aim, an important factor was the extent in which LIFFE acts first to grab the new market. If LIFFE was able to win such a head start in euro contracts and was successful in rolling over open interest in its euro-mark and *Bund* contracts into the euro, then market share could be maintained. However, simultaneous head-to-head competition would split business within exchanges, without any clear concentration in LIFFE. The announcement by LIFFE that existing Euro-mark, short sterling and Euro-lira contracts would settle on euro-rates after 1999 in the event of German, UK and Italian participation in EMU already provided the exchange with a head start over continental rivals. Also an early establishment of appropriate settlement facilities could enhance London's chance of dominating the market.

The extent to which LIFFE's competitive position could be influenced by UK non-participation seemed limited to the City of London, since it was hard to see how regulatory or other discriminatory barriers could be erected by participant states to stem the growth of LIFFE outside the EMU area. Also in the OTC markets there was no scope for competitive threats in the event of the UK remaining outside EMU. Legal issues appeared more significant due to a risk of litigation connected to contracts involving the ECU and national currencies subsumed into the euro during the transition.

The Impact of EMU on Some Key City Services

Fund Management

A very lucrative service strongly developed by the City's merchant banks is fund management. London is the world's largest fund management centre with over £1,800bn of institutional equity holdings in 1997. Total assets under management in the UK exceeded £2,2000bn in 1997, on behalf of institutional and private clients in the UK and overseas (British Invisibles 1999). Its success owes much to the surging growth of the United Kingdom pension funds, but also to a favourable regulatory environment and to the pool of highly skilled labour (BBA *et al.* 1996).

According to the Institutional Fund Managers' Association, the direct impact of EMU on the industry was likely to be fairly limited. It is true that the extension to the whole EMU area of currency matching rules, requiring up to 80 per cent of assets to be denominated in the currency in which the liabilities arise, would increase the scope of asset diversification in the common currency area, thereby also increasing the opportunities for banks with fund management capabilities (Levitt 1996a). However, UK fund managers could benefit from the impact on currency matching rules even in the case of non-participation in EMU. The only downside of non-participation would be that UK fund managers could not gain from the improved transparency of pricing and performance that would be associated with the single currency area.

Corporate Banking

Another field merchant banks have made mostly their own is that known as corporate banking. This involves a number of services to the corporate sector. These include advising companies on a range of matters (among which the conduct of take-over battles is the most important) providing, more generally, professional banking help for 'merger and acquisition' (M & A) activity, handling share offers, devising methods for restructuring or arranging underwriting facilities (Reid 1988).

Corporate banking is extremely competitive in the City of London, where companies may find undisputed expertise and professionalism. However, competitive pressures from within the single currency area were expected to increase further with the entry of the UK, since corporations would be likely to rationalize treasury operations and existing banking relationships in the EMU area. Also competitive pressures from outside might increase as a consequence of the imposition within EMU of a relatively onerous regime, for example reserve requirements, on the banking industry.

Against this background, it was essential for British banks to provide efficient payments and related services from the start of 1999. The impact on corporate banking would clearly be less if the UK did not participate in EMU, but to maintain their competitive position British banks ought to be prepared to offer adequate euro service all the same (BBA *et al.* 1996).

Insurance

London is one of the largest insurance markets in the world. For international insurance London is the world's largest market, with net premium income of £9.6bn in 1997.

Since UK insurers are much more involved in the US market than their European counterparts and the most of the London Market business is conducted in dollars, EMU impact on current business was judged to be fairly limited. In the event of British participation, some concerns arose over the possibility for euro/$ exchange rate to be more volatile than £/$ one. There was also the risk that EMU led to lower exchange rates, reducing the insurance companies expected returns from premiums on non-profit business.[29]

---

[29] In fact, in these cases premiums are usually kept down by reliance on high investment returns.

If the UK entered EMU, insurance companies had to address also costs arising for modifying computer software, particularly in the payments and claims systems. On the other hand, if the UK opted out of EMU, little preparation would be required, namely, the mere conversion of other participants assets and business into euros. As regards insurance funds management activity, the same considerations of general fund management applied.

The City of London and EMU: A Difficult Relationship?

From the analysis above it clearly emerges how the establishment of a single currency area in Europe posed direct competitive threats to the City of London by itself, irrespective of UK participation. In particular, in an EMU-area, the elimination of trade barriers in many relevant City's markets (as, for example, in securities dealing, particularly in the equity market, or in derivative markets) as well as the development of new financial instruments denominated in the common currency, would certainly increase the other European financial centres' chances to grow by grasping the new market opportunities. Thus it would undermine the City of London's until now undisputed financial leadership in Europe.

It is true that British participation would at least eliminate the possibility for the EMU countries to adopt protectionist measures, like conditioned access to TARGET, or the ending of currency restrictions on the investment of institutional investors only in the EMU area. However, it is also true that much more threatening consequences might derive to London as an international financial centre from British entry in EMU.

Indeed, the peculiarity of London as a financial centre is given precisely by its unique international orientation. London is the most international of the leading financial centres and has the largest share of many global markets. The London Stock Exchange has a greater turnover of foreign equities than all other centres combined, £359bn and 59 per cent of global turnover in 1994. It is also estimated that at least 60 per cent of Eurobonds are issued in London, and an even higher proportion, 75 per cent, of secondary bond trading takes place in London. The London foreign exchange market is the largest in the world, with a daily turnover of $637bn in April 1998, which is higher than that of New-York and Tokyo combined. At February 1997 there were 565 foreign banks in London, two thirds of which coming from non-EU countries, more than in any other city in the world. Foreign currency deposits in the UK banks account for £1,021,080 million, well exceeding sterling ones. London ranks second to the USA in exchange traded financial futures and options, but LIFFE was established only in 1982 and its share of world market had increased from 7 per cent in 1988 to 17 per cent in 1994. It is also the world's largest international insurance market, with net premium income of £9.6bn in 1997, as well as the global clearing centre for gold forwards trading and financing. Further, the Baltic Exchange is the world's largest ship-broking market (British Invisibles 1996a). Finally, UK financial institutions, predominantly based in the City of London, earned a net £20.4bn through overseas transactions during 1994 (British Invisibles 1996c).

British participation in EMU would certainly undermine this leading international role of the City of London by first of all imposing restrictions on the working of its markets and institutions, and, generally, by submitting the City of London to exogenous controls. Instead, also in the new British regulatory environment controls for the wholesale money markets are only represented by a discretionary supervisory role of the Bank of England while capital markets after the Big Bang are self-regulated through the endogenous organizations of the Securities Investment Board (SIB) and of the SROs.

Moreover, EMU would affect the City's international primacy by eliminating the possibility for London to develop as the main off-shore market in euro or in euro-denominated assets,[30] an activity which, the UK being inside EMU, would certainly be developed by one of its major world competitors. Finally, it is necessary to take into consideration the domestic economic consequences of joining a monetary union. These are usually included in the all-embracing expression of 'loss of sovereignty', but, in the case of the City of London, have the clear-cut meaning of the loss of the ability to influence domestic monetary and exchange rate policies, with all that it implies in terms of loss of domestic political power (Levitt 1996b).

Given this analysis of the consequences of EMU on the City's markets and activities, it should not be particularly surprising that, as Paul Richards, Director Public Finance of HSBC Samuel Montagu, put it, already in November 1996[31] the working assumption within the City of London was that EMU would go ahead without Britain's joining it in the first run. Also Sir Douglas Wass, Chairman of Nomura International *plc*, thought, in November 1996, that the British government would not even try to enter EMU from the outset. This was demonstrated by the fact that both British

---

[30] In its December 1997 report on the euro, the Bank of England clearly claims: 'The introduction of the euro represents an opportunity for London rather than a threat. There will be a vigorous euro-euro market in London, just as there is a vigorous euro-DM, euro-franc, euro-$ and euro-yen now.' See Bank of England (1997), p. 12.

[31] Which means exactly one year before the new Labour government actually stated that the UK would have not joined EMU on January 1, 1999.

leading parties had committed themselves to run a referendum on the issue,[32] a referendum which, in the opinion of other authoritative City's voices was very likely to be lost and, thus, it would be an easy way out.[33]

However, as pointed out by Sir Michael Butler, Director of Hambros Bank Ltd and also EU adviser to the Labour party, in a lecture at the London School of Economics on 11 November 1996, even if it wanted, the British government, any British government, would certainly not be able to enter in 1999. This happened because first, it was not in the EMS, second, the criteria might not be fulfilled and finally, there was the need for much legislation and regulation to be passed before entering EMU. Therefore, since the government would have other priorities, it would be very difficult to join from the beginning. Moreover, fixing parities and having a single monetary policy abruptly would be, in the opinion of many City representatives, extremely risky, 'a leap in the dark', as Sir Michael Butler told the House of Lords Select Committee on the European Communities (House of Lords 1996).

According to Malcom Levitt, the first risk of EMU was the threat to the Single Market as a whole. In fact, far from favouring the process of achieving a European Single Market, the progress towards an EMU restricted to a limited number of countries could instead run the risk of creating a protectionist area, particularly in the field of financial activities. This would threaten the progress achieved with the passing of the Single Markets directives on financial services and insurance. On the other hand, however, in the opinion of the City, if EMU countries relaxed their monetary and fiscal stance after joining either the new European currency will be very weak, or the union will collapse, but, if this happened, European political stability itself will face a serious threat. Moreover, this risk was made more likely by the capacity of financial markets to anticipate it, and thus to pose a risk-premium on exchange rate even within EMU.

There was then also the opposite danger, namely, that the economic policies within the EU will become pro, rather than counter cyclical, that is, they will not be able to cope with recessive pressures, and, instead, they would favour them. Regarding this, it was held extremely important that the Stability Pact included a more flexible approach than the one eventually adopted in order to counter cyclical effects, unless EMU led to a genuinely low inflation rate which would almost automatically imply lower interest rates. However, this seemed very unlikely to the City of London, and even if it happened, it had to be perceived by the business community as a per-

---

[32] *Interview with Sir Douglas Wass*, Chairman of Nomura International plc, London: 18 November 1996.

[33] *Interview with Duncan McKenzie*, Economic Adviser to the British Invisibles, London: 14 November 1996; see also Talani, L. (1996b).

manent effect, and not as a merely temporary event, otherwise it would not favour long-term investment decisions.

Finally, there was the problem of the relationships between those countries with a tradition of fiscal stability, and those with no such a tradition as regards the reduction of inflation rates and the reduction of their public deficits and debts, the real threat being that they will not be able to maintain their stances. Regarding this point there seemed to be a genuine concern in the British financial sector over the economic performance of the other member states as they did not want to risk that the degree of economic prosperity reached in the UK might be threatened by EMU. In particular, concerns were expressed over the so-called 'pension issue', that is, the possibility that demographic pressures in the other EMU member states would also jeopardize UK ability to pay pensions which is much higher than in the other countries thanks the extraordinary development of the pension fund instrument. Consequently, Mr Richards considered it vital, to avoid serious risks being triggered by EMU, to stress the importance of 'sustainable convergence.' This meant not just meeting the convergence criteria, but creating the conditions to keep them fulfilled also after joining EMU. Sir David Scholey, Chairman of SG Warbourg Group since 1984 and Director of the Bank of England since 1981, 'could see some very unpleasant consequences' (House of Lords, 1996) if member states were generally unable to sustain the convergence criteria, as the pressures which could not be spilled over on exchange rates, would be taken out on the real economy. Also Sir Michael Butler, if EMU was really going to happen, would prefer it to start with a very small number of countries. It would be even better to use an evolutionary approach, as the one proposed by him and by Richards in the Hard ECU plan, and put off to a later moment the idea of fixing parities and pooling monetary policies, an idea that also met the support of other City operators.

Despite the scepticism still often expressed within the London financial circles towards the EMU project as a whole,[34] as well as towards the Maastricht way to it, from the publication of the European Commission Green Paper on EMU, and, generally, from 1995 onwards, the British financial institutions started thinking that EMU could actually became reality. Consequently, they started considering the issue seriously and establishing working groups to assess its consequences.

The key issue at stake was the impact of European Monetary Union on the City of London with the UK outside. In the opinion of Sir Douglas Wass,

---

[34] Cristopher Johnson, former Chief Economic Adviser to the Lloyds bank and now UK adviser, Association for the Monetary Union of Europe, claims:
'Meme si la City reste sceptique a' l' égard des merites de l'euro'. See Johnson, C., 'La City de Londre face a l'Euro', forthcoming.

'nobody in the City is concerned about the negative impact of EMU if the UK remains out of it', since the other European countries, as Frankfurt, Paris or even Amsterdam, do not have the same facilities as London whether it remains out of EMU or not. As, moreover, most of the City's business, and, certainly, the greatest part of Nomura International business, is in foreign currencies, mainly dollars, Yen, DM and Ecus, and not in sterling which has lost much of its international role, Britain's refusal to join EMU would not affect the City of London's activity.

According to Sir Peter Middleton, a Deputy Chairman and Director of BZW of Barclays Bank since 1991, as well as a Treasury official, the City 'would not be greatly affected one way or the other'. He considered 'London, New York and Tokyo as hubs from which a series of spokes go to other financial services which feed into them and actually give them strength rather than take it away' (House of Lords 1996). Also the Governor of the Bank of England seemed fairly convinced that 'the attractions of the City as a financial centre depend on a much broader range of issues than the currency we operate in', and that, in the event the UK stayed out, there might be even 'positive benefits' for the City of London (ibid).

Gavyn Davies, partner of Goldman Sachs since 1988 and principal economic commentator of *The Independent* since 1991, shared the Governor's view and declares himself 'not pessimistic about our ability to become a dominant force in the euro market in the same way that we have become a dominant force in the dollar market throughout the world'. He thought that the issue of the relationship between sterling and the euro was not central in determining the outlook for the City, 'what is much more central is getting the regulatory structure of our financial markets right, and getting that structure to continue to induce foreign firms to operate in London as the prime international centre. It is not clear to me that that need may be any more difficult if we are outside the single currency (ibid).'

On the contrary, according to Malcom Levitt, the real threat for the banking community was a government which decided to enter from the very beginning. This was considered a nightmare for the British banking sector. Indeed, it was undeniable that if EMU effectively started in 1999 the City ought to be ready to offer services in euro in its wholesale markets and to modify its structures consequently. However, British banks would incur much higher costs if the UK decided to enter from the beginning, because this would entail changing all the processing, settlement and accounting of retail payments through every medium all over the country. This was a very definitive step, from which it was very difficult, and extremely expensive, to get back if something happened and EMU collapsed or the British government decided to withdraw. Indeed, changing the currency would require changes in every element of a bank's information technology operations, with a total cost to the banking sector of £9.7bn as estimated by the Cap

Gemini Sogeti (CGS) the Europe's largest computer services company. Thus, although the banks had started to study the impact of EMU on their structures and organization already in 1995, they were not going to change the retail payments system.

In the opinion of McKenzie also, the risk of financial activities' fleeing from London to Frankfurt with the realization of EMU had been greatly exaggerated. Just looking at the position of London in the exchange markets, international banking or in lending, as well as generally in the dealing markets, it was possible to understand how its leadership was not seriously threatened by the process of EMU. Moreover, London was prominent because it was not influenced by domestic politics, the kind of advantage which was likely to be at risk inside a common currency area. Even if EMU posed some question marks, McKenzie thought that there were clearly going to be many pressures on the City of London from many external sources, and EMU was only one of these. It was therefore not adequate to speak about the impact of EMU on the City of London as a whole, while it was necessary to effect a sector by sector analysis.

Generally, however, there were not going to be major changes in the City with the UK out of EMU. As pointed out at length in the City of London's reports and publications, the main challenge for London if the UK remained out was represented by the risk of protectionist stances of the hard core EMU countries. Regarding this, there was a widespread agreement within the City of London that the British authorities would answer by putting the stress on the Single Market and claiming that also informal discrimination between ins and outs was illegal, as they had already started doing in relation to the debated issue of the conditions of access to TARGET for non-EMU countries (House of Lords 1996: 33; see also Bank of England 1996; and BBA *et al.* 1996).

However, according to Sir Douglas Wass, in the City of London people did not believe that the core countries would find a way to damage the financial activities of the out countries, also because this would have a negative impact on their own banks. Moreover, apart from the challenges, British refusal to join EMU might well entail some positive consequences, if, for example, the single currency area was subject to reserve requirements since, as the Governor of the Bank of England was keen to point out: 'I do not believe for a moment we would wish to impose (them) if we were on the outside' (House of Lords 1996: 22). The extent to which the euro was able to capture new markets, in fact, was very much dependent on the regulatory system inside the EMU area and if it was too strict, London would certainly have a competitive advantage with respect to Frankfurt and Paris.

In summing up, it seems that the British government's decision to remain out of EMU in January 1999 put the stress on two major sets of issues.

First, whether the EMU-area would impose restrictions which would make it particularly advantageous to be out, such as the imposition of non interest bearing minimum reserve requirements with the ECB. Second, how to develop competitive wholesale markets denominated in euros within the City of London even if the UK did not join, the main underlying assumption being that the impact of EMU on the City's wholesale financial markets would be momentous in any case.

As regards the first set of issues, it was still not certain whether these minimum reserve requirements would be imposed within the EMU-area, but it was clear that Germany, and the Bundesbank in particular, believed that this was necessary to control the implementation of monetary policy within the EMU-area. If ECB eventually imposed minimum reserve requirements, this would turn to be a major advantage for the City of London. Indeed, some people within the City of London tended to believe that, with the imposition of minimum reserve requirements, the City of London would be able to establish an 'Euro-euro' market, an offshore euro market in both currency and bonds. The main flaw of this hypothesis was that, while the US authorities were not concerned about the establishment of a Euro-dollar market in London, the European System of Central Banks would be extremely keen to try to avoid the establishment of an Euro-euro market outside the EMU-area. It remained to be seen, however, whether the ESCB would be able to do it, which, indeed, was a very difficult question to answer.

In the opinion of many within City, the chances for similar issues to be solved positively for the City of London, would be much enhanced if the UK government took an open position towards EMU, stating that the UK would not join EMU from the beginning, but 'when the time is right'. This is, indeed, the position eventually adopted by the Labour party at the end of October 1997, when ruling out early British entry in EMU.

Concluding on this first point, in the City of London before the establishment of EMU there were two prevailing opinions. On the one hand, those who believed that staying out was a competitive advantage. On the other hand, those who thought that this competitive advantage would be somehow offset by the other countries by, for example, limiting access to TARGET or not imposing minimum reserve requirements, both limiting the scope or the creation of a 'Euro-euro' market. The second set of issues concerning the City related to the preparation for EMU starting from the assumption that, in any case, the City would be more competitive (inside or outside EMU) if it was well prepared. On this point there was a general consensus within the City of London.

According to Sir Michael Butler, 'the City will need to prepare (for the introduction of the euro) even if we are not going to join if British banks and other financial services companies are not to lose business to their competitors' and in its written evidence, the BBA and APACS argued: 'regardless of whether the United Kingdom is in or out of EMU, City institutions, including banks, will need to be prepared to offer customers a full range of euro products in the wholesale financial markets. This will necessitate the banking and payments industries having in place the right mechanisms for trading, paying and settling in euro (House of Lords 1996: 32).'

The preparations included first, a great interest and active participation of the City of London in the decisions taken in Brussels over the legal framework for the use of euro. Second, the establishment of a wholesale payment system in euros in the City of London. Third, preparation of the computing systems to enable the banks to operate also in euros in the wholesale markets. Lastly, other changes to the wholesale markets. It was true that these preparations started relatively later in the City of London than in Paris or in Frankfurt. However, it was also true that there were no preparations for EMU going on in the retail business.

Things might actually be different after the establishment of EMU and, according to Sir Michael Butler, if EMU was a success, UK interests, as the interests of any other country, would suffer a lot if it remains outside. Indeed, underlined Sir Michael Butler, if the euro was created in 1999 all banks would use it, and it was an illusion to believe that Britain would have an independent monetary policy. UK interest rates would be European ones plus 1 or 2 per cent as a premium for the risk of not being part of EMU. Moreover, all countries, like Japan or Korea, which are now investing in the UK, would be much more tempted to invest in the countries belonging to EMU. Thus, in his opinion, there was no doubt that in the long run there would be a discrimination in favour of those banks inside the EMU and against Britain if it stayed out and that the City of London would suffer, but this was not likely to happen immediately and not if the government is committed to enter at a later stage.

More generally, Sir Douglas Wass identified three possible scenarios for the development of EMU. The first was the 'optimistic scenario', according to which EMU is a success: the EMU countries find it easy to maintain the Maastricht criteria, the ECB does not implement recessive monetary policies, and the euro is broadly accepted and traded. In this case, but only in this case, the non member countries would decide to enter. In the second scenario, the first pessimistic scenario, the participating countries cannot sustain the Maastricht criteria without implementing recessive policies leading to low or negative growth and to high unemployment rates, whereas the non participating enjoy a relatively more prosperous economic situation. In this scenario, the non-member countries would not ask to participate but, although there would be some discontent in EMU, nothing would happen.

In the last, pessimistic scenario, however, the situation described above, would cause anxieties in the EMU countries, and the system could break down, with even some political consequences, as the victory of extremist parties in the French or German elections, as happened during the 1930s. This would be extremely dangerous and very damaging for the process of European integration as a whole. On the likelihood of these three scenario, it is still difficult to make forecasts, but Sir Douglas considered the first scenario more as an hope than as a true possibility.

In conclusion, as the Thatcher government's 'wait and see' attitude towards the Exchange Rate Mechanism of the European Monetary System perfectly matched the British financial sector preferences for a set of monetarist practices inconsistent with the pegging of the exchange rates, also the present British government's 'wait and see' attitude towards the Maastricht way to EMU conceals a balance between the pros and the cons of EMU for the City of London which is still pending on the cons side. That the preferences of the British financial community might change in the course of the process leading to EMU is, of course, a possibility implicit in the approach adopted here.

However, from the overall picture coming out from the analysis of the impact of EMU on the City's markets and institutions, as well as from the declarations of some of its authoritative officials, it is possible to infer that at the moment of the making of EMU the City of London still preferred the British government to avoid committing the UK to EMU in any way. Thus, the new Labour Government's announcement at the end of October 1997 that the UK would not be joining EMU in 1999, seems perfectly in line with the preferences of the British financial system towards the issue.[35] Further, the inclusion among the economic tests for British participation of the impact of the EMU on the London financial markets confirms the sensitivity of the subject for the City of London. However, since the success of the City of London has always been linked to its ability to adapt to the changing environment, its markets and institutions will certainly be able to grasp the business opportunities coming from the establishment of a single currency area even remaining outside it.

Of course the City of London is not the only powerful sector within the European Union political and economical area, and of course many other power conflicts within groups of interest of the other EU member states at the domestic, as well as at the European level, will have to be analysed to give a credible answer to the many questions the process of European

---

[35] As already pointed out, on October 27, 1998, the Labour Chancellor announced that the UK would exercise its opt-out from stage 3 of EMU and would accordingly not be a participant on 1 January 1999. See Bank of England (1997).

monetary integration still poses, but this may only be the subject of another research project. As far as this one is concerned, it has reached the point in which it is necessary to stop, and leave the field open to more authoritative interventions.

5

The Joy of Flux: What Europe may Learn from North America's Preference for National Currency Sovereignty

STEPHEN CLARKSON

Whatever Europe has learned from America over the centuries when the 'new' world has stood as a beacon to the old, it seems hardly conceivable that its great experiment in monetary union has classes to take from across the Atlantic Ocean on currency policy. Indeed, Charles Goodhart, the respected scholar of currency union, has stated that 'the combination of a single market and floating exchange rates is untenable' (Goodhart 1995: 478), implying that it is the North American Free Trade Agreement (NAFTA) that has lessons to ingest from Europe, not the reverse.

Few doubt the overall benefits of a single market within the European Union (EU), but there is reason to doubt that a single market with no exchange controls, and with free movement of factors, will be compatible with the ability of its constituent members to vary exchange rates autonomously and sharply (Goodhart 1995: 478). In short, Goodhart believes North America's three members will not long be able to enjoy the luxury of separate national currencies if they want to secure their continental market.

We thus start our reflection with a paradox. The members of NAFTA arguably comprise a more integrated economy than that of the EU—whether integration is measured by the hard indicators of capital and even trade flows,[1] or by the softer measures of corporate structure (Blank 1995: 5–72)

My research was generously supported by interviews with Mostafa Askari (International Monetary Fund), Tom Bernes (International Monetary Fund), Bernard Bonin (Bank of Canada), Javier Guzman-Calafell (International Monetary Fund), John Murray (Bank of Canada), Charles Siegman (Federal Reserve Board), Robert Solomon (The Brookings Institution), and Ted Truman (Federal Reserve Board). Aimée Downey assisted in the research. The text has profited enormously from detailed comments by Eric Helleiner (Trent University) and Jim Stanford (Canadian Auto Workers) and from a critical reading by Tim Lewis and E.A. Safarian.

[1] Given Canada and Mexico's overwhelming dependence on the US in terms of both trade and foreign direct investment, North America can be considered to be more economically integrated than the European Union (see Box 1).

Box 1. Intraregional trade and foreign direct investment in North America (1990)

Intraregionl trade

For Canada: exports to the US as a percentage of total exports: 72.66; exports to Mexico as a percentage of total exports: 0.37; imports from the US as a percentage of total imports: 62.88; imports from Mexico as a percentage of total imports: 1.24.

For Mexico: exports to the US as a percentage of total exports: 73.12; exports to Canada as a percentage of total exports: 2.42; imports from the US as a percentage of total imports: 70.80; imports from Canada as a percentage of total imports: 1.27.

For the US: exports to Canada as a percentage of total exports: 21.10; exports to Mexico as a percentage of total exports: 7.22; imports from Canada as a percentage of total imports: 18.14; imports from Mexico as a percentage of total imports: 5.96.

Source: Blank (1995: 15).

Intraregional foreign direct investemant (FDI)

For Canada: FDI in the US as a percentage of total outward FDI: 62.7; FDI in Mexico as a percentage of total outward FDI: 0.2; FDI from the US as a percentage of total inward FDI: 62.5.

For Mexico: FDI from the US as a percentage of total inward FDI: 63.1; FDI from Canada as a percentage of total inward FDI: 1.4.

For the US: FDI in Canada as a percentage of total outward FDI: 20.9; FDI in Mexico as a percentage of total outward FDI: 1.9; FDI from Canada as a percentage of total inward FDI: 7.9.

Source: DeBlock and Rioux (1993: 22).

and cultural homogeneity.[2] Nevertheless, despite the historic steps taken in the past decade to harmonize trade and investment policy through economic integration agreements painfully negotiated first between Canada and the USA and then with Mexico, these partners show no sign of taking Goodhart's admonition seriously. No serious consideration has been given to the introduction of a North American Monetary Union (NAMU) with a continental bank that might in some way parallel the European Monetary

---

[2] While Quebec's use of French and Mexico's use of Spanish preserve some degree of linguistic heterogeneity on the continent, the homogenization of cultural values broadly defined to include consumer products, professional athletics, and movie or television consumption is far greater than in Europe where diversity is entrenched by the distinct national history and language of each member state. In one crucial dimension, labour mobility, North America is markedly less integrated than Europe.

Union (EMU) and the European Central Bank (ECB). Exploring this paradox should not just shed light on the specific features of North American integration but also bring into sharper relief some of its implications for the institutionalization of the EMU.

As a subject for analysis, currency union appears to belong squarely in the domain of economics, but as this book's title suggests, politics cannot long be kept out of the discussion. Economists may have framed the debate in the academic literature, but it is politicians who have to take the legislative steps necessary for bringing the scholars' abstractions to concrete fruition. And, if the monetary union project comes to grief, it is in the political domain that the pigeons will come home to roost. Accordingly, we will first look at the somewhat arcane debate in the economics literature about currency policy options in North America before considering the more political arguments based on national interest. This will let us examine the relevance of the one continent's experience for the institutional deficits likely to result from monetary union in the other.

The View from Economics

As the first non-conforming member of the Bretton Woods club—Canada let its dollar float as early as 1950[3] as can be seen in Fig. 5.1—it is not surprising that orthodox Canadian economists developed some comparative advantage in debating the merits of a floating versus a fixed exchange rate. There are five principal arguments in favour of fixing (and so against floating) the Canadian exchange rate—and joining a North American currency union would simply be an extreme version of such pegging.

Fixer 1. Fluctuations of the exchange rate have had damaging economic effects in Canada.

Fixer 2. Price stability would result from pegging a weaker Canadian to a stronger and more stable American coinage.

Fixer 3. Adopting the American dollar would generate huge savings in debt servicing due to the lower interest rates that Canadian governments would have to pay.

Fixer 4. Sheltering Canada's currency from speculative attacks provoked by intemperate mood changes among callow bond traders would reduce uncertainty for entrepreneurs and so increase both trade and investment flows.

---

[3] Canada managed to escape the discipline of the Bretton Woods system's fixed exchange rate stipulations, allowing its dollar to float from 1950 to 1962 and, following a period of pegging to the American dollar, from 1970 onwards.

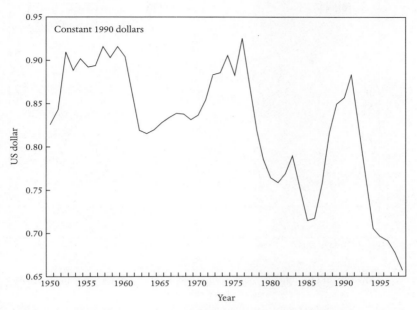

FIG. 5.1. Canadian dollar real bilateral exchange rate in terms of US dollars (1950–95).
Source: Bank of Canada.

Fixer 5. Exporters, importers, and tourists would save the transaction costs involved in having to change from one currency to the other—a significant factor in an economy whose bilateral trade with the USA runs at C$1 billion per day.[4]

Each of these arguments put forward by the faction we will call the *Fixers* in favour of a pegged currency or a currency union has been challenged by the school we might name the *Floaters*. To wit

Floater 1. Evidence that currency fluctuations have been damaging to the Canadian economy is inadequate.[5]

Floater 2. The price stability argument is not so much conjectural as conjunctural: recently, Canada has achieved lower inflation rates than the USA,

[4] The European Monetary Commission estimated in 1990 that the elimination of transaction costs under EMU would amount to a savings equal to approximately 0.4% of EU GDP (Bayoumi and Eichengreen 1993*a*: 2).

[5] Lafrance and van Norden (1994: 54) cite earlier studies by Farrell, DeRosa, and McCrown (1983) and Belanger and Gutierrez (1990). Côté (1994) concludes that the effects of increased volatility on trade are ambiguous. The reductions in trade as a result of exchange rate variability are minimal and hedging allows avoidance of these at little cost. Also, such variability can have a positive effect by creating profitable trading and investment opportunities for business.

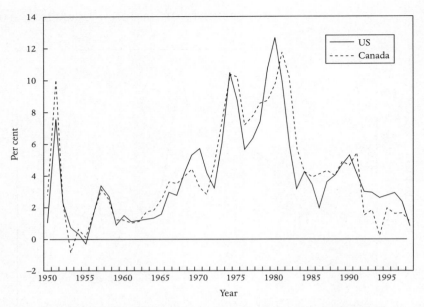

Fig. 5.2. Canadian and US inflation rates as reflected in the consumer price index (1950–95).
Source: Bank of Canada.

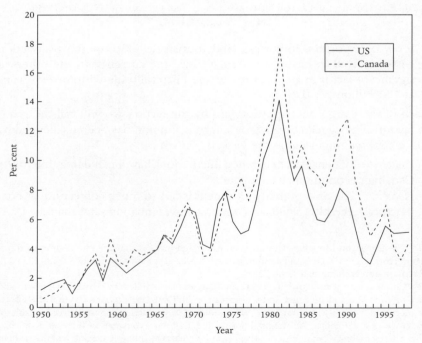

Fig. 5.3. Canadian and US short-term interest rates (1950–95).
Source: Bank of Canada.

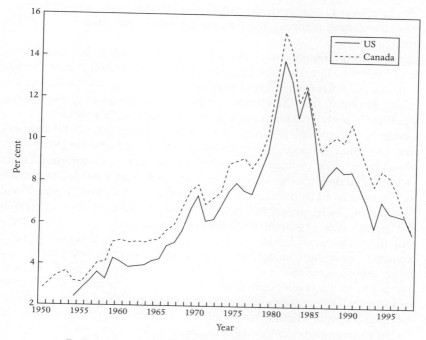

FIG. 5.4. Canadian and US long-term interest rates (1950–95).
Source: Bank of Canada.

so that linking up with the Federel Reserve System at this historical moment
would entail taking on higher inflation rates (see Fig. 5.2).[6]

Floater 3. By the same logic Canada, with its lower short-term interest
rates, would currently suffer higher, not lower debt-servicing costs by adjusting to American levels (see Figs 5.3 and 5.4).[7]

Floater 4. Historically, speculative pressures were a greater concern for
Canada under the Bretton Woods system of fixed but adjustable exchange
rates. Nowadays, bracing oneself against possible speculative attack is
more of a problem for a badly than a well-managed economy, though
policy-makers' awareness of their vulnerability to global capital markets'
capricious moods seems to have mitigated the problem considerably.[8]

---

[6] Canadian inflation has been lower than the American level for the 1990s as a whole.
The increase in consumer prices between 1994 and 1995 stood at 2.8% in the US compared
to 2.2% in Canada. *International Financial Statistics Yearbook (IFSY)*, 1996.

[7] Although central bank lending rates have been historically higher for Canada than for
the US, they have fallen below US rates in the last two years (*IFSY* 1996).

[8] Murray, van Norden, and Vigfrisson (1996: 35) conclude that there is little support for
the excess volatility argument. Most of the broad movements in the Canadian dollar can be
explained by changes in market fundamentals and not aberrant speculative activity.

The prospect of currency meltdown is more pressing for economies emerging from state planning systems or hyperinflation than for relatively normal systems.

Floater 5. Transaction costs cannot be argued away but they can be put in perspective. The question becomes whether eliminating these charges is worth the costs involved in giving up currency flexibility. It is in praise of this flexibility that the Floaters' logic is more compelling, particularly when their analysis focuses on how best to respond to shocks.

Floater 6. Economies are subject to major unanticipated disturbances that are either economic or political in nature, and that originate both from either inside or from outside the system. They can, for instance, be victims of supply shocks in which the availability of a needed commodity can be blocked by political cataclysm (civil war) or natural disaster (flood or drought), or its price can fluctuate widely as did that of petroleum in the Organization of Petroleum Exporting Countries (OPEC) crises of 1973 and 1979. Demand shocks can be equally disruptive, particularly for a resource exporting country like Canada. As foreign markets pass up and down the curve of the business cycle their import needs oscillate, causing shocks to the staple-exporting economy. The gyration in world prices for individual commodities produced by changing demand for, say, wheat can spell boom or bust for monocultural regional economies such as the Canadian prairie provinces which are heavily dependent on the export of a few staples. The jagged curve of Canada's terms of trade reflects these commodity price fluctuations (see Fig. 5.5).[9] According to the Floaters, a flexible exchange rate remains an important device for governments trying to cope with shocks, whether generated internally or externally (Lafrance and van Norden 1994: 58). This currency elasticity affords a degree of policy independence which is not worth sacrificing in order to gain the relatively minor advantages offered by pegging.

Enlarging the field of vision from Canada alone to Canada and the USA, Floaters have little trouble showing that the North America defined by these two economies does not match their strict criteria for what should constitute an optimal currency zone.[10] Shocks in the US economy are distinct from shocks in Canada. Being a net importer rather than an exporter of resources is but one index of the US economy's different industrial structure, and helps to explain why it responds differently from

[9] Historically, Canada's terms of trade variability relative to other G10 countries has been moderately large, averaging 22.3% between 1979 and 1989, and suggesting a comparatively high degree of volatility (Fenton and Murray 1993: 508).

[10] See Lafrance and van Norden (1994) and Bayoumi and Eichengreen (1993b). Both studies conclude that Canadian supply shocks are negatively correlated to those affecting the US economy, which is not an optimal currency zone either: the 1990–1 recession affected the east and west coasts but not the interior states.

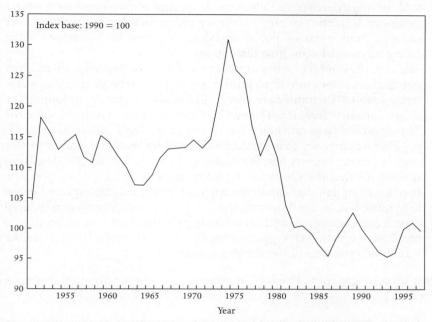

Index base: 1990 = 100

FIG. 5.5. Canadian terms of trade as expressed by the commodity price index (1950–95).
Commodity price index (US$) divided by the US GDF deflator.
Source: International Monetary Fund.

the Canadian economy to the same external shocks. And if economic regions react asymmetrically to such disturbances they, by definition, do not form an optimal zone for the purposes of forming a currency union (Lafrance and van Norden 1994: 52). For the area comprised by Canada plus the USA we come, in short, to another paradox. The Canadian economists who have been the most powerful advocates of economic integration between the two countries have all defended the notion of a floating Canadian dollar in the name of national, macroeconomic autonomy, despite Canada itself not constituting an optimal currency zone—Johnson (1970), Eastman (1971), Ronald Wonnacott (1987), Laidler and Robson (1990), Lipsey (1992), and Purvis (1992).

Floater 7. The Floaters' argument about shock therapy goes further. A government's loss of exchange rate flexibility following incorporation in a currency union raises the question of what alternative policy tools are available for helping an economy adjust to major disturbances. With its central bank neutralized as the prime economic shock absorber, the country's treasury has to bear an increased load. This imposes a greater strain on fiscal policy which has, in any case, become a counter-productive tool of macroeconomic adjustment as capital becomes increasingly footloose. Imperfect or not, a currency union member's capacity to alter tax rates and levels of public spending becomes its last resort when facing substantial economic disruptions.

Floater 8. Beyond the policy argument in favour of flexibility, there is the practical consideration of what price would have to be paid to join a currency union. The immediate cost to the smaller economy in joining the larger currency zone is presumed by Floaters to be substantial since the former would have no choice but to accept the high conversion rate for pegging its currency that would be dictated by the latter. Italy's experience in gaining re-entry into the Exchange Rate Mechanism (ERM) in 1996 reminds us that the *demandeur* typically has a weak bargaining position. Benefits from membership in the currency union may be expected in the long term, but, in the short run, the cost would be experienced in reduced export competitiveness and deflationary pressure. Bonn's decision to give the East German Mark parity with the Deutschmark clearly hurt the economic prospects of the Eastern *Länder*.

Not surprisingly, these Floaters' arguments encounter refutation from our Fixers:

Fixer 6. In as regionally and sectorally heterogeneous an economy as Canada's, the utility of currency flexibility as a shock absorber can be questioned. Where the country's staples-producing region may suffer from a fall in commodity prices, its manufacturing region may prosper: a 'correction' of the currency may help one region but harm the other and, for this reason, is too blunt an instrument to respond to regionally specific changes in economic conditions.[11] The Fixers' argument becomes either that Canada, with a highly diversified economy, does not need exchange rate flexibility, or that the instrument is too insensitive to cope with its enormous regional variations (Harris 1992). In other words, it matters that Canada is not an optimal currency zone.

Fixer 7. Fiscal policy would certainly become more important as an instrument of adjustment to external shocks following entry into a currency union, but it is not the only adaptation mechanism available for policymakers. Since the locus of industrial policy is increasingly moving to the provincial and municipal levels (Wolfe 1997), made-in-the-region policymaking is likely to be more responsive to local conditions, including the geographically specific fallout from general shocks. Other factors—

---

[11] The absence of a significant correlation between supply shocks to western and eastern Canada suggests the ineffectiveness of currency flexibility for Canada (Mundell 1961).

including other types of government policy—could or would also come into play. Many tools of microeconomic policy can be targeted by subnational jurisdictions to stimulate an economic region or sector in distress. While NAFTA prohibits some policies (particularly those that discriminate against foreign-controlled corporations) and the World Trade Organization, (WTO), subsidy code rules out others (particularly those targeted at export promotion or import substitution), high unemployment or low income can justify government intervention that the WTO would otherwise deem protectionist.

Beyond the direct intervention of government, market forces can also work independently of exchange rate responses to mitigate the impact of shocks. Wages, if they are flexible, cushion the impact of external disruptions. As trade unions lose power in response to globalizing forces and as wage rates consequently become less 'sticky', wage flexibility makes economies more responsive to shocks, particularly where unemployment levels are high. Labour mobility—which can be encouraged by industrial adaptation policies—can also help depressed or manic regions adjust to (mis)fortune.[12] Foreign capital may also help an economy respond to shocks, whether positive or negative, though some types of foreign capital move faster and other types of capital are economically more productive. The inflow of speculative financial flows can only provide short-term relief while at the same time increasing an economy's vulnerability to future destabilization. Direct foreign investment can actually create economic activity, but transnational corporations' strategic decision-making is too slow for shock-buffeted economies to count on this factor as a means of achieving rapid adjustment.

Fixer 8. Establishing the entry cost of a currency is a political decision to be sure, but does not necessarily work to the detriment of the new entrant. The entry level for the Canadian dollar and the Mexican peso to NAMU would have to be negotiated. It is not obvious a priori that, if the USA did want the monetary union, it would impose an economically—and so politically—unacceptable cost on its neighbours.[13]

---

[12] Newfoundland, as the weakest economy in the Canadian federation, is the one province to have experienced an outflow of population in the last five years: its population declined 2.9% between the censuses of 1991 and 1996 (Mitchell 1997). But this argument is double-edged: it can be used against rather than for currency union. With its own currency, Floaters could argue, Newfoundland would have been able to adjust to its economically depressed condition by devaluation and so create jobs through the resulting growth of exports.

[13] Within each country, of course, there are conflicting interests with producers, exporters, and the tourist sector favouring a low exchange rate while the financial sector, importers, and tour operators tend to prefer higher levels.

Fixer 9. Perhaps the most telling argument among Canadian Fixers over the years has been the scornful dismissal of the Bank of Canada's policy capacity as the 'thirteenth district' of the Federal Reserve Board. For all its architectural splendour (the Bank of Canada building in Ottawa is a sublime superimposition of a 1970s romantic modernist glass cage around a massive 1930s art deco core) and for all the competence of its professional economists (sometimes dubbed the best and most orthodox economics faculty in the country), the Bank of Canada's margin of autonomy, Fixers maintain, is strictly constrained by its position in the shadow of the globe's financial hegemon.

The Floaters will then counter these arguments

Floater 9. Such, at least, was a view widely held among monetary policy sceptics in the 1970s. More recently, the Bank of Canada's critics have implicitly made the opposite case. If they were complaining in the early 1990s about a 'made-in-Canada recession', economists were crediting the Bank of Canada and John Crow, its steely, zero-inflation governor from 1987 to 1994, with the capacity independently to steer a route of monetary austerity more stringent than the Fed's (von Furstenberg 1995: 23–4). Floaters concede that the Canadian system is closely interlocked with the American, but affirm that, although its room for manoeuvre is limited by the financial instruments the Bank of Canada trades (primarily short), its capacity for autonomy is effective precisely because the volume of North America's capital flows is so large that the Canadian section of the market is sensitive to the interest rate fine-tuning which the Bank of Canada can still practise. High Canadian/American capital mobility and easy asset substitutability mean that monetary policy can effectively, if indirectly, massage exchange rate levels through manipulating interest rates, and affect the market's judgement about resulting price stability. It is this capacity for sophisticated monitoring and adjusting which would be lost to the national economy from currency union.

Mainstream Floaters find support from more radical, structuralist economists who deem exchange rate flexibility since 1970 to have 'played a crucial role in protecting the competitiveness and viability of Canadian industry despite the notable rise in Canada's unit labour costs over the period relative to those in the US.'[14] Labour laws and employment policies being more generous north of the border than in the USA, the depreciation of the Canadian dollar has helped the weaker economy sustain a stronger welfare state (Stanford 1995). Beyond the economic priesthood there has also been a general recognition in the business press that the Canadian economy has only been able to survive the American competitive onslaught triggered by

---

[14] Letter from Jim Stanford, 9 June 1997.

free trade because the Canadian dollar ultimately fell far enough that labour remained competitive despite the country's richer social wage.[15]

If the main thrust both of neo-classical and structuralist economists defended a Canadian dollar delinked from the American, what can be said about the 1990s, when the definition of North America was expanded to include Mexico? Is sauce for the Canadian goose also sauce for the Mexican gander? The consensus among the Floaters is overwhelmingly affirmative. For economies that react to external shocks asymmetrically a floating exchange rate offers a fast, flexible response mechanism (Lafrance and van Nordern 1994: 56). Despite Mexico's catastrophic experience with exchange rate crises under an adjustable peg, Floaters maintain that the basic thrust of this argument holds there too.

Mexico strikes even the amateur observer as a third world economy.[16] Even if its state-sponsored import substitution industrialization and the autarchic, monopolistic structures that were erected after World War II have been rapidly dismantled in the past decade, it is patently vulnerable to much higher rates of inflation, unemployment, and currency volatility than its gringo neighbour.[17] Having had a peso fixed at the rate of 12.5 to the US dollar for two decades from the mid 1950s, it devalued in 1976 to 22.6 to the dollar. A few tumultuous years of oil price appreciation with the consequent increased inflation, foreign capital influx, external deficit growth, and ultimate debt crisis in 1982 resulted in a peso worth one-150th of a dollar. Five more years following the fall of world oil prices left the exchange rate at 2,281 pesos to the dollar. An even greater peso crisis was in store following continuing high inflation which, together with rising US interest rates, massive intervention by the Banco de Mexico to maintain a high exchange rate, and the influx of long- and short-term foreign capital in anticipation of the new North American Free Trade Agreement, produced a peso so overvalued by 1994 that it was poised for a further disastrous crash (see Fig. 5.6).

Given this roller coaster history it might be thought that Mexico would be the first to apply for currency union for the same reason that France, since the early 1980s, has wanted identification with, if not actual membership in, the Bundesbank: Mexico would instantly gain the international credibility of its hegemonic neighbour along with its level of price stability. Because of Mexico's state-controlled union movement, wages can 'flexibly' respond to

[15] Canada's tariffs being twice the American level, it stood to lose more market share at home from free trade than it stood to gain market share in the US.

[16] Mexico's per capita GNP in 1994 before the last crisis, was $7,019 compared to $20,257 for Canada and $25,572 for the USA (L'État du Monde, Paris: La Découverte 1995). Mexican statistics are so notoriously unreliable that other observers' estimates setting Mexican GNP per capita at one-tenth US levels are equally credible.

[17] Since 1990 consumer price level changes have varied between 26.7 and 35% in Mexico compared with 5.4–2.8% in the USA (IFSY 1996: 111–12).

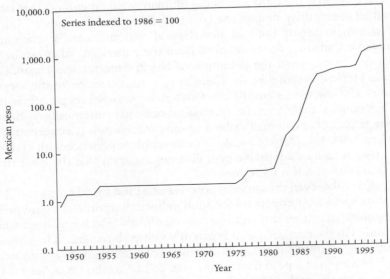

FIG. 5.6. Mexican peso exchange rate in terms of US dollars (1950–95).
Source: Bank of Canada.

a shock, allowing the economy rapidly to achieve a new 'equilibrium' without having to resort to devaluation (Lalonde and St. Amant 1995: 105).

For banking professionals, however, fixing Mexico's exchange rate would be extremely risky. For one thing, the period between the announcement of the plan to form a currency union and the actual moment of consummation would be perilous: a lone currency pegging to a stronger one requires very substantial international reserves to defend itself from the speculative rushes that would be unavoidable until the irrevocable had happened.

Moreover, the differences between the Mexican and American markets' reactions to shocks are far greater than those between the Canadian and the US economy. Supply shocks account for more output fluctuation in Mexico than in any US region. Apart from its response to shocks, their nature in Mexico is different. Although there is a common component to North American supply shocks,[18] the size of real demand and monetary shocks is greater for Mexico,[19] leading to larger price shifts and greater changes in real

[18] For example, disruptions in the international petroleum market would affect Mexico, western Canada and the US northwest, all energy-producing regions in North America (Bayoumi and Eichengreen 1993a: 23).

[19] A real demand disturbance for Mexico could be a response to a shift in the government's fiscal policy or a change in the level of world demand for petroleum. Monetary shocks could be changes in net foreign capital unflows or an increase in the domestic money supply in response to the public's desire to increase cash holdings (Lalonde and St. Amant 1995: 108).

balances.[20] What is more, political shocks can be even more disruptive to the economy. In the course of a single calendar year rural uprisings, political assassinations, and spectacular kidnappings linked to the ruling party's authoritarianism and the narcotics business shook the confidence of global capital markets and, combined with dubious monetary policy, culminated in the currency crisis of December 1994 (Weintraub 1997: 54–68).

Once in NAMU, Mexico's problems would not be over. It would still suffer external economic shocks, whether those generated in the American economy through its fluctuating demand for Mexican products or from global economic changes. It can expect to continue to be shaken by those internal tremors that form part of the current process of radical economic liberalization, with its resulting widespread urban and rural poverty under conditions of reduced government control and increased violence (Teichman 1997a). In either case, membership in a currency union would make it harder to offset the forces raising the Mexican level of unemployment. Blocking imports by higher tariffs to counteract a critical current account deficit and stimulating specific sectors with interventionist industrial policies targeted to promote Mexican companies are policies no longer available to the government under the restrictive provisions of NAFTA. Devaluation can at least stimulate exports, but with exchange and interest rates fixed not by the Banco de Mexico but by a continental central bank, the government would be forced to rely on fiscal policy, a tool even less useful for helping a developing economy react to external disruption than it is in a highly industrialized economy.

As in the Canadian case, this argument for currency autonomy can be questioned. The 1994 crisis was itself the product of a misguided, albeit autonomous, policy aimed at keeping the peso's exchange rate defiantly high.[21] However much these arguments can be contested, our opening paradox is nevertheless reaffirmed: policy-makers who find in NAFTA a key to transforming Mexico from a third to a first world economy consider NAMU to be a formula condemning Mexico to remain a weak regional sister, the Newfoundland of North America.

Politics and Calculating the National Interest

Referring to the fate of Newfoundland shifts the debate on to a different plane. If this bankrupt British colony floating by itself in the cold waters of the North

---

[20] The greater severity of demand and monetary shocks in Mexico leads to increased swings in unemployment and national income.

[21] Mexico spent over $20 billion during 1994 to prop up the peso. *The Washington Post*, 1 Jan. 1995 (Teichman 1997b: 21).

Atlantic could never have been thought to qualify as a member of an optimal currency zone with the nine provinces comprising the Dominion of Canada in 1948, we must introduce the factor so far excluded from our analysis: politics. Prestige and patriotism—one dare not speak of a Canadian version of Manifest Destiny—motivated Canadian politicians to accept the burden of the fiscal transfers needed to bring Newfoundland's infrastructure and standard of public services up to the Canadian mainland's norm. Since a slim majority of Newfoundlanders considered the promise of these material gains to be worth the sacrifice of currency and policy autonomy, there was the making of a deal.

The case for or against currency union, in other words, cannot be left solely in the hands of neo-classical economists and bankers. At some point the national and social values of the potential partners have to be addressed. If we are to understand why North America has not moved to currency union, we must come to grips with the way each country sees its national interest.

Mexico

We have already seen that the Floaters' economic critique of currency union has an implicitly political subtext: currency autonomy is necessary if the Mexican government is to have any hope of navigating through tumultuous seas. Thinking more broadly of the Mexican political culture, with its deeply anti-Yankee nationalism born of bitter military experience with US territorial expansion and direct American intervention in Mexican affairs over the years, the subsuming of the peso into a super-dollar can only be contemplated as an ultimate giant step in a long process of cultural integration in which Mexicans' national identity had become compatible with a superimposed North American consciousness.

The United States

Washington aims to maximize continental economic and policy integration but minimize the three states' institutional integration. Even though its neighbouring governments have less and less actual control over their important economic policy levers, it is in the hegemon's interest not to accept responsibility for their social and cultural problems.

Washington's concern about the peso is indirect: will instability on Mexico's currency market have a contagious 'tequila effect', destabilizing other currencies, including the American? Will exchange rate swings swamp the effects of tariff reductions achieved by NAFTA? The American interest in the Mexican peso is therefore to achieve a stable exchange rate with smooth rather than catastrophic adjustments to future shocks. American politicians keep a watching brief on Mexico's performance, but in the current circumstances of its underdevelopment and overpopulation, currency union is a nightmare, not a dream. The American goal is to extend the market's sphere (which it dominates) while reducing the reach of political institutions (where Mexican and Canadian policies could voice their demands). If currency union brought NAFTA a step closer to labour market integration, NAMU would nullify one of the chief objectives Washington had hoped NAFTA would achieve: a more prosperous Mexican economy generating enough employment for its own burgeoning population to reduce migratory pressure towards the north. Taking on the burden that could imply massive transfers of population over the Rio Grande from the south to the north, and perhaps massive transfers of social support funds from the north to the south, is not a US prescription for life, liberty, or the pursuit of happiness.

While discrete parts of the American economy may suffer from the import competition exacerbated by a peso devaluation, there is no national resonance for a battle cry against Mexico of 'competitive devaluation!' analogous to France's angry response to Italy's depreciation of the lira in the early 1990s. Washington's apparent unconcern about competitive devaluation even relative to Germany and Japan is also due to the key American state agencies that deal with exchange rate policies being institutionally insulated from the industrial sectors that can suffer from global currency volatility (Henning 1994). When the Canadian dollar is low, there are specific interests in the American political economy (forest cutters, grain farmers, auto workers, steel makers) who complain of unfair competition. But the US economy is so diversified that these losers are balanced by other winners (notably the consumers of lower priced imports). High levels of US corporate control in Canada also ensure that no powerful political force develops a platform to attack Canada's competitive advantage allegedly derived from exchange rate depreciation.

The Canadian economy has such high levels of American ownership and technological mastery, is so complementary to the US economy's needs, and is such a large market for US exports that political Washington has little sense of threat from it. There might be some public satisfaction from the thought that the domain of the US dollar would be expanded to cover the whole of the continent, but the American public would not likely be willing to pay for this increase in pride with any increase in financial burden.[22] American politicians' tenacious determination to retain every possible speck of national

---

[22] There is no evidence that Americans would respond to Canada's and Mexico's closer integration in the US economy in a way analogous to West Germany's sacrifice to ease the absorption of the former German Democratic Republic. Public transfer payments from the Federal Republic to East Germany in 1991 amounted to DM10 billion, approximately two-thirds of East German GNP (Friedmann 1992: 144).

sovereignty would make it very hard to sell the idea that Canada and Mexico should be granted membership in a continentalized Federal Reserve Board.

Canada

For their part, Canadians seem to have no more political desire for such an eventuality than their neighbours. France may want a European central bank in order to have some control within the ECB's virtual-reality Bundesbank, but Canadians have no illusion that even a seat on the board of the Fed would give them 'any more influence than Atlanta has', as one observer put it, referring to the insignificant role played by Atlanta in the deliberations of the present Federal Reserve Board. The disparity of power is too great for Canada to have a comparable rivalrous ambition—as France nourishes towards Germany—to keep the larger neighbour constrained through participation in its currency policy. Nor is there much potential for alliance with the rest of the hemisphere to offset American hegemony, a 21st-century version of Britain's alliance against Napoleon. Although such a Lilliputian notion flickers at the back of Canadian policy-makers' minds when they think of the ultimate implications of a Free Trade Area of the Americas creating a bloc from the Arctic to the Antarctic, this fantasy belongs more to the realm of social science fiction than to that of practical politics. There is no disastrous war within living memory whose resurgence needs pre-empting. There is no sense that NAFTA is a continental political system in the making, one in which a common identity should be affirmed with a common banknote in every pocket from Chiapas to the Klondike.

But times change. About twenty years ago no one but the long-shot candidate for the presidency, California's Governor Ronald Reagan, could talk seriously about a 'North American accord' linking not just Canada and the USA but including Mexico. Is it possible that, twenty years from now, NAMU could be not fancy but fact?

The prime precondition among neo-classical economists for NAMU is for the North American economy to approximate an optimal currency zone. While it would be unnecessary for all of the continent's regional economic differences to have become homogenized in terms of their mix of resource, manufacturing, and service industries, their developmental disparities would need to have narrowed. Most important in this regard would be a successful transition by the Mexican economy to first world status. What would further condition symmetrical responses in Canada, the USA, and Mexico to common economic shocks would be a continuing continental integration through transnational corporate restructuring. Trilateral harmonization in the market place could generate such low tolerance for any currency fluctuations among market players that they might press to have NAMU put back on to the policy agenda.[23]

Approaching the condition of an optimal currency zone might not even be a necessary let alone a sufficient condition. Washington would need to be impelled—possibly by a change in the global balance of forces—to consider NAMU in its national interest. The USA retrenches continentally when threatened globally (Clarkson 1997: 4–6). In the mid 1980s, the USA embarked on the course that ultimately led to NAFTA because of its apprehended decline in global hegemony. If by the 2010s, the euro has successfully challenged the US dollar as a reserve currency, Washington might again look to North America as a means to buttress its competitive position on global capital markets.

It is hard to envisage such continuing economic integration taking place without pressures for a parallel political deepening of the NAFTA system. Such an institutional consolidation of the North American regime would not have had to achieve full political integration just as the EU does not need to have become a United States of Europe to consummate EMU. Many assume that making currency union acceptable in the USA would require a monetary authority that was still politically accountable to Congress. Others believe the policy rigidity created by NAMU would require labour mobility across national boundaries as well as mechanisms of redistribution so that losing areas could be compensated by winners. Whether labour mobility and regional economic equalization need to be part of a currency union, can, of course, be contested. The EU has only very minor degrees of both since cultural differences restrict labour migration and the EU budget for regional development is modest. NAMU would probably have to be brought into being without either.

At this point we can ask whether NAMU would ever be necessary. If Europe is the implicit model for this analysis, it can be argued that North America is already demonstrating some of the characteristics that the project of monetary union in Europe is designed to achieve. It took the Maastricht criteria —negotiated behind closed doors and imposed on the EU's reluctant member states over massive protests in the streets of Paris and angry obstruction in the council chambers of Rome—to push member-state governments in the direction of a neo-liberal orthodoxy which has already been achieved in Ottawa and Mexico City by other, less institutionalized means. A change of generation within the Institutional Revolutionary Party's technocratic elite has brought fervent neo-liberalism to the commanding

---

[23] 'The lure of lower financing costs for private businesses, caught up in the dynamics of NAFTA-inspired economic integration and the disruptive effects of real exchange rate swings on competitiveness, will cause monetary union to be given a second look in the Americas' (von Furstenberg 1996: 40).

heights of the government and the Banco de Mexico (Teichman 1997*b*: 14–22). The Bank of Canada shifted to monetarism in 1974 well ahead of Paul Volcker's conversion of the Federal Reserve System. Ottawa's Department of Finance—chastened by Moody's unfavourable credit ratings—pushed the national deficit relentlessly down to zero, whatever the cost to the country's social and cultural fabric. In effect, bank, treasury, and finance officials in the three countries already form a continental chapter of the global epistemic community of financial officials—reading the same books, thinking the same thoughts, convening in the same conferences, and persuading their respective publics that low inflation has priority over low unemployment as the number-one policy priority.

Implications for EMU

To extract the lessons for Europe of the divergent North American currency experience, let us rephrase our opening paradox. Although the world currency market—with its high-tech, 24-hours-a-day, instant transmission of billions of funds—is the most advanced aspect of globalization, exchange rate autonomy is touted as a prime expression of national identity not only by the continental hegemon but by its neighbours to the north and to the south. Bankers north of the 49th parallel and south of the Rio Grande concede that, as economic integration among the three countries continues to deepen—with pressure on the two peripheral countries to harmonize their industrial standards and even their tariffs up or down to US levels, exchange rates can be expected to fluctuate less and long-term interest rates converge more. They concur that policies straying from orthodoxy will in any case be rapidly punished by globalized capital markets. Nevertheless, contrary to Ohmae's prognostication that globalization has made obsolete the traditional instruments of central banks,[24] North American banking officials cling to their currency sovereignty.

It would appear that we hold in our hand the key to explaining some of the most intriguing differences between the process of integration on the two continents. If we translate our paradox into global finance's 'unholy trinity'—capital mobility, exchange rate stability, and monetary policy autonomy—we can put our contrast of the two continental systems into a more analytically fruitful light (Cohen 1996: 280). All members of NAFTA

---

[24] '[A]s the workings of genuinely global capital markets dwarf their ability to control exchange rates or protect their currency, nation states have become inescapably vulnerable to the discipline imposed by economic choices made elsewhere by people and institutions over which they have no practical control' (Ohmae 1995: 12).

and the EU have opted for capital mobility, but North American states are willing to sacrifice exchange rate stability in order to retain what for them is the greater good of monetary policy autonomy. In contrast, those states joining EMU are willing to abdicate monetary policy autonomy in order to achieve what for them is the higher value of exchange rate stability.

Thus, dogma reigns in its distinctive fashion on both shores of the Atlantic Ocean. On its eastern beaches open economies are believed to be too vulnerable to tolerate the disruptive threat of the very currency volatility which, on its western shore is held to be a stabilizer vital for the survival of separate socio-political regimes. In North America so much trade is carried on within the continental corporation that exchange rate stabilization is low on the transnational corporations (TNCs) political agenda. In Europe it is maintained that the TNCs are a driving force urging EMU, even if they too are shielded against uncertainty by their intra-firm accounting practices.

The elites driving EMU to fruition seemed to want a common currency less for economic reasons than to pursue a multiple—though not necessarily coherent—political agenda: neo-liberal pressure to restrain the welfare state, the Fortress Europe drive to consolidate Continental power in its global context, the Franco-German effort to remain hegemonic within the EU, the 'Club Med' countries' striving not to be left behind, and neo-functionalist hopes to achieve a supranational Europe with a common identity for its citizens. Because currency notes and coins are not just one of the most widely produced consumer goods but as a consequence among the most powerful vehicles producing national identities (Helleiner 1998: 6), one can hypothesize that North America is likely to remain a mirror image of the European Union. Whereas the euro is expected to strengthen the community-wide self-consciousness of European citizens, North American elites prefer to leave national identities intact while unobtrusively acting as co-ordinated managers of a continental dollar zone in which Canada and Mexico follow the US lead in most important monetary policy shifts, unless they want to be even more neo-conservative than the Fed.

An enormous territory encompassing widely different geographical characteristics, the Canadian federation itself falls far short of qualifying as an optimal currency zone. Interprovincial currency rigidity has only been tolerable for the past fifty years because a relative powerful central government was able to compensate regional losers through massive equalization transfers, whether by investing in economic development projects in poor provinces or by guaranteeing a high nationwide level for social support policies.[25] The implication of Canada's national experience for Europe is that

[25] The irony of this phenomenon can be seen in Quebec's nationalist movement which declares that an independent Quebec would still use a Canadian dollar even though economists believe that, for its economy to survive the shocks it could expect post independence,

establishing a single currency for a Continental economy whose member states demonstrate widely differing characteristics and levels of welfare will necessitate the capacity, both institutional and fiscal, to make very significant transfers to compensate losing regions for their economic misfortunes. Otherwise, the burden of bearing the impact of adverse shocks will fall on workers in Europe's still quite immobile labour markets.

In North America, with high market autonomy and capital mobility but low institutionalization of political functions, currency autonomy remains a useful vestige of nation-state sovereignty. Held up in the light of North American integration, EMU appears dangerously homogenizing—an ambitious and highly risky project being driven over uncongenial economic ground. The implication for EMU is that it may become impossibly difficult to sustain relatively generous social policies and labour market structures when the member states are subjected to the policies of a democratically unaccountable continental central bank inspired by a neo-liberal philosophy. If this prophecy comes true, countries with a rich *acquis social* may come under strong pressure to recapture their currency autonomy or to break the Maastricht rules prescribing fiscal policy conformity in order to protect their unique policy traditions.

Canada participates actively in such multilateral global institutions as the WTO and the OECD. Of greater relevance for its currency concerns are the secretive monthly sessions of the Basle Committee on Banking Supervision within the Bank for International Settlement, the surveillance work done in the International Monetary Fund, and the highly visible annual pow-wows of the G7 (Coleman and Porter 1993). It may be that a middle- to large-sized power (Canada currently boasts the world's seventh largest GDP) enjoys more influence on global currency matters through its participation in these many-membered global institutions than it would in a three-member continental currency union in which its GDP represented but 8 per cent of the total continental product. The implication is that those in the UK may be right who fear not only that monetary union will deprive it of a policy lever it needs to adjust to economic disturbances (Talani 1997). Its voice on currency matters may be heard more effectively in the global fora as a nation state than as one of fifteen in the councils of the European Central Bank, particularly if participation in the latter precludes direct participation in the former.

Whether the cure of integration via monetary union imposed from above is worse than the disease remains to be seen. But the prevailing orthodoxy

Quebec would need to manage its own currency. Both Rousseau (1978) and Fortin (1978) conclude that the benefits of an autonomous monetary policy under a separate currency regime are fewer for small, open regional economies which are highly integrated with the national economy. Fortin (1978: 63) maintains that monetary isolation would adversely affect Quebec sovereignty by destabilizing the value of the new currency relative to the Canadian dollar.

concerning EMU has such momentum that North America's market integration generated without currency union is unlikely to be of much interest in Europe unless or until disaster strikes. At that unhappy point, when other formulae for continental cohabitation would again be considered, the North American experience in abstaining from monetary unification might become pressingly relevant. Meanwhile, continental integration driven from below by market forces proceeds apace in North America in telling contrast with the European model driven by the brave faith that efforts exerted from above can transcend its historic national divisions.

6

Policies, Institutions, and the Euro: Dilemmas of Legitimacy

AMY VERDUN AND THOMAS CHRISTIANSEN

The establishment of the single currency and the creation of a set of new European monetary institutions are likely to transform the European, if not the global, economy. But European Monetary Union (EMU) is more than an economic project. In fact, the rationale for EMU has often been emphasized as being political rather than economic. Moreover, the decisions surrounding EMU are widely regarded as contributing to political integration even though it is clear that the term 'political integration' means different things to different people. As is the nature of European integration more generally, economic means are being used towards a political end (i.e. the 'ever-closer union') set out in the Rome Treaty's preamble. In this view, economic arguments have been used to support or to refute the move towards monetary union. However, ultimately the debate about the economic costs and benefits of a single currency came secondary to the political interests vested in EMU. Political arguments have ranged from the democratization of European monetary policy—wrestling control over the setting of continental interest rates from the Bundesbank—to the geopolitical—creating a powerful counterweight to the dollar and yen on the global financial markets.

Accepting the underlying political nature of the monetary union project, this chapter seeks to question the foundations of its legitimacy. In doing so, we suggest that current and future problems of legitimation of the single currency can be explained as follows. On the one hand, EMU rests on the creation of a set of powerful institutions with direct and executive authority in an area of policy-making (i.e. monetary policy) which is generally regarded as elementary to the governance of a modern economy and society. On the other hand, the establishment of important and autonomous institutions at the European level precedes the emergence of a political community in which such decisions, or, more significantly, the procedures for the taking of such decisions, can be grounded. Indeed, as remarked at the outset, EMU is specifically designed to contribute to the emergence of such a polity.

This leads to a situation in which the legitimacy of EMU decision-making is positively lopsided. In the domestic context, policy-making is grounded in the first instance in the legitimacy of public institutions. These are in turn legitimized either through the procedures of representative democracy or because they are directly embedded in the belief system of the polity. At the European level, and in particular in the context of EMU, the picture is reversed. The policies of monetary union have not been developed by a set of public institutions that are embedded in the wider polity. Instead, policies are designed to bring a set of public institutions into being which are in turn expected to contribute significantly to the development of the Euro-polity.

Given this image of a lopsided legitimation of EMU it comes as little surprise that the project has been seriously criticized at every stage in its evolution. The domestic stability policies designed to bring countries' economies and public finances in line with EMU membership requirements had no recognizable institutional reference point for the wider public. Given the absence of a European institutional framework within which these domestic policies were chosen, there remained little that could prevent an all-out public attack on them. Equally, as soon as the main new European institution related to EMU came into being—for example, during the nomination of the President and the members of the Governing Council of the European Central Bank (ECB)—it again became clear that the project is open to attack. The controversy surrounding the appointment of the first president demonstrated that individuals, their nationality, their personal background, etc., influenced the legitimacy of the project more than trust in the set of new institutions (e.g. see *Financial Times* 5 May 1998: 2). The wider criticism is that any European institution of this kind will suffer from the lack of either democratic procedure, or of a wider political community which might otherwise provide the automatic legitimation which public policy-making enjoys in constitutional democracies (see Forder and Oppenheimer 1996; Gill 1997; Gormley and de Haan 1996; Kenen 1995; Patomäki 1997; Teivainen 1997; Verdun 1996, 1998a; Wincott 1992).

This chapter approaches this subject in the following manner. The first section looks in some detail at crucial aspects of the monetary integration path. It explains the logic of its institutional construction but also the problems related to the choice of this particular institutional set-up, such as its incomplete institutional design and the limited popular acceptability of the EMU project. In the second section, a model of the legitimation of European policy-making is developed. This model is sensitive, both to the complex conceptual nature of legitimacy in general, as well as the specific circumstances of the European integration process. The third section relates these problems to the wider legitimacy concerns over EMU. The conclusion draws these strands together in search of a comprehensive treatment of the dilemmas of EMU.

The Legitimacy Crisis of Monetary Integration

Economic and Monetary Union was put on agenda in the mid 1980s after having laid dormant for more than a decade. It emerged in the wake of the signing of the Single European Act (SEA). When it became clear that the Internal Market programme boosted the European economies and the European integration process it was considered important that the integration momentum was maintained. Moreover, member states wanted to find a European 'response' to globalization and financial market integration (Verdun 1995). In addition to these more general reasons, there were also specific power-political reasons for its relaunch. The European Monetary System (EMS) worked well during the mid and late 1980s but was based on the dominance of German monetary policies. Moreover, there was the widely held belief that monetary policy could only be effectively dealt with if it was conducted by a credible monetary authority. The extent of the credibility of the monetary authorities in question depended on their reputation, the degree of politically responsiveness of the central bank, as well as whether they had a clear policy objective.

Hence, in the late 1980s when EMU came on the agenda, it was clear that there was only a limited window of opportunity for it. An EMU would have to satisfy a number of criteria. First, it would have to replace the *de facto* German hegemony by copying it and institutionalizing it within a European framework. Second, it needed to be primarily based on a 'monetarist' notion of EMU. In other words, a parallel development in the economic sphere was considered unacceptable (Verdun 1996). Third, it had to be non-exclusive in theory but exclusive in practice (i.e. member states all needed to be granted the right to join if their policies and policy outcomes were sufficiently converging); at the same time, however, there needed to be criteria that could be used to determine which countries would be ready to join EMU once it became fully operational.[1] Fourth, EMU needed to provide an answer to the problem that globalization and financial market integration increasingly reduced member states' room for manoeuvre. During the 1980s monetary authorities had learnt that monetary policy was likely to be unsuccessful if policies in neighbouring countries—in particular that of the Federal Republic of Germany—were not taken into consideration. A common monetary policy would be even more effective.

---

[1] In retrospect it can be judged that many member states circumvented being excluded from EMU by adopting policies which rigorously dealt with their budgetary debt and deficits as well as their inflation levels. These harsh policies in turn often were subject to popular attack.

These criteria for creating EMU made it necessary that it would have a particular type of institutional set-up. When in the 1970s EMU was first studied it was then still considered important that, besides a European Central Bank (modelled after the US Federal Reserve Board), there be a flanking institution which could be held responsible for co-ordinating macroeconomic policy-making. A so-called 'Centre of Decision for Economic Policy' (CDEP) was envisaged in the first concrete EMU blueprint (Werner Report, EC 1970). This supranational institution was to instruct member state governments on the direction of their macroeconomic policies. Moreover, this institution could be held responsible to the European Parliament.

This economic component present in the Werner Report was absent in the EMU blueprint drafted in the 1980s (Delors Report 1989) for good reasons. First, there was no belief that such an institution was really necessary. But, second, even if it was a useful institution in theory, it would still be impossible to find a common ground which could be considered the basis on which such an institution could work. Policy-learning had happened regarding monetary policies in the 1980s, but regarding the conduct of macroeconomic policies there were still important differences between the member states. Also any clear co-ordination of macroeconomic policy-making would imply the need for a European political community, which is clearly still absent.

The strong motivation of national governments to create EMU was driven by the desire to institutionalize at the European level the monetary regime that a number of 'important' countries had started to adhere to during the 1980s. It was soon discovered that anti-inflationary monetary policies were less effective if they were pursued without consideration of those pursued in other European Community (EC) countries. In fact, they were most effective if they copied German monetary policies. Hence, the institutionalization of these anti-inflationary policies became very important. This instrumental, almost functional process of European monetary integration, leads us to question whether this politically unquestioned transfer of sovereignty over monetary policy-making incurs problems of legitimacy or accountability. In examining this question, let us look at the situation in Germany, where the central bank has been independent for decades.

The German central bank, the Bundesbank, has been politically independent since its creation in 1957, or indeed since 1948 when its predecessor the Bank deutscher Länder was set up (see Kennedy 1991; Marsh 1992). Since its foundation, citizens of the Federal Republic have held a positive attitude towards the independent conduct of monetary policy-making (i.e. keeping the political control over monetary policy outside the hands of elected politicians). There is also general support for the objective of keeping inflation rates low. This aim is supported widely by citizens, as well as by organized interests, such as trade unions and employers' organizations. They all accept that prices and wages should not rise too much (see Hall 1994; McNamara and Jones 1996; Sturm 1989).

Most of the other European countries have not had this particular background. In most countries the central bank has been subject to instruction from the government (see Busch 1994; Hasse 1990; Louis 1989). Also, in most countries the fear of inflation has not been so profound as has been the case in Germany. Anxiety related to inflation came about in part due to the fact that the German population had witnessed hyperinflation in the inter-war years. In addition, they had been subject to Nazi domination. Hence they were very eager to leave the monitoring of monetary policies to an independent central bank. In West Germany it was accepted that a monetary institution could be put in place first, and that political legitimacy for such an institution could logically follow afterwards, that is, after it would become clear that the institution successfully managed monetary policies.

In the 1980s a similar process occurred in the EC. It was believed that anti-inflationary monetary policies could be institutionalized, and that sovereignty over monetary policies be transferred to a European institution. However, there are three important differences between the situation in West Germany described above and that of the EC in the 1980s and 1990s. First, in the 1980s there was not an unambiguous full public support for the conduct of anti-inflationary policies in the EC, even though there was at least one important historical experience, namely the failure of the Miterrand socialist experiment in the early 1980s[2] that gave support to the low inflation policy objective. A second main difference was that a formal European institutional framework (a European System of Central Banks, ESCB) would only be created towards the end of the 1990s (i.e. to prepare the launching of the single currency). During the 1980s and 1990s when the decision to focus on low inflation and exchange rate stability had been made there had only been an *ad hoc* European institutional framework. Decisions to devalue or revalue currencies within the EMS framework were prepared in the monetary committee which advised the Council of Ministers of Economic and Financial Affairs (ECOFIN). This committee operated in an ambience of secrecy. The ECB was only envisaged to become fully responsible over monetary policy once the single currency had been launched. The European Monetary Institute (EMI), the predecessor of the ECB, was only responsible for preparing the introduction of a single currency, thereby merely fulfilling an advisory role. Third, the conduct of an independent monetary

---

[2] President François Miterrand experimented with socialist policies in France at a time when other countries were moving towards neo-liberal and anti-inflationary monetary policies (Hall 1986). The financial markets attacked the French franc, making it almost inevitable that the it would drop out of the EMS. Miterrand subsequently radically altered his policies, and *de facto* moved towards the conduct of a German-type monetary policy.

policy would be introduced within the framework of the European Union, which falls well short of being a federal state.

Another concern related to the creation of EMU was that the main players in the intergovernmental negotiations leading up to the Maastricht Treaty, which set out the EMU provisions, were monetary experts representing the member states, as well as leading experts in the field. Hence, EMU consisted only of those elements which were considered important to monetary experts and to policy-makers who had been concerned with monetary policies. There were no concerns about how other policies would be affected by the decision to create EMU in Europe, nor did it reflect the possible concerns of the community at large.

Since the signing of the Maastricht Treaty, which stated what EMU would consist of and how it could be obtained, member state governments and the general population have been concerned about the possible outcome. The fear was that there would be a leaping process of European integration. On the one hand, member states' monetary policies would be centralized and managed by the future ECB. On the other hand, there was nothing arranged regarding any flanking body (e.g. an 'economic government') or a European institution for macroeconomic policy-making (even though the French negotiators on many occasions tried to convince the others of the need to have such a government).

EMU was monetarist because that is what the leading monetarist elites considered to be the most acceptable design. Central bank independence was a 'must'. Furthermore, it needed to replace the asymmetric EMS system which was strongly based on German monetary policy. The choice for this particular regime was in part motivated to ensure policy credibility, and to ensure a culture of stability (Winkler 1996).

There was far less concern for accountability and legitimacy. As was shown above in relation to Germany, an independent central bank can be the appropriate body to deal with policy-making of this nature; provided there is political support for such an institutional set-up. But it is problematic, if the majority of the citizens affected by the decision is uneasy with either the overarching aim of reaching low inflation at any cost, or the idea that the central bank is not politically accountable and should be if the effects of the policies are inequitable (for a discussion of central bank independence see Kaufmann 1995; for a discussion of the Westminster model vs. the Bundesbank model see Busch 1994).

More generally, the problems lie not so much with the principle of having a non-hierarchical or non-majoritarian mode of governance as such, provided there is strong consensus that the institutions who have been given a certain mandate have full support of the political community at large (see Majone 1996, 1997). In the US, there have been similar modes of governance. Independent regulatory agencies monitor areas of policy-making, thereby falling largely outside the control of parliaments. There can be perfectly good reasons to accept this type of monitoring. Yet, when projected on the European case, problems may occur regarding the legitimacy of the monitoring role of these agencies, if it is felt that these agencies are operating in an ambience of secrecy outside the public control, when it is unclear why they should have been given the mandate to control the policy-making process (Shapiro 1997).

All in all, the choice for the kind of EMU created is clearly related to the above motivations of ensuring credible policies, and taking the conduct of monetary policy out of the hands of elected politicians. The problems of legitimacy can occur because the public at large feels insufficiently 'connected' to the political process. Questions arise about why the new institution would be the appropriate body to make decisions regarding monetary policy, and who would control the new central bank if the outcome was unsatisfactory.

In addition, EMU could theoretically, have been designed differently. For example, it could have included further political integration or the creation of at least some sort of economic government, that could have been responsible to the European Parliament (as was proposed in the Werner Report). Another possibility would have been to have more fiscal transfers, embark on fiscal federalism (see Tondl, Chapter 9), and have a European body (or the European Council) be clearly responsible for determining redistributive politics. EMU could have been blocked altogether, and the choice could have been to strengthen exchange rate cooperation, falling short of the introduction of a single currency.

Let us now summarize why this particular EMU regime was created. First of all, EMU was a reaction to the success of the German model, and the initial apparent success of the EMS. Those who designed it wanted to deconstruct the dominance of Germany, but were not necessarily interested in creating a truly balanced EMU. Second, the particular feature of the independent central bank was to create a European institution that was credible and acceptable. Democratic principles would be adhered to regarding the selection of the governing council and the president, as well as an annual presentation of a report to the European Parliament. It was strongly believed that no other regime or institution would be capable of effectively pursuing monetary policy. Third, the design was meant to safeguard credibility vis-à-vis the markets. Fourth, the absence of support for further (political) integration (EC 1993) explains why there was opposition to the French proposal for an economic government. Fifth, there was enormous divergence among the member states. Therefore there were no alternatives to this type of EMU; it was to be based on the principles and practical experiences of the EMS, and force policy convergence through a fulfilment of the convergence criteria. Sixth, in the course of the 1980s and the 1990s there had been a change in general monetary policy beliefs: experts became convinced that monetary policy was most effective if it was geared towards a clear objective, such as safeguarding price stability. Finally, there was a widely held view that the economic effects of EMU would strengthen the integration process, and facilitate its further creation, even towards further political integration. It is this inherent logic of the European integration process which points to the dilemmas of legitimacy discussed here. It is thought that once EMU provides successful economic effects, its institutions will gain credibility and legitimacy. This in turn, will help create the political community.

There are serious problems with both this method of European integration (the so-called Monnet method of integration), as well as with the particular design of EMU. Let us start by focusing on its particular design. First, obviously not all the above assumptions and reasons for creating EMU are indisputable. For example, economists are not convinced that an independent central bank will automatically safeguard low inflation (Lohmann 1996; Winkler 1996). Second, the costs and benefits of EMU will not be equally spread. The problem is that it is difficult to see who will be held responsible for the outcome, and whether a more equal spread of the costs and benefits will be ensured by the European Union (EU) institutions. The creation of a new institution brings with it a need for even greater reassurance to member states and the population that no one (individual states, groups, particular industry sectors, etc.) will suffer disproportionate costs as a result.

Third, the effects of EMU are not guaranteed. Economists are still debating whether they will be positive or indeed negative, whether on the economy of the EU as a whole, and/or on individual parts. Fourth, to understand what EMU is all about involves understanding a number of technically complex ideas; the public at large, and indeed policy-makers and national politicians, easily feel intimidated by this. They feel frustrated that they cannot fully comprehend what is at stake and what they need to know in order to make a balanced judgement. Fifth, the political symbolism of currency for national identity implies that individuals will feel close to this subject. It has a significant effect on the expression of nation-statehood and identity (e.g. see Risse 1998). Sixth, the lack of communication from elites to the public about why EMU is necessary makes the public at large quite sceptical about the plans. An interesting case is that of Dutch public opinion, which went through a major turnaround in 1997 from being one of the most supportive of EMU to being on average almost opposed to EMU. This phenomenon coincided with the first public debate on the merits and costs of EMU.

All the above feeds the public opinion that such an important decision could not be taken without it being done fully legitimately. In part it requires a full consultation of the public at large. If the feeling arises that it was an elite-driven programme which might cost some more than others, then this legitimacy is already at risk. Legitimacy will be particularly problematic if the people do not feel that they can turn to a particular European institution with complaints or be able to seek compensation if individual citizens, sectors, or even member states were to be affected negatively. Thus it becomes clear that the legitimacy of EMU depends on the institutions' capacity to generate positive economic outcomes. How can the EU create a new monetary regime, which might cost some more than others, when it is not willing or able to discuss redistributive matters? Nor will it be clear who will be held accountable for any imbalance. The design of EMU, in fact, makes it clear that the only new institution that will be created, the ECB, cannot be held politically accountable for the consequences of fulfilling its mandate. In fact, the current ECB statutes explicitly state that no one may even *try* to persuade it to change its policy (Treaty on European Union, Art. 107). Moreover, to change the mandate of the ECB requires a change of the Treaty. Thus, the mandate is securely ingrained. Any possible discontent would have to be addressed by EU political institutions at large. As it currently stands, it is not at all clear who could be held politically accountable for the overall regime, the distribution, and for possible complaints and imperfections of EMU once it is fully operational. Thus, it can be considered to be illegitimate. The *economic* effects are assumed to be the reason why EMU will be desirable; the *political* institutions, but the political community, and indeed the polity which would underlie it were not fully developed prior to its inauguration.

Public acceptance or rejection of EMU depends on many factors. *Eurobarometer*, the EU public opinion poll, has shown an overall public support for the single currency throughout the EU as a whole. Opinion polls are held twice a year, and only once in the period 1993–7 was there less than 50 per cent majority in favour of the single currency (in Spring 1997 47 per cent was in favour of the single currency while 40 per cent was opposed; *Eurobarometer* 48: 44, Fig. 3.11). Thus the problem with public acceptability does not lie in the absolute percentages of support or opposition to EMU. The problem emerges when the data are analysed in parts: in particular, when the attitude per country is examined. The citizens of eight countries showed an overall support of the single currency on average, with roughly 60 per cent in favour, versus 25 per cent opposed, and the remaining holding no opinion (*Eurobarometer* 48: 45, Fig. 3.12). By contrast, in the seven other member states there was no clear majority in favour of the euro. In five (Germany, Sweden, Finland, Denmark, and the UK) the percentage of those opposed to the single currency was much higher than those in favour (in the last four countries approximately 32 per cent in favour vs. approximately 60 per cent against). Opposition to the euro in fact occurred in the countries that are not taking part in the euro (i.e. Denmark, Sweden, and the UK). Yet there are two countries in which the population on the whole is against the introduction of the euro, but which are nevertheless still participating.

Eurobarometer also shows that demographic factors appear to influence support for or opposition to the single currency. Women are typically more resistant than men, as are individuals aged fifty-five or over. Similarly, manual workers and individuals with fewer years of education are less supportive than white collar employees, managers, and the self-employed.

So far, it remains a guessing game to understand why individuals differ in their attitude towards the single currency. There is some evidence explaining why the Germans and Finns would be on average more opposed to the introduction of the euro than citizens of other countries. In Germany, the role of the Deutschmark as part of national identity has been very strong. Also, the mark has been a very successful stable currency. Hence, it is somehow a special situation (see Risse 1998; Verdun 1998b). The Finnish economy, by contrast, has traditionally relied on devaluations. Participation in EMU is part of a large-scale restructuring process, inducing high social costs in that country (see Moses 1998). As regards the demographic differences throughout the EU, it seems that those with less understanding of it, or who would like to know more about it, are resisting change. These indications may suggest that part of the problem lies in asking the general public to accept a major change without an underlying sense of the need for such a change.

Legitimizing Governance in the Modern State

Clearly, the legitimacy of the single currency project has been contested. EMU is easily and frequently under attack, and support for the project in the eyes of the public appears difficult to maintain. Obviously, at first much of the debate took place in the vacuum of uncertainty surrounding a currency which had as yet to be established. Much of the pros and cons were debated in terms of events—failure or success—which were promised or feared. Since its launch, the apparent weakness of the euro has provided additional argument for those questioning the legitimacy of the project. But for now, no reassuring history provides 'lessons' which could be used by either side of the argument. As a result, the debate is won by those who manage to paint the picture of a post-EMU situation most convincingly and with the greatest confidence.

The single currency's problems in achieving a broader public acceptance are usually explained in terms of this uncertainty about future developments. We seek to show here that this is only a very superficial take on the underlying dilemma facing the legitimation of monetary union. Uncertainty and history play a role in this, but these factors are only symptoms indicating more substantial problems with the way in which public policy and institutions are grounded. In this perspective, EMU appears as a project confronted with unique challenges, not because it is a new policy or novel set of institutions, but because the making of a policy and the creation of institutions has preceded the development of a societal consensus about European monetary policy.

Similar things might be said about the Common Agricultural Policy or structural policy, and indeed we can see how these policies still continue to suffer from a legitimacy deficit. But there are important features which distinguish them from EMU: they have been gradually expanded and have, in the process, acquired support among a discrete segment of the European population. These groups, indeed entire nations and occupations, are strongly affected by one or other of them, and will mobilize for or against policy change accordingly. In contrast to EMU, the wider population has little stake in these policies and will hardly mobilize on either side of any argument. Even more important, these policies are being pursued by existing European institutions, which have already established themselves as legitimate actors in these fields. Consequently, any disagreement is not bound to lead to queries about the very existence of such a policy, as we witness in the case of EMU. There may be argument over the extent of such a policy—the funding committed to it and the procedures under which it is being dispersed—but neither institutions nor the policy as such will face existential questions in the process. Indeed, while EU politics remains distinct from those on the domestic level, we have here features of the policy-making process which are not fundamentally different from what one would expect within the state.

EMU is a different story and presents entirely unknown challenges not only with regard to substantive issues, but also to the question of its legitimation. In seeking to understand the special nature—and the particular problems—of the single currency, a brief look at the nature of legitimate governance more broadly is called for. A starting point here may be very basic dictum that in a liberal democracy public policy is determined by citizen preferences. In modern states, this only rarely occurs directly. Instead, the institutions of representative democracy ensure that elected governments fulfil the demands of 'most of the people, most of the time'. Various theories of public administration and of state theory criticize this as a naive perspective on public policy-making, and that sectional interests or bureaucratic inertia may well exert disproportionate control over the policy process. Yet it seems defensible to argue that when specific issues become politicized, popular opinion—via political parties, parliamentary elections, or referenda—will reassert democratic principles. The key here is the *potential* of removal from office of those who are seen as failing to deliver on the expectations of the majority.

Thus, in a representative democracy, the people might not have direct control over policy choices, but they will have a degree of control over those executing policies. Public administration, to the degree to which it is hierarchically organized and subordinated to the elected executive, is ultimately accountable to citizens. There might be disagreement over the degree to which practice matches these ideal-typical expectations, but what matters, in our view, is the public's *perception* that the institutions of the state are responsive to majoritarian decision-making. It is this perception (if not entirely out of line with reality) which provides policy-makers with legitimacy. And it is the legitimacy invested in *institutions* that permits these to pursue policies which might well be unpopular or even lacking in majority support.

This is why under conditions of representative democracy, the legitimacy of institutions rather than that of policies is the key to stability and continuity.[3] But democratic accountability has been only one way of legitimizing institutions. In a number of areas in which economic performance, technical expertise, impartiality, or long-term continuity are at stake—issues which Majone (1996, 1997) has identified as being essentially about efficiency rather than redistribution—non-majoritarian institutions have wielded significant political power. Rather than from the affirmation of their policies on the electoral circuit, such institutions take their legitimacy from a broader societal acceptance that the general will is best served by removing such decisions from the partisan floor of politics. The prime examples of this type of institution are, of course, independent central banks, but one could also name cartel offices, audit offices or, in a wider definition, supreme courts.

But any belief that the policies of such institutions are purely technical and/or non-partisan rather than political is flawed. Monetary policy, to take the example at hand, is highly political and does have serious redistributive effects. Why else are trade unions and employers regularly at odds over the setting of interest rates? Handing the enormous power to take such decisions autonomously to independent institutions must surely be a gamble. The answer to this puzzle lies less in the rationality of achieving a Pareto-optimal resource allocation, but in the way in which the institutional arrangements respond to a wider societal understanding and thereby manage to remain 'unquestioned'. What is crucial to non-majoritarian institutions, such as the Bundesbank, is the link between key experiences in the history of the polity—here the traumatic nature of hyperinflation after both world wars—and the consensus over the best structural response to prevent such a recurrence.

---

[3] Even those who have, in the 1970s and 1980s, criticized representative government as undemocratic since it was seen as delivering policies which were ostensibly opposed by the majority of the population, attempted to remove the legitimacy of institutions and to return to single-issue, direct action, and movement politics. The result, though, tends to be a recognition of the necessity to maintain a degree of representation. Thus, anti-establishment groups have developed into Green parties in most electoral systems of Western Europe and, as such, have become fairly established and indeed frequently serve in government.

In a nutshell, this is what can be called the societal embeddedness of public institutions. Their legitimacy does not require the regular affirmation of a popular vote, since they themselves are an accepted cornerstone of the polity. What this argument emphasizes is the legitimating role of the polity itself—something so self-evident that it is often left out of the equation. But elements, such as culture, history, beliefs, and identity, all play a crucial part in the legitimation of public institutions, whether majoritarian or not. Indeed, we can even go so far as to say that a functioning polity constitutes the precondition for effective democratic procedures. The recognition that the 'people can only decide once it has been decided who are the people' is not new, and is certainly of central importance to the whole question of legitimacy. In this respect, the degree to which institutions are embedded in, and seen to be a 'natural' part of, polities does have substantial consequences for their legitimacy.

Take as an example the British parliament: in popular folklore it is the 'Mother of Parliaments' and the cornerstone of a political system seen to be founded on the concept of parliamentary sovereignty. Over the past few decades much political discourse in Britain has centred on the defence of the 'sovereign powers' of parliament. Clearly the parliament at Westminster is seen as a core institution of the British polity, even though most observers agree that its actual significance has waned dramatically, and the view that office of the Prime Minister can be likened to 'elective dictatorship' is not at all recent.

What this shows is that the legitimacy of public policies as traditionally seen within the nation state is actually a very complex phenomenon. It rests on the way in which, over time, institutions interact with society—not only in the immediate sense of producing policies and policy outcomes which win majority support at the polls, but also, and more fundamentally, in the wider of sense of linking up with, and making sense of, the identity of a polity. Public institutions embedded in this sense within society are regarded as legitimate, and while governments may change, institutions—the state—remain static. This, in addition to the effectiveness of the democratic process linking citizen to public institutions, is what can be seen as having contributed to the maintenance of stability and continuity in the modern states of Western Europe.

We can sum up this argument by saying that legitimate public policy-making rests on the link between institutions and their polities (their degree of societal embeddedness), on the link between policies and institutions (the effectiveness of the electoral process), and on the link between policies and their social and economic effects (output–orientation) (see Figure 6.1). It is the interaction of these elements that ultimately constitutes legitimate government, and it is against this domestic background to policy legitimation that the efforts of legitimating monetary union in the EU ought to be evaluated.

The EMU Legitimacy Crisis Reconsidered

So what light does this general picture of political legitimacy shed on the question of monetary integration? Above, we have sought to show that much of the public and political debate surrounding EMU has concentrated on the policy aspects of the single currency project. In the main, we have identified three different arguments calling the legitimacy of the project in question: first, criticisms about its effects, or anticipated effects; second, criticisms about the kind of policies which will follow from the introduction of the single currency; and third, about the institutional accountability of monetary union—or the lack of it.

As a result of such a framing of the issue, much of the discussion about monetary union has been concerned with the economic, and to some extent with the institutional, consequences of the project. The discourse about EMU, by supporters as well as critics, has essentially been output-oriented. The ambition here is to convince the general public that EMU is good/bad because it will bring economic benefit/hardship. Indeed, there is little dispute among the two sides that EMU will have a significant economic impact. The difference is simply that for some there is the prospect of a cost-saving exercise that will make EU producers more competitive, while for opponents that is precisely what carries with it the spectre of higher unemployment.

While this is very much the way in which EMU has been debated in the UK, in Germany the concern has been more the actual policy which is to underlie the single currency. Governmental elites as well as the media and the public at large have focused on the issue of 'stability'—the question as to whether the European Central Bank will seek to maintain the high degree of price stability which has been the hallmark of economic growth in post-war Germany and, during the past decade, in Western Europe more generally. Here, the issue is policy—the economic effects of such stability-oriented policy-making, whether positive or negative, are taken for granted and remain largely undebated.

A final critique of the EMU project—arising out of concern both for effects and policies—centres around the accountability of the institutions charged with monetary policy-makers. Here, the concern is that the ECB will be too much/too little guided by political preference. In one perspective, the ECB is seen as 'undemocratic' since its decisions will not be guided by electoral preference, while any other attempt at creating such a linkage (e.g. via the Euro-X Council), is dubious as it endangers the 'institutional independence' of the ECB.

What is remarkable about this abbreviated summary of the legitimacy problems of the single currency project is the way in which questions over effects, policy-making, and institutionalization dominate the discussion. If one were to assume that establishing the single currency is merely the further development of the emerging Euro-polity—simply one more aspect of communitarized governance—then it would be striking that almost no reference is made to the underlying polity in order to justify the creation of a single currency. But that, it seems, is an assumption one is not to make. Arguments about EMU are not made with reference to the demands of the Euro-polity. Indeed, quite the reverse seems to be the case. Rather than legitimizing the single currency with reference to a wider polity that requires such an instrument, EMU is the tool through which the architects hope to achieve such a polity.

Monetary integration as the conduct of political integration with other means? The image is not far-fetched, since the entire history of the European Community has been one of pursuing the goal of political integration through the means of economic integration. Political union was the ultimate object of the 'founding fathers' of the Community, as it was of Delors' 'relaunch' of integration. As part of this relaunch, single market and single currency were identified as the most promising agenda in order to move integration forward—important agenda in their own right, no doubt, but ultimately vehicles for the political project of unifying the European Union.

One could summarize the analysis so far by saying that the debate about the anticipated effects of monetary policy is determining the construction of a novel polity. In other words, policy output is legitimizing—or de-legitimizing—polity formation, something which, as we have sought to argue above, is precisely the opposite of what has occured in nation states. In domestic systems one would rely on the embeddedness of institutions within a settled polity in order to legitimize policies (whatever their effect). The single currency is not only facing the debate about the pros and cons of its anticipated effects and institutional design without the legitimating safety-net of such societal embeddedness, but in fact is expected to provide the main driving force towards achieving it. No wonder that it is creaking in the seams under the strain of such a task. The effects of a certain policy precede the actual creation of such a policy, which in turn precedes the establishment of the relevant institutions. And the work of these institutions—ECB, Euro-X Council, and Commission—precedes the formation of a polity which will have some sort of societal consensus over the values to be pursued through political institutions and public policy. Figures 6.1 and 6.2 indicate this contrasting state of affair.

What this stark contrast between the legitimation of public policy in domestic systems and in the European system indicates is not that EMU will automatically find it impossible to achieve popular acceptance. But it does suggest that its legitimacy is much more fragile—open to questioning and attack—than that of national monetary policies. The output orientation of much of the debate about the benefits and the costs of EMU signifies that

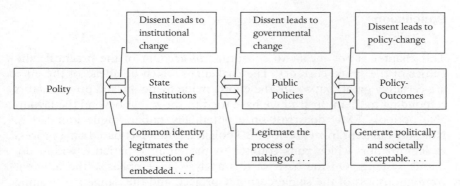

FIG. 6.1. The process of legitimation of the modern state.

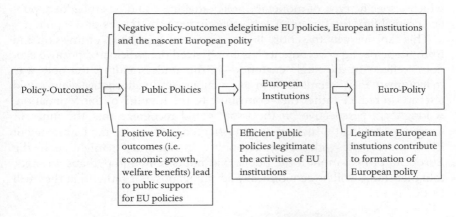

FIG. 6.2. The process of legitimation in the case of EMU.

policy-makers regard its economic and social effects as the strongest, perhaps even as the only, possible legitimating aspect of the single currency. Such a perception makes it hostage to the economic fortunes of the day and, should these turn out to be negative, jeopardizes not simply the effects of the policy, or the policy, or the institutional framework—the perceived failure of the single currency would undeniably endanger the future of the Euro-polity as a whole. Policy failure in domestic systems might not necessarily spell the end of specific institutions, and it would hardly affect the legitimacy of the polity itself, but in a European system in which policies are used to legitimate institutions and thereby help to build the a polity, policy failure may have potentially disastrous effects on the legitimation of the entire project.

Conclusion

This chapter is not meant to constitute an account of the practical difficulties of the single currency. The challenges which lie ahead of the euro are certainly great, but so are the efforts made by public and private actors responding to them. Instead we have tried to show that beyond the favourable outlook, EMU does rest on a potentially rather fragile foundation. Not only different from previous EU policies, but in fact based on a process of legitimation which runs counter to the entire experience within domestic systems. On the basis of this analysis we emphasise the inherent contentiousness of the single currency project, and the dangers of waning public acceptability should the promised economic and social effects not be sustained. With little, if any, legitimacy held by the new institutions charged with managing the single currency, and in the absence of a polity within which a specific type of monetary policy-making could be embedded, public acceptability rests more or less squarely with the results of the policy.

This explains why the entire line of argument from the Commission and from participating governments has emphasized the anticipated positive economic effects of the single currency—in this understanding, the only way to legitimate EMU seems to be in this manner. Yet an alternative view would attempt to reduce rather than contribute to the fragility of this foundation. A long-term perspective on the issue would recognize that the inherent dangers of relying on such an output-oriented strategy for the legitimacy of EMU and for the wider European polity. In response, it might serve the European project more if the public was not simply, and perhaps wrongly, told that things will be economically advantageous, but rather that they will be different.

7

The Role and Status of the European Central Bank: Some Proposals for Accountability and Cooperation

CHRISTOPHER TAYLOR

Ever since the Maastricht Treaty was signed, concerns have been expressed about the European Central Bank's unique role and status, based on the exceptional strength of its policy mandate and independence, and the absence of counterbalancing European Union (EU) institutions. Some commentators have drawn attention to the weakness of its democratic accountability;[1] others have focused on the dangers of separating the responsibility for monetary policy from that of fiscal policy, which raises what is known in the literature as the 'assignment problem'—the assignment of the main instruments of macroeconomic policy to different and possibly conflicting objectives.[2] This chapter examines these interrelated issues further, explaining why democratic accountability and policy cooperation will matter in European Monetary Union (EMU) context and why the Maastricht model falls short, despite its virtues. Consideration is given to what are widely regarded as the two other main paradigms of central banking independence, the US Federal Reserve System and the 'New Zealand model'. Although neither has been adopted for EMU, they offer instructive comparisons. Finally, proposals are offered for strengthening the democratic and cooperative elements in the Maastricht model, while respecting the treaty constraints and the objectives of the key players.

The author is grateful to John Arrowsmith for helpful discussions.

[1] For a review of the literature on the democratic deficit of EMU with particular regard to the ECB, see Verdun (1998a).

[2] See Meade and Weale (1995) for a theoretical exposition of the problem in an EMU context.

The Maastricht Model

Independence and Accountability

The relevant features of the Maastricht design for the new European System of Central Banks (ESCB), of which the European Central Bank (ECB) is the head, can be summarized as follows.[3] The ESCB's policy mandate, set out in Art. 105 of the treaty[4] and repeated in Art. 2 of the ESCB statute[5] is, intentionally, both narrow and exclusive. It sets the maintenance of price stability as the 'primary objective' of the ESCB, and of no other body. Although the ESCB must support 'the general economic policies in the Community with a view to contributing to the achievement of the object-ives of the Community', its support must be 'without prejudice to the object-ive of price stability'. However, although the objective is narrow, it is not specific; the interpretation of 'price stability' is left to the ECB, with respect to both the measure of prices used and its permitted rate of change. The reference to the 'economic policies *in* the Community' (emphasis added) is also very unspecific. It deliberately encompasses the policies of individual member states as well as those of the Community, but they are mentioned only briefly in the treaty, in Arts. 102a and 103 which relate to policy co-ordination. Members' policies must contribute to the 'objectives of the Community' (in Art. 2), but these too are framed only broadly. They include, for example, 'sustainable and non-inflationary growth respecting the environment' and 'a high level of employment and of social protection'.[6] Clearly, such objectives are open to very wide interpretation.

Within its sphere of competence the ECB/ESCB's independence, specified in the treaty's much-quoted Art. 107, is absolute and comprehens-ive: 'neither the ECB, nor a national central bank, nor any member of their decision-making bodies shall seek or take instructions' from Community bodies, from a member government, or from 'any other body'. Community institutions and governments 'undertake to respect this principle and not to seek to influence members of the decision-making bodies . . . in the

---

[3] The European System of Central Banks comprises the ECB and all the national central banks (NCBs) of the EU, although only the NCBs in the EMU-area will share in the system's policy-making and operational activities. The ECB is the system's directing and co-ordinating body, and has legal identity, whereas the ESCB has no such identity. See the comprehensive and detailed account in Kenen (1995).

[4] Treaty on European Union (1992).

[5] 'Protocol on the statute of the European System of Central Banks and of the European Central Bank', in Treaty on European Union (1992).

[6] There is no injunction on the Community or member governments to adopt the ECB's objectives or assist in their achievement.

performance of their tasks'. It would be difficult to envisage more blanket protection from political interference for the new central bank.

In contrast, the treatment of ECB accountability is sparse. Its Executive Board of president, vice-president, and up to four directors is to be appointed by common accord by the governments of EU member states, at head-of-government level, on a recommendation from the EU Council (in this context ECOFIN, the economic and finance ministers' Council), for non-renewable eight-year terms; the European Parliament is to be consulted but may not reject an appointment. The national central bank governors who will comprise the rest of the ECB Governing Council (its senior policy-making body) are to be appointed in accordance with their national procedures, but their terms of office must be no less than five years. A member of the ECB Council may be removed only if he 'no longer fulfils the conditions required for the performance of his duties or if he has been guilty of serious misconduct' (ESCB Statute, Arts. 11.4 and 14.2). This wording implies that dismissal could result only from serious personal incapacity or wrongdoing, and not from dissatisfaction with policy, for which the ECB Council has collective responsibility. Thus, the only avenue by which external control can be exercised over the ECB's policy actions is through the appointment of governors and executive directors; once elected, they have total discretion to pursue their mandate, for relatively long terms in the latter's case.

The ECB Council's proceedings are to be confidential, although it may decide to publish the outcome of its deliberations. Although it must publish reports on its activities at least quarterly and address annual reports to the Community institutions on its activities and on monetary policy, which are to be available to any interested party, there is no treaty guidance on their content (ESCB Statute, Art. 15). The ECB president and directors may be heard before the competent committees of the European Parliament, at its invitation or on their own initiative (Treaty, Art. 109b); but they cannot be compelled to attend, as Harden (1992) points out. The ECB president must be invited to participate in ECOFIN meetings when its discussions are relevant to the ESCB's objectives and tasks; and the president of ECOFIN and a member of the Commission may participate in ECB Governing Council meetings and submit a motion for its deliberation, but not vote (Treaty, Art. 109b). There is thus provision for regular reporting by the ECB at Community level, and for top-level contact between the ECB and ECOFIN, but such encounters need not go beyond bland reporting and superficial exchanges if the ECB does not wish it. The ECB is not obliged to answer specific questions, or take account of views presented to it, much less act on them. Moreover, the treaty makes no provision for accountability at national level. It is silent on links between national central bank (NCB) governors and their national parliaments, but the blanket protection of Art. 107 applies, and would empower the ECB Council to ignore national parliaments' criticism if it chose. It would presumably also empower NCB governors to refuse to attend their respective parliamentary committees, although they would probably not risk a refusal.

Thus, if 'accountable' means not merely 'liable to give an account', as in standard dictionary definitions, but also 'subject to a degree of control by another body', which seems closer to political usage, the ECB's accountability must be judged very weak. This is by no means an inevitable corollary of strong independence. Instead, a natural presumption might be that 'the greater the degree of central bank independence, the stronger and clearer should be the accountability for the exercise of the authority delegated to it' (Guitian 1995). That would be consistent with the concept of 'stewardship', in which the steward performs a role or task under his master's authority, and with the 'principal–agent' relationship, discussed more fully below.

Separation of Policies

The treaty confers total and exclusive responsibility for the definition and implementation of monetary policy on the ESCB/ECB, more specifically the ECB's Governing Council, given its powers to instruct national central banks (ESCB Statute, Arts. 3, 8, 12.1, 14.3, and 16). The clear implication is that monetary policy is assigned to price stability, and the ECB must treat other objectives as subordinate. It is also clear that responsibility for fiscal policy remains with national governments, subject to the quantitative limits in the excessive deficit procedure (Treaty, Art. 104c), reinforced by the Stability and Growth Pact agreed at the Dublin Council in December 1996. However, the position on exchange rate policy for the euro is less clear. The treaty confers responsibility for any 'exchange rate system' involving the euro, and for 'general orientations' regarding the exchange rate, on national ministers acting through the ECOFIN Council—more specifically, the group of EMU-area ministers within the Council (Treaty, Art. 109).[7] But the management of the exchange rate lies with the ECB, since it controls the relevant instruments. Moreover, in setting policy for the exchange rate, ECOFIN can only act (by qualified majority) on a recommendation from the Commission or the ECB; it must consult the ECB (and the Parliament in the case of a 'system'); and its policy must be without prejudice to the objective of price stability. So the ECB will be in a strong position to resist ECOFIN guidance on exchange rate policy if it sees a conflict with its main objective, and the hurdles to be cleared if ECOFIN is to prevail in this respect are high (Kenen 1995: 32).

Relations between the euro and other EU currencies are to be governed by the reformed exchange rate system, ERM 2, also agreed at Dublin in 1996.

---

[7] Now often referred to as 'Euro-X'.

Under these arrangements, EU states outside the EMU-area are expected to peg their currencies to the euro, at central rates and with fluctuation bands to be mutually agreed between ministers of EMU-area states, the ECB, and ministers and central bank governors of non-EMU states. Although decision-making is to be by consensus, it was made clear at Dublin that 'the division of responsibilities will need to respect the independence of the ECB and the non-EMU-area NCBs (European Council 1996, Annex 1, para. 14). This implies that the ECB will have a decisive influence on the setting of central rates and other key decisions under ERM 2, if it is to support currencies under pressure through action having monetary consequences in the EMU-area (such as non-sterilized intervention in foreign exchange markets).

Rationale of the Maastricht Model

As is widely recognized, the ECB/ESCB's key features—the strength of its mandate and independence, the weakness of its accountability, and the assignment of monetary policy to price stability, derive from the German model of central banking and reflect the extent to which it dominated the treaty architecture. Not only was it necessary for other states to defer to the strong preferences of the German government in order to secure its agreement to move to EMU, given the size of the German economy and the Deutschmark's role as the ERM's anchor currency; also important was the perception that the German approach to macroeconomic management has been outstandingly successful for over thirty years—a view that has become part of policy-makers' conventional wisdom.

Underlying this approach is the belief that price stability is a necessary condition for sustained economic growth, and promotes maximum sustainable growth. The ascendancy of this view dates from the major inflation episodes of the 1970s, when the German economy coped relatively well with the two major oil price shocks through pursuing non-accommodating monetary and fiscal policies. This contrasted with the Anglo-Saxon economies, whose policies tended to accommodate the oil price increases, and where domestic inflation rose more and output stagnated more, given their 'sticky' price environment. The rationale is that inflation distorts relative prices, rates of return, and effective tax rates, and so leads to inefficiency in resource allocation, particularly long-term investment decisions; and encourages 'stop–go' policies. The belief in price stability as a growth-promoting condition has been supported on the whole by empirical research, although the issues are still not entirely resolved.[8] The widely accepted conclusion

---

[8] A review of the theoretical arguments and empirical evidence on the costs of inflation can be found in Briault (1995).

remains that there is no stable long-term trade-off between inflation and unemployment, although a short-term trade-off probably does exist, the strength and stability of which is still open to much debate.[9]

Also increasingly accepted since the late 1970s is the view that price stability is most reliably achieved through the agency of a central bank with a high degree of autonomy. The rationale is that governments seeking re-election tend to pursue over-expansionary policies in order to win popular support, but the benefits from such policies generally turn out to be short-lived and sooner or later boost inflation. Even when governments declare that they will refrain from short-sighted policies, there can be high interest rate penalties if financial markets suspect that the temptation to indulge in 'time-inconsistent' policies will prove too strong.[10] The solution is either to 'tie the government's hands' through commitment to an inflation target, or to remove monetary policy from the political arena by assigning it to an independent central bank. Where credible governmental commitments are hard to achieve, perhaps because of a history of broken promises, central bank autonomy is the preferred course.[11]

There is a body of research which suggests a negative correlation between central bank independence and inflation (or inflation variability) in industrial countries (although not in developing countries). However, the research has its critics, partly on the grounds that independence is hard to measure, the index numbers used being arbitrary, and that the observations are rather few; and partly because the causality is disputable.[12] Moreover, it has not been possible to show a clear relationship between central bank independence and *output* growth or stability; indeed, there is some evidence that independent central banks achieve better inflation performance at the expense of output stability, because they encourage rigid price expectations among economic agents (Briault 1995). Thus, although there is a plausible economic case for central bank independence, it is 'better seen as suggestive, rather than definitive' as Guitian (1995: 15) observes.

Furthermore, it is recognized that there could be dangers in delegating authority over monetary policy to the central bank, if central bankers have private objectives (such as reappointment to well-paid jobs or aversion to public criticism) which may induce them to pander to an incumbent government's short-term objectives, thereby recreating inflation bias. This has

---

[9] Even the longer-term Phillips curve now seems to be making something of a come-back in continental economies (see Sinclair and Horsewood 1996).

[10] A comprehensive review of the earlier literature on time inconsistency and the credibility of monetary policy can be found in Blackburn and Christensen (1989).

[11] For a discussion of the theoretical case for and against central bank independence in the context of monetary control, see Cukierman (1994).

[12] See Eijffinger and Schaling (1993) for a discussion of the evidence in favour of central bank independence. For some criticisms, see e.g. Posen (1993), Lohmann (1996).

become known in the literature as the 'principal–agent' problem in central banking (e.g. Fratianni, von Hagen, and Waller 1993). One suggested solution is to appoint a central banker who is more inflation-averse than the average voter (Rogoff 1985), but his true priorities may be uncertain or may change, and so lead to suboptimal results. Another solution, preferred by Fratianni *et al.*, is to give central bankers a high degree of legal personal independence (e.g. through long-term non-renewable contracts), possibly linking their remuneration to prescribed objectives for inflation and output stability. However, as these authors point out, contract specification may be difficult because the parameters of social objective functions are unlikely to be constant, so such arrangements cannot guarantee superior monetary policy outcomes.

Nevertheless, given the compelling need to secure German acquiescence, and Germany's perceived economic success over a long period, it is hardly surprising that not only the essence but much of the detail of the German approach was adopted by the Delors Committee (1989) which produced the blueprint for EMU; by the EC central bank governors' committee in its draft statute for the new central bank; and eventually in the Maastricht Treaty itself. The result was the creation of an institution which has been described by Kenen (1995: 42) as 'more independent than any central bank—even the Bundesbank—and thus less accountable'. Unlike the Bundesbank, the European Central Bank's powers and tasks are enshrined in an international treaty, which can be amended only with the consent of every EU state, a notably difficult hurdle. And its objective of maintaining price stability is less vague than that of the Bundesbank, whose function is defined as 'regulating the amount of money in circulation and of credit supplied to the economy, using the powers conferred on it by this Act, *with the aim of safeguarding the currency*' (emphasis added).[13] Moreover, as Verdun (1998a) points out, citing Kenen (1995) and Thygesen (1989), the German provision resides not in the constitution but in the Bundesbank law, and so is less difficult to amend.

The Case for Stronger Accountability in EMU

The case for central bank accountability rests on the view that the conduct of monetary policy cannot be a purely technical exercise, and therefore 'above politics', because it involves important and complex value judgements. This is likely to be true even for well-integrated economies, but the problems are more difficult in EMU because it embraces (initially) eleven sovereign states with differing economic structures and objectives. The elements of the argument in an EMU context are as follows:

[13] Bundesbank Act, para. 3, cited in Kennedy (1991).

1. Despite the conventional economic wisdom, the control of inflation cannot be a purely technical exercise entrusted to central bankers on the ECB Council, and thereby entirely outside political control. The ECB's role involves the *formulation* as well as the implementation of the single monetary policy, with pervasive economic and social effects, and is therefore unlike the administration of justice, with which it is sometimes compared.[14] Granted that price stability generally provides the best environment for growth in the long run, monetary policy will still have substantial implications for output and real incomes so long as there are important short to medium-term trade-offs between inflation and activity. Accordingly, there will be scope for legitimate disagreement between experts, for example on the optimal mode and speed of response to shocks or cycles affecting the general price level. All central banks are from time to time obliged to make choices which involve, not only technical judgements about policy implementation, but also value judgements about its welfare effects on different groups of citizens—by income, age, region, etc.

2. Such value judgements are likely to be particularly onerous for the ECB Council because the EMU area includes countries which still differ markedly in their structures, institutions, and objectives. Despite its advantages, the single monetary policy will inevitably be less adapted than national policies to cope with the local effects of asymmetric shocks or non-synchronized business cycles. Even when shocks are symmetric, differences in national financial structures will imply differences in the *transmission* of monetary policy, so a given monetary action will have unequal national effects on banks' lending rates and the supply of credit, and thence on investment and activity. National differences in wage and price flexibility will also mean that a given monetary action will have unequal effects on labour costs and activity across EMU. So too will the large differences observable in institutional features like pensions provision, which may become an important source of friction between economies where pensions are substantially funded privately and those where entitlements are still largely met from public revenues (Corby Report 1995).

3. In a heterogeneous group of countries there are likely to be greater differences in the economic preferences of broad groups of citizens than in

---

[14] Reasons grounded in public administration have been put forward for questioning the analogy between monetary policy-making and the administration of justice. Writing on the possibility of an independent European central bank a decade before Maastricht, a legal adviser in the Netherlands Ministry of Finance argued that the monetary authorities 'help prepare, determine, and implement government policy, thus making them part of the executive', which is answerable through government to parliament for policy, whereas the judiciary pursues the different function of ensuring that 'the actions of the executive accord with the norms set by the legislature', for which independence from the legislature is necessary. See Schokker (1980: 34–5).

a single country, reflecting international differences in age, income, occupational patterns, etc. Policy choices will arise not only from the aggregate inflation/activity trade-off that commonly features in game-theoretic models, but also from the disaggregated redistributive effects of monetary policy actions, which are less easy to model. Thus, even aside from asymmetries in shocks and cycles, policy transmission mechanisms, market responses, etc., the ECB's policy actions might benefit large groups of citizens at the expense of others, producing tensions across national boundaries that might ultimately threaten EU cohesion.

4. As has been extensively recognized in the EMU debate, the comparatively small scale of the EU central public budget means that the automatic fiscal transfer mechanisms that normally operate in federal states to cushion the regional effects of economic disturbances will be largely absent, except possibly for small states that benefit disproportionately from the structural funds. Thus there will be little scope in EMU for fiscal transfers to ameliorate the national welfare effects of centrally set monetary policy. The potential for monetary policy to generate regional tensions, in any given external environment and assuming unchanged EU institutions, is therefore larger with EMU than without it.

5. In contrast, the heavy local weight of national budgets means that member governments will be able through fiscal policy action to affect both activity *and the general price level* in their own economies—and perhaps in the EMU area as a whole, in the case of larger governments. Such actions may not be constrained by the ceilings on fiscal deficits in the Stability Pact if, for example, they comprise shifts in the mix of revenue between direct and indirect taxation, or if governments balance their budgets in the long run, as may happen if the fiscal rules are taken seriously.

6. The formation of EMU has meant transferring control over monetary policy from national authorities to an international authority. However persuaded citizens may be of EMU's long-term benefits, the new central bank is bound to seem more remote than their own authorities, geographically, politically, and culturally. Especially if the benefits are not uniformly spread, and the mechanisms for cushioning redistributive effects are minimal, strong popular demands for influence on the conduct of monetary policy could redevelop. Few such demands are apparent now but that is hardly surprising, given the newness of the venture and the uncertainties about its long-term effects. In states still to join EMU and where joining will be subject to a referendum, like the UK and some Nordic countries, it will be surprising if democratic accountability does not feature as a key issue.

The contrary arguments, insisting on full policy independence for the ECB/ESCB, resemble those for the 'German model': the introduction of popular control over monetary policy in EMU would seriously jeopardize the hoped for price stability benefits.[15] At the political level, any watering down of the German model would risk losing that country's allegiance to EMU. Any serious proposals for strengthening ECB accountability have to address those objections.

The Case for Stronger Policy Cooperation in EMU

The case for improved machinery for policy cooperation in EMU is based on the view that the sharp division of policy responsibilities between the ECB and ministers could lead to policy conflict and error, if the respective players have different objectives and neither takes account of the other's priorities. This is demonstrated in an emerging analytical and empirical literature.

Fiscal Policy

As the Commission and others have conceded (EC 1990: 165), the non-availability of monetary policy as an instrument for dealing with asymmetric shocks and cycles in EMU increases the onus on fiscal policy to stabilize activity. It is not hard to envisage circumstances in which an exogenous shock would induce the ECB and national finance ministers, acting independently, to take mutually conflicting policy action. The clearest instance would be a shock which has the immediate effect of raising domestic prices and reducing output in the EMU-area, such as a surge in world commodity prices. In response, an ECB intent only on maintaining internal price stability would be obliged to raise interest rates to avoid accommodating inflation, while finance ministers, concerned with the level of activity, might relax fiscal policy to counteract the output fall. Independent action by each would make the others' task more difficult, and might induce successive policy 'retaliations'. The result could be increasing deviations from target levels of inflation and output, which might become unstable if the policy conflict persisted. The precise outcome would depend on the nature of the authorities' social objective functions and the parameters of the key economic relationships involved. However, it can be shown that, on reasonable assumptions about objectives and structure, and for a variety of exogenous shocks, non-cooperative solutions under EMU (with exclusive assignment of monetary and fiscal policy to different objectives), would result in larger losses in terms of deviations from target levels than cooperative solutions,

[15] See Neumann (1991) for an uncompromising theoretical defence of full statutory autonomy for the ECB, in the monetarist tradition.

and, for some types of shocks, worse than non-cooperative solutions without strict policy assignment (Hughes Hallett and Ma 1996).

Admittedly, there are features of the Maastricht model that aim to prevent conflicts of this kind. If interpreted strictly, the limits on fiscal deficits in the 'excessive deficit procedure', reinforced by the Stability Pact, imply that few governments will have large room for discretionary fiscal expansion unless they are in unusually deep and prolonged recession or they normally run budget surpluses. In addition, the rules against direct monetary financing of budget deficits (Treaty, Art. 104) aim to discourage government borrowing that could undermine the price stability objective. However, the 'no monetary financing' rule is mainly cosmetic: it would not prevent a government from selling debt to the private sector, and the ECB would be obliged to absorb excessive debt in the secondary market (thereby indulging indirectly in monetary financing) if it did not want interest rates to rise, as Kenen (1995: 41) and others have pointed out. The deficit ceilings are a potentially stronger constraint on fiscal excess, but there remain doubts about their enforceability in practice, given that it would depend on political decisions in the ministers' Council. In any case, the ceilings are a poor substitute for effective policy cooperation, because they make little allowance for differing national objectives and circumstances.

Exchange Rate Policy

Conflicts can also be envisaged between governments and the ECB over policy for the euro exchange rate. The ECB proposes to focus on domestic monetary variables as intermediate targets in its pursuit of price stability, and although it may not be indifferent to the euro exchange rate, the latter is no more than a subsidiary indicator of monetary conditions. In contrast, EMU-area governments are very sensitive to the euro's level, especially in an international environment of low inflation, for then nominal exchange rate movements imply changes in real exchange rates and thence competitiveness. Even though the EMU-area collectively is not much more open to trade than the USA and Japan, large competitiveness movements may have significant effects on the EMU group's output at the margin, and the effects are likely to concentrated in the smaller peripheral economies, which are more open to external trade and less diversified than the core economies.

If and when the euro emerges as a global currency rivalling the dollar, and assuming the ECB manages fairly soon to establish a good reputation for inflation control, the new currency could (paradoxically) be subject to heightened instability, initially appreciating sharply against the dollar, and subsequently depreciating as economic fundamentals take over (Alogoskoufis and Portes 1997). EMU-area ministers will be concerned to minimize such instability, especially if other EU currencies, notably sterling, weaken sharply against the euro. But their inclinations might well conflict with the ECB's commitment to the internal inflation objective. Without effective cooperation, a series of suboptimal policy responses, perhaps also involving fiscal policy, could develop.

Other Models of Central Bank Independence[16]

The US Federal Reserve

Comparisons between the ECB and the Federal Reserve System (Fed) in the USA seem both relevant and inevitable. Much attention in the EMU debate has focused on the USA as the world's principal established monetary union, and the Fed is often held to be one of the most independent central banks—ranking only after the Bundesbank and the Swiss National Bank according to formal indicators (e.g. Grilli, Masciandaro, and Tabellini 1991).

Nevertheless, the Fed's independence is not easy to categorize, since it is affected by many checks and balances. Its governing body, the Federal Reserve Board is, by statute, explicitly independent of the Executive in determining and implementing monetary policy. Even so, Congress, from whom its powers are delegated, retains the right to instruct it—and indeed has come close at times to doing so (Skanland 1984, cited in Swinburne and Castello-Branco 1991). A number of other features contribute substantially to Fed independence. A major factor is its regionally decentralized structure, which makes for a dispersed system of senior appointment and advice, and distances it from control by the Executive.[17] Five of the twelve members of the Fed Board are drawn (on rotating one-year terms) from the presidents or first vice-presidents of the twelve regional Federal Reserve Banks, in whose appointment neither the US President nor Congress play a direct role. The other seven members of the Board are appointed by the President and confirmed by the Senate, for (staggered, non-renewable) fourteen-year terms, and there are provisions ensuring a regional spread of representation. The President also appoints, and the Senate confirms, the Chairman and Vice-Chairman from among the Board, for (renewable) four-year terms, after which they may resume ordinary membership of the Board.

The long, non-renewable terms of the majority of Board members, together with the staggering of appointments, help to shield it from short-term political influence. However, the US President may remove a Board member 'for cause', a non-specific ground that could include dissatisfaction

---

[16] The account in the next two sections draws heavily on the comparative IMF study by Swinburne and Castello-Branco (1991).

[17] In this respect, if not in many others, it closely resembles the Bundesbank.

with Fed policy. Finally, financial independence from government is also a factor making for policy independence, although by no means peculiar to the US system (Swinburne and Castello-Branco 1991: 35–6).

The checks and balances mean that although the Fed's independence is substantial and it can initiate unpopular policies, 'its ability to sustain a generally unpopular course over a long period is limited' (Akhtar and Howe 1991: 350). Apart from the checks and balances in appointments, several other factors are important in providing accountability. The Fed is required to pursue the *government's* goals, which extend to several economic objectives, not necessarily the same in the short as the long run. Under the relevant legislation (the Humphrey Hawkins Act 1978), these include striving for economic growth near potential, combined with 'reasonable price stability'. The Act does not set policy priorities, nor assign a particular goal to the Fed, which has to aim for balance, according to its best assessment of the short- and long-term effects of its actions. The plurality of goals means that the Fed has to be prepared to work regularly with others, including the Executive, to co-ordinate policies and balance objectives.

Second, the Fed is required to observe a very open routine of reporting and consultation. The Board has to report semi-annually to Congress on economic trends and its monetary plans, and Board members are required to make frequent appearances before Congressional committees and must respond to Congressmen's enquiries on monetary policy and exchange rate policy.[18] In addition, the minutes of the Federal Open Market Committee (FOMC), the system's regular decision-making body which meets at least eight times a year, and of which Board members comprise the voting body,[19] are published six weeks after the event. Although not in themselves highly informative, the fact that there is a public record of decisions increases the sense of accountability felt by FOMC members. All this generates a lively public discussion and helps keep the Fed to its mandate. However, the Fed cannot be held to particular quantitative targets, underlying or intermediate, even on the occasions when it stresses them, as it did in the early 1980s.

Third, Congress can influence the Fed by passing, or threatening to pass, new legislation. In the period 1979–90 Congressmen introduced some 200 Bills containing over 300 proposals substantially involving the Fed, many of them addressing the independence or accountability of monetary policy; and a quarter of them were 'serious' in that they led to Congressional hearings (Akhtar and Howe 1991: 356). The fact that none were passed in this period

---

[18] In 1990, the Fed chairman appeared 24 times before Congress, and other Fed governors and top officials, 22 times (Akhtar and Howe 1991: 353). Such appearances are frequently televised and the transcripts are publicly available.

[19] The other Fed presidents attend and may participate, but not vote.

does not mean they had no effect on Fed policies. Akhtar and Howe comment that 'historically, legislation or the threat of legislation has played some role in circumscribing the Fed's independence, at times, during periods of crisis' (e.g. in providing for the Fed to finance public sector debt on favourable terms in wartime (Akhtar and Howe 1991: 356)). Kenen (1995) too attaches importance to the power of Congress, and also that of the German parliament, to amend their respective central bank statutes as a way of asserting long-term accountability.

The New Zealand Reserve Bank

The shift to central banking autonomy in New Zealand is a relatively recent development which has attracted global attention because of its novelty and boldness. The key legislation (Reserve Bank of New Zealand Act 1989) was part of a package of reforms aimed at root and branch liberalization of a hitherto heavily regulated economy with one of the poorest growth and inflation records in the OECD. Previously monetary policy had been 'notably politicized and short-term' and attracted much of the blame for New Zealand's poor inflation record from the mid 1970s (Wood 1994).

The Act gave the Reserve Bank of New Zealand (RBNZ) the single goal of price stability and the responsibility for formulating and implementing monetary policy in accordance with published quantitative targets directed to that objective.[20] The targets are agreed between Reserve Bank governor and finance minister, and have so far comprised a specific inflation target (initially 0–2 per cent per annum for the Consumer price index, amended to 0–3 per cent in December 1996), accompanied by specific exemption clauses, all set out in a 'policy targets agreement'. The exemptions are designed to allow the RBNZ to deviate from its inflation target temporarily and exceptionally in the event of certain specified shocks to the price level, to the extent of accommodating the shock's direct effects but not the second-round effects. In addition, the government may *override* the statutory objective temporarily (for up to one year), or negotiate revised policy targets, provided its actions are laid before parliament and approved. The RBNZ is also required to consult with government and any other parties which can assist in the achievement of its objective. Nevertheless, it is entirely free to decide how it should operate monetary policy to achieve the target: 'In this sense, the Bank is truly independent of Government' (Brash 1993).

The provision of exceptional exemptions and overrides to central bank policy targets in New Zealand reflected in part that economy's exceptional openness to international trade, and its reliance on primary commodity exports.

---

[20] 'The primary function of the bank is to formulate and implement monetary policy directed to the economic objective of achieving and maintaining stability in the general level of prices' (RBNZ Act, section 8).

New Zealand is specially prone to terms-of-trade shocks which feed quickly into domestic prices and activity, so rigid adherence to non-accommodating monetary policy could be highly inappropriate at times there. For this reason also, it was felt sensible to express the target in terms of a low inflation rate rather than a stable price level.

However, rationalization of the government override goes beyond the individual circumstances of the New Zealand economy. It is argued that, by recognizing the government's ultimate responsibility for the inflation objective and providing a formal channel for government to influence policy, the arrangement is likely to be more sustainable in the long term, and therefore more credible, than a more extreme form of central bank independence (Swinburne and Castello-Branco 1991: 23). The transparency arrangements are vital in this context because they offer a strong safeguard for the central bank against covert government manipulation of the targets. In contrast, situations of full central bank independence, with all government intervention formally barred, are vulnerable to covert deals between government and central bank, and may actually encourage it.[21] In addition, an override with transparency provisions gives some protection from the possibility that parliament will change the statutory objective under pressure of adverse developments, or if the consequences of adhering to the original objective appear too painful (Wood 1994: 15). In these respects the New Zealand model may possess more long-term credibility than an approach without overrides.

Formal accountability is strong in the New Zealand approach. In essence, there is a 'performance contract' between finance minister and governor, which incorporates the policy targets to be achieved during the governor's tenure. It therefore focuses on the governor individually, in line with the solution recommended in the literature on the 'principal–agent' problem. The New Zealand Act also defines the duties of the central bank's Board of Directors, whose role is to monitor the governor's performance and that of the RBNZ as whole, on behalf of the minister; the Board is not a policy-making body in the sense that the Fed Board is (and the Bundesbank Council was before EMU). The government appoints the governor and deputy governor (on an RBNZ Board recommendation) and a majority of the four to seven non-executive directors, with other Board members representing the government explicitly (though not members of the government). Governor and directors are appointed for (staggered, renewable) five-year terms. The government can remove the governor, deputy governor, and/or directors for unsatisfactory performance in relation to their respective defined roles. Failure to achieve the inflation target would be a ground for dismissing the governor.

---

[21] Even in Germany, the government can request the Bundesbank to defer a policy decision by up to two weeks.

Public monitoring of performance in relation to targets is carried out through the RBNZ's six-monthly policy statements to the finance minister, which are tabled in parliament; through its annual report, also tabled; and through the minister's power to impose periodic external 'performance audits' on the Bank. There are no formal limits on the RBNZ's ability to finance government (or indeed on the Fed's in the USA). But, unlike almost all other central banks, the RBNZ's public policy functions are financed under an agreement between finance minister and governor, ratified by parliament, and the governor's salary has to be consistent with the price stability objective—although, contrary to an initial proposal, it is not linked directly to his performance. These arrangements attempt a compromise between operational efficiency and autonomy.

New Zealand's economic record since the RBNZ reforms has been distinctly more successful than its previous one. The reduction in inflation was sharp, from an average of around 15 per cent in the mid 1980s to an increase in the 'underlying' consumer price index (CPI) of below 2 per cent (the top of the target range) in mid 1993. Although much of the fall had already occurred before 1989, the reduction soon afterwards was of the order of five percentage points. The fall in interest rates was even larger: nominal five-year interest rates fell from 13 per cent in 1990 to 7 per cent in 1993, suggesting a small fall in real rates. There was a penalty in the form of a rise in unemployment of some four percentage points after 1989, but the trade-off was 'no worse' than the average since 1970 (Wood 1994). The inflation fall was faster than the RBNZ expected, and the output recovery was initially modest and not sufficient to reduce unemployment much. Wood's conclusion in 1994 was that 'there is some evidence of the Act giving credibility to the low inflation policy and that credibility brings benefits. But the evidence for the latter is not strong' (Wood 1994: 31). The governor was reappointed after what was deemed a successful first contract period. There was only one, minor, revision to negotiated targets in the period, when a new government came to power in 1990. No move to change the arrangements emerged in the 1993 election.

Subsequently, New Zealand's GDP picked up satisfactorily overall: unsustainably rapid growth in 1993–4 gave way to steadier growth in 1995–6, and unemployment then fell by around three percentage points. Empirical investigation using survey data on price expectations in New Zealand concludes that the targetry approach has secured a significant reduction in price uncertainty there (Fischer and Orr 1994). However, underlying CPI inflation rose somewhat in 1994–5 and exceeded the 0–2 per cent inflation target. It subsequently remained close to the upper limit and monetary policy has been kept tight in an effort to prevent further breaches. The governor defended the raising of the upper limit to 3 per cent in 1996 as a step to release the RBNZ from an excessively active policy remit, and by no means a relaxation of the attachment to price stability by the new (coalition) government (Brash 1997). The governor's second term was then widely held to be a success, and none of the main political parties wished to change the 1989 Act.

The success of the New Zealand model has led to imitation elsewhere, principally in Australia and Canada, and latterly also in the UK. In 1993, a House of Commons select committee recommended that the Bank of England should be given autonomy in the conduct of monetary policy, with policy targets agreed with government and parliament, but subject to a temporary and exceptional governmental override, much on New Zealand lines (House of Commons 1993). At about the same time, a committee of independent experts chaired by Lord Roll also concluded in favour of Bank of England independence on New Zealand lines, although with power for the Bank to set its own targets, and also with provision for a temporary government override 'in extremis', subject to parliamentary approval (Roll Committee 1993). One of the first actions of the new UK Labour government on coming to power in May 1997 was to grant operational autonomy to the Bank, to pursue a quantitative inflation target set by government, with a temporary emergency override subject to parliamentary approval.[22] These new arrangements continue in operation and a bill to give them statutory backing was introduced in the House of Commons in October 1997 (House of Commons 1997). Thus, in Anglophone economies at least, the New Zealand model is gaining acceptance.

Implications for the ECB

Following Guitian (1995), the main alternative approaches to central banking independence can be classified according to their key characteristics. He distinguished two main models of *de jure* independence: 'model A'—allowing no formal government directive or override on monetary policy; and 'model B'—allowing a directive or override, subject to certain explicit conditions. He included the laws of Germany, Switzerland, Chile, and the ECB/ ESCB among others in category A, and New Zealand, Australia, Canada, and the Netherlands among others in category B. (No doubt the UK would also now be in this latter group.) He included the United States in model A, but it seems more appropriate here to split model A into two subgroups, one embodying an explicit statutory objective for monetary policy,

---

[22] Letter from Gordon Brown, Chancellor of the Exchequer, to Eddie George, Governor of the Bank of England, *Financial Times*, 7 May 1997.

as for the Bundesbank (A1), and the other with no explicit statutory objective, as for the Fed (A2).[23]

Although the ECB, as constituted, is firmly in category A1, it is still worth considering whether features from the other models could be added, to strengthen accountability and policy cooperation, while retaining enough of the basic model to command anti-inflation credibility and German support. Potential modifications can be grouped under five headings in the following sections.

1. Appointments and Dismissals

In models where the terms of office of governors and directors are particularly long, as for the Fed Board (fourteen years), appointments tend to be subject to confirmation by a democratic body. Given that ECB presidents' and directors' terms will be eight years, about double the (renewable) four-to five-year terms of governors in model B, and of Fed Board chairmen, there seems a good precedent for making their appointment subject to confirmation by the appropriate EU body, which would logically be the European Parliament. Furthermore, on the analogy with models A2 and B1, there is a case for making ECB presidents and directors liable to dismissal for *unsatisfactory performance* in relation to their statutory objective, although this would ideally require more precise definition of the ECB's objective (see below). Whereas giving such powers to ministers might be hard to reconcile with the treaty's independence provisions, a power of dismissal for serious failure to meet treaty-based targets would appear more acceptable if lodged with the Parliament, to be exercised only as a last resort, requiring a large voting majority. There are EC precedents for such powers in relation to the Commission, in that the Parliament may, by passing a vote of censure with a two-thirds majority, compel the members of the Commission to resign as a body (EEC Treaty, Art. 144); and at Maastricht, appointment of the Commission as a body was made subject to a vote of approval by the Parliament (Treaty on European Union, Art. 158.2). The fact that the Parliament felt it necessary to press for the removal of certain Commissioners for serious administrative shortcomings in early 1999, and was able to compel the Commission to resign as a body, is a dramatic confirmation

---

[23] A further group might be distinguished, having no formal statutory objective for monetary policy, but allowing powers of government override or direction—'model C'. A number of central banks would come into this category, including the Bank of England before the grant of autonomy, and several of the other large EC central banks before the Maastricht-inspired drive to independence.

(if one were needed) of the case for a strong reserve power of dismissal over the Community's senior executive body, and of its practical effectiveness. Adoption of similar powers with respect to the ECB's Executive Board would seem equally appropriate. Their 'nuclear' character would ensure that they would rarely if ever be used, but they would nevertheless reinforce the Parliament's status as the democratic body to which the ECB is ultimately answerable.

2. Reporting, Auditing, and Hearings

The emphasis on open monitoring and reporting is much stronger in models A2 and B than in A1. It is particularly (and perhaps excessively) strong in the Fed model, where it serves to provide the markets and the interested public with a regular indication of policy priorities as seen by the Executive and Congress, in the absence of explicit statutory targets; and to provide the legislature with a way of bringing its views to bear on Fed performance, in the absence of contractual arrangements of the kind that operate in New Zealand. While it would probably be undesirable to subject ECB presidents or directors to parliamentary interrogation with the frequency and intensity of the US system, the risk that the reporting process in EMU will prove inadequate seems too great to ignore. The European Parliament should accordingly be empowered to *require* periodic attendance by a member of the ECB Executive Board before its specialist committees (e.g. after each meeting of the ECB Governing Council); and to require the production of written and oral evidence. And national parliaments should be able to exercise corresponding powers over their respective central bank governors without fear of breaching Art. 107. If treaty amendment to provide such powers is not feasible, the next best solution would be for the ECB Governing Council to declare on its own initiative that a cooperative approach is to be followed on attendance and provision of evidence at parliamentary hearings, both centrally and nationally.

An open approach should also be adopted in relation to the dissemination of relevant official reports and proceedings involving the ECB, including the minutes of ECB Governing Council meetings. The treaty would permit this, but the onus will be on the ECB to be forthcoming, offering maximum transparency consistent with the responsible conduct of monetary policy. A similarly high degree of openness should extend to audits of the ECB's internal operations, which should go beyond routine accounting. External efficiency audits of ECB management are provided for in the treaty, through the agency of the Court of Auditors (Art. 188c, and ESCB Statute, Art. 27), and this feature should be fully utilized.

3. Targets and Overrides

If accountability is to be effective there must be explicit, pre-set, objectives against which the steward/agent accounts for his/her performance to his/her master/principal. It follows that central bank accountability can be exercised more reliably and efficiently if the central bank is set unambiguous objectives at the beginning of the accounting period. This is illustrated by a comparison of models A2 and B. In model B, the RBNZ has a clear quantitative objective, grounded in statute and incorporated in the governor's contract, against which his/her performance can be judged, with minimal room for cross-purposes or obfuscation. In model A2, the Fed's statutory objectives are far from explicit, and the objectives it follows may change, depending on the Fed's appreciation of the economic situation as it evolves through time. This inevitably makes the task of monitoring and assessing performance laborious and uncertain, as shown by the remarkable frequency of Congressional hearings involving the Fed chairman or senior officers.

If weight is put on the efficiency and transparency of the accountability process in EMU, the case for having a pre-set quantitative target for the ECB's primary objective is strong. And if so, there is also a strong case for providing that governments should be involved in selecting the target, even if the decision finally rests with the ECB. Given that early treaty amendment on such matters is unlikely, the next best solution is for the ECB to adopt a quantitative inflation target and announce it publicly. The EMI made such a recommendation in its proposals for the monetary policy framework of stage 3 (European Monetary Institute 1997, chapter 1), and the ECB has followed its advice. This is to be welcomed, but it is unfortunate that the target is apparently to be fixed without reference to governments or outside experts.[24]

If the ECB has indeed set its face against consulting EMU-area ministers on the price target, such an attitude is hard to reconcile with political reality. EMU will function smoothly only if the ECB's final objective commands the active support of participating governments; they have to share the

---

[24] It might be argued that the choice of the precise quantitative definition for price stability in EMU is hardly a controversial question, and that the range of 0–2% for the permitted rise of the consumer price level suggested by the EMI is unlikely to be much challenged. But experience in New Zealand and elsewhere shows that the selection of 0–2% for the annual inflation target may in some circumstances oblige the central bank to pursue an unduly active monetary policy, e.g. when world commodity prices are volatile. Although the EMU-area as a whole is less exposed to external price shocks than small- to medium-sized open economies, an upper bound of 2% might prove difficult for the ECB to observe at all times if the euro turns out to be as volatile a currency as the US dollar has been for several decades. At the very least, an element of flexibility in interpreting the ECB's final objective should be looked for.

same target, in a medium- and long-term perspective, if conflicts are to be avoided. This reality is hinted at some places in the treaty, even in the crucial Art. 107, which defines independence in terms of the ECB and national central banks 'exercising the powers and carrying out the tasks and duties *conferred upon them by this treaty*' (emphasis added). The implication is that *specification* of those powers, tasks, and duties is a responsibility of governments via the Council of Ministers, and what governments confer they may surely amend—or even revoke *in extremis*.

The message from model B, supported by the literature on the 'principal –agent' problem, is that where formal targets are adopted, they should be accompanied by arrangements which link incentives for central bankers to their performance. In EMU this could be done by introducing provisions for dismissal of ECB presidents and directors on grounds of failure to meet their target, perhaps in conjunction with a mid-term performance review, given their long appointment terms. A dismissal proposal could be by qualified majority of EMU ministers on the Council, but should be subject to confirmation by the European Parliament, as outlined above, in order to ensure transparency and give protection from political short-termism.

Model B also exemplifies the case for a temporary government override when formal central bank inflation targets are adopted, against the possibility of major unexpected shocks requiring temporary adjustment to the normal inflation objective, or temporary changes of political objective. Such provisions are also supported in the 'principal–agent' literature, provided they are temporary and transparent. It might be objected that the New Zealand override is necessary only because of that economy's exceptional susceptibility to terms-of-trade shocks, but similar arrangements have been adopted elsewhere, and there may be good additional reasons for them. Guitian (1995: section IV) points to a number of circumstances in which Model B may be preferable to A: where the constitutional tradition is against vesting power in unelected officials; where there is a strong public economic awareness and debate supported by a free and active press; or where there are liberalized and developed financial markets, able to play an effective disciplinary and informational role and so provide an effective check on government meddling. The first two circumstances certainly apply in some EU states, and the pursuit of free and competitive financial markets is an important single market objective, endorsed in the treaty.

A formal government override might seem too radical a departure from the treaty, difficult to reconcile with ECB independence. Yet if it is accepted that the ECB's objectives are those laid down by governments, it would seem highly desirable to provide for temporary departures from a quantitative inflation target, with safeguards against abuse. Those arguments apply *a fortiori* if the ECB sets the target without consulting ministers.

4. Parliamentary Amendment of ECB 'Tasks and Duties'

The enshrinement of the ESCB/ECB Statute in an international treaty means that it cannot easily be subject to surveillance by national parliaments, whichever model of independence is adopted. An element of 'long-range' accountability could however be provided for EMU by giving the European Parliament the right to approve, on its own initiative or that of other Community bodies, amendments to the ECB's tasks, although not to its basic objective. At present, there is provision for parliamentary approval of Council amendments to a number of the ECB's lesser tasks and duties, as well as to the allocation of ESCB income (Treaty, Art. 106.5), and to possible 'additional tasks' in the field of prudential supervision (Treaty, Art. 105.6). But the Parliament cannot initiate such amendments, and it has no powers to amend the ECB's main tasks even where active compliance by member states is involved, such as calls for foreign exchange reserves, or banknote issuance. Given that ECB-authorized banknotes will be the only ones to have legal tender status 'within the Community' (Statute, Art. 16), it would seem particularly appropriate for the Parliament to exercise a degree of long-term surveillance over this function.

Any extension of amending powers to the Parliament, as well as powers of approval or dismissal over the ECB Executive Board, would of course have to address the question of restricting voting rights to MEPs from states participating in the EMU-area, but such a development should hardly be controversial, given the fact of an EMU without some member states.

5. A Forum for Policy Consultation

A number of the foregoing proposals imply ongoing consultation between EMU-area finance ministers and the ECB Council, especially the adoption of formal targets and overrides. And even the modest existing provisions for amendment of ECB tasks and duties presuppose some such consultation. Yet, owing to the treaty emphasis on independence, the provisions for government–ECB consultation are minimal, as noted earlier. Under the treaty, any such consultation must take place in ECOFIN and in the 'Economic and Financial Committee' (of supporting officials) which replaced the Monetary Committee when stage 3 started. Admittedly, these are not ideal fora, given that several member states do not participate in EMU. Accordingly, EMU-area questions are dealt with informally by the group of ministers known as the Euro-X Council, meeting on the fringes of ECOFIN. This group has no basis in the treaty, and no formal powers to consult the ECB president or directors, although it may presumably do so informally if the latter agree.

Moreover, the possibility of policy conflicts also discussed above underlines the need for an effective forum for regular consultation between

EMU-area finance ministers and the ECB/ESCB on their respective policy plans. On these twin grounds, there seems a strong case for creating a Stability and Growth Council (SGC) for the EMU-area, with equal membership from Euro-X and the ECB Governing Council (not necessarily all members thereof). This kind of body was advocated by the French government in the discussions leading to the Dublin Council but not agreed then, reportedly owing to implacable German resistance.[25] The SGC would, in addition to being responsible for administering and enforcing the 'excessive deficit procedure' in the EMU-area, periodically review the mix of monetary and fiscal policies in that area, assessing their combined impact on activity and growth, both in aggregate and nationally, with particular reference to short- and medium-term stability. It would also discuss exchange rate policy for the euro, and its consistency with monetary and fiscal policy. The SGC might choose to publish 'opinions' on monetary policy, as well as on fiscal policy, but could not normally insist on ECB action. However, it might have power to impose, by qualified majority vote among EMU-area ministers and in predefined emergencies, a temporary override over the ECB's price stability target, subject to endorsement by the European Parliament. It should also have power to issue, on ministerial authority only, policy orientations for the euro, taking up the functions which the treaty assigned to ECOFIN.

Conclusion

The foregoing modifications to the Maastricht blueprint, if largely adopted, would strengthen ECB accountability and reduce the risk of policy conflict and error, without sacrificing the treaty's basic thrust. The stronger powers for the European Parliament over ECB appointments and dismissals, and amendment of its tasks and duties, would reduce EMU's democratic deficit, giving the Parliament a degree of long-range influence over the new central bank without implying short-term political interference. The strengthening of the inquisitorial role of parliaments in relation to the ECB, both at the centre and nationally, would also boost democratic involvement and sharpen the policy debate, while avoiding the frenetic atmosphere that sometimes characterizes Congress/Fed relations. Involvement of ministers in setting the ECB's price stability target would add to the efficiency and transparency of the accountability process and strengthen policy coherence. The provision of a strictly temporary override exercisable by ministers, subject to European Parliamentary approval, would underpin the new regime's

---

[25] However, the original Weigel proposals for the Stability Pact did contain a suggestion for a Stability Council, although with a rather narrow remit. (See the report in the *Financial Times*, 2 Oct. 1995.)

long-term sustainability and its credibility. A Stability and Growth Council would bridge the worrying institutional gap in policy formulation at the heart of the new regime.

Among the changes, the introduction of an override might be judged too radical a dilution of ECB independence. But there is growing support for such devices both in the practical world of central banking and in the theoretical literature. Targets and overrides would improve the quality of monetary policy decisions and reinforce government loyalty to them, particularly at moments of stress. In the circumstances of EMU, with markets aware that the allegiance of participating governments to the rules of the game may come under intense pressure at times, this would contribute to the regime's long-term sustainability, and thence to its credibility now and later. Ultimately, if EMU is to be successful, the ECB's targets must be those of participating governments, and remain so. If governments cease to share them, and are not in a position to ensure that monetary policy adapts to major adverse shocks, the consequences for the EMU-area and for the European Union generally could be serious. In some states, the temptation to resort to expansionary fiscal policies to counter rising unemployment could ultimately become irresistible, with adverse implications for euro interest rates. *In extremis*, political pressures to desert the monetary union could develop. Markets will be aware of these possibilities, and will penalize EMU as a whole, or the states most affected, if policy cannot respond flexibly. It can indeed be argued that the modifications outlined above, far from weakening the credibility of the new institutions created at Maastricht, would actually strengthen it.

In the tense period before the start of stage 3 it was clearly unrealistic to expect significant amendments to the EMU blueprint. But, as the European Monetary Institute showed in its recommendation for published quantitative targets, there was still scope for development within it. Now that EMU is finally launched, the atmosphere may be more receptive to second thoughts about its more problematic features. The treaty is not set in stone for all time; judicious amendment should be possible in the light of experience. Since the beginning of modern central banking near the end of the 18th century, there have been alternating long-term swings of the pendulum between autonomy and political involvement (Capie, Goodhart, and Schnadt 1994). The swing to central bank independence that has so far characterized EMU may not be the end of the story.

8

National Wage Determination and European Monetary Union

COLIN CROUCH

One of the biggest questions raised by the introduction of a single currency zone to a region with widely differing levels of productivity and subject to differing liabilities to external shocks concerns the kinds of adaptations that can be made by the labour market. Securing real-wage reductions when a national economy becomes uncompetitive is a painful social process, and one of the main functions of currency devaluation has been to reduce this strain while achieving a rapid, across-the-board reduction in export prices.[1] Are there any alternatives to massive deflation and direct wage cuts which might be used in such circumstances once a single currency zone has been established? This question leads us naturally to consider the scope for action by labour market institutions—associations of employers and workers, collective bargaining arrangements, the industrial relations system in general—to shape wage changes.

In a period dominated by neo-liberal political economy, this seems a dated question, ruled out *per definitionem*. On the other hand, the recent revival and reform of neo-corporatist policy arrangements in a number of individual European states suggests that neo-liberal theory and policy practice may be parting company at this point. In the following discussion I shall review the current state of theory about the capacity of institutions to affect labour market behaviour, and briefly examine the prospects for the emergence of a Europe-wide system of industrial relations. I shall then consider the past experience of individual national systems—especially that of Germany

[1] This deals only with the case of national competitiveness problems; shocks and endogenous deteriorations can also take place within particular industries or geographical regions of a country. It is assumed in economic theory that these problems will be dealt with by workers moving from one industry or region to another, and that the costs of such mobility are significantly lower than those across nation-state boundaries. This is only partly true, as persisting regional unemployment in many countries testifies. To that extent, the problem of national competitiveness is not so unique and one might ask why the special protection of devaluation should be so important to it. One answer is that it is at this level that political outcomes are mainly determined, and therefore where governments particular want to have available a ready policy instrument.

given similarities between the role of the Bundesbank and that envisaged for the European Central Bank (ECB). Finally, I shall examine what evidence we have of the potential capabilities of industrial relations behaviour at individual national levels.

Institutions and Labour-market Theory

A widely noted, subtle and useful theory of the labour market within the neo-liberal camp was that propounded by Calmfors and Driffill (1988). They proposed an inverted U-curve for understanding labour-market policies. The vertical axis of their graph measures the real wage; the horizontal axis measures the degree of co-ordination of economies. According to the authors two *opposite* conditions will be associated with the containment of real wages: either purely free, self-clearing labour markets where no organizational forces can interfere at all (zero centralization); or the case where centralized organizations of capital and labour, representing a whole national economy, have the ability and incentive to fix wage levels in a non-inflationary way (maximum centralization). This follows the theory of encompassing organizations developed by the late Mancur Olson (1982). Starting from the classical position of economic theory that economic interest groups which are able to organize themselves will use their organizations in a rent-seeking manner, internalizing all goods and externalizing all bads on to the general unorganized public, Olson saw the possibility of exceptions where a group was so large that its own membership constituted a significant part of the general public. This could erode the distinction between internal and external. In terms of practical industrial relations systems, this implied fully centralized national bargaining arrangements, or what has become known in the political science and sociology literature as neo-corporatist arrangements. These form the opposite pole of the Calmfors–Driffill U-curve. The Nordic economies provided the starting point for that limb of the theory (as they did for Olson's encompassing concept), but the argument can be applied to other cases too.

Soskice (1990) subsequently criticized the specification of full centralization as imposing a theoretically and empirically unnecessary condition for achieving wage restraint. He argued that what was required was that those involved in wage setting had means of *co-ordinating* their action, and a variety of mechanisms short of or different from centralization of bargaining might achieve that. While this analysis led him to generalize excessively about the kinds of economy which embodied co-ordination, the basic theoretical point about the requirements of a wage-fixing system it is to embody restraint is sound. Centralization is clearly one means of providing co-ordination, but there can be functional equivalents. Henceforth I shall therefore talk of co-ordination unless centralization is specifically intended.

The intriguing aspect of the Calmfors–Driffill thesis is its specification of two opposed extreme conditions for labour-market stability: an absence of co-ordination or complete co-ordination. Given that extreme conditions are more difficult to sustain than intermediate compromises, interesting questions are raised about what must be the very frequent cases of economies unable to sustain either extreme and landing in the middle of the U-curve. It is easier to follow this if we invert the curve to make it a normal, not inverted U. This is simply done by changing the sign on the vertical indicator: the extreme (high) ends of the U then become associated with a high level of capacity for real wage *containment*; the bottom of the curve with lack of such containment. This enables us to talk about economies which are unable to remain near either pole and start to slip down the side of the U. For the rest of this chapter I shall use the Calmfors–Driffill U-curve in this cosmetically revised sense.

In the case of neo-corporatist labour markets a slip down the side of the U would mean that, while they remained organized (i.e. there were significant trade unions), the capacity for co-ordination was being lost. The prediction is of increasing problems with inflation. This would describe the Nordic cases in the 1980s. The same argument can be applied on the other side: previously pure labour markets become distorted by organization (or by regulation), and cease to be self-clearing. Following Olson's thesis, as organization continues to grow, inflationary crises will become worse. The general policy lesson is that, once the slide has started, the actors in a system face a choice. If they wish to avoid inflation they must either restore the conditions that previously obtained when they were at the top of their preferred limb of the U; or, if that seems impossible or undesirable, they must try to move to the other, opposite pole. This is likely to mean that they must plough their way right through the trough of the U and up the other side. The reason for this in the case of a decision to switch from pursuing the neo-liberal pole to the neo-corporatist pole is that elaborate institutions need to be constructed in order to establish neo-corporatism. While they are being built they might take an organizational form that is as yet incapable of co-ordination, landing them in the trough of the U-curve. In the case of the opposite movement, from neo-corporatism to neo-liberalism, labour market institutions need to be deconstructed. Apart from dictatorships,[2] governments and others are likely to find this a slow process, involving some time being spent in the trough. In practice, most economies in the 1980s and 1990s have been somewhere near the trough. Neo-corporatist strategies

---

[2]   The paradigm case of a shift to almost pure neo-liberal policies remains that of the Pinochet dictatorship in Chile (Drago 1998).

became difficult to maintain and slid down from an optimal level of co-ordination; labour markets were very 'sticky' with a combination of organization and regulation of employment conditions.

Economies were saved from high inflation in the 1970s by one or both of two *dei ex machina*: persistent and strongly deflationary policies; or periodic devaluations of the national currency. The former has become the main distinguishing feature of the period which then flowed and which still characterizes most Western European labour markets. It enables inefficiently organized and regulated labour markets to persist without either being dismantled completely or pressed to adopt neo-corporatist discipline, but at the cost of persistent high unemployment.

Devaluations also secure a form of national wage restraint without the need for neo-corporatist agreement. In this way, they enable a set of national labour-market actors to dump the strain and conflict of reaching agreement on to other economies, whose relative costs are forced to rise. The strategy is not risk-free. If a country has more than very rare recourse to it, it experiences low confidence in its exchange value in financial markets—as happened to Sweden by the early 1990s. This pre-empts the devaluation strategy and leads to increases in export costs which might themselves prove inflationary. Further, such devaluations can spark a round of competitive devaluations among the economy's trading partners, seeking to recoup competitive advantage. This can become self-defeating for all involved.

If neither deflation nor repeated devaluations are acceptable long-term policies, there seems no alternative but to climb out of the trough of the U. But in what direction? Here, the preference of the dominant neo-liberal economic policy community (including Calmfors and Driffill) is clear: labour markets must be thoroughly deregulated and de-organized so that countries can congregate around the free-market pole, achieving simultaneous low inflation and low unemployment, though at the cost of a drastic weakening of labour protection, the virtual disappearance of trade unions (possibly also employers' organizations), and almost certainly a major increase in inequality. These are costs which, from the perspective of neo-liberal economics, are well worth paying. Chile, the USA, and recently the UK are held up as cases which have already largely achieved this position, and incentives to European governments to do the same are built into the architecture of the Treaty of Maastricht (consolidated in the Amsterdam Treaty) and the constitution of the European Central Bank. Indeed, as Visser (1998) among others has argued, breaking down labour-market institutions has been one of the explicit aims of at least some European political forces in advocating monetary union. In this way European Monetary Union will both remove the devaluation option and give powerful incentives to the European economies to plough right through the trough of the U, dismantling labour-market institutions, until they emerge at the top of its free-market pole.

The OECD *Jobs Study* (1994b: 20–2)—which set the subsequent pattern for labour-market policy throughout the advanced capitalist world—explicitly addressed the question of paths from the trough of the U. Using the Calmfors–Driffill analysis it argued that achieving the level of economic centralization necessary to secure non-inflationary stability through the neo-corporatist option could take place only under very special conditions; these conditions were highly unlikely to obtain in the decentralized, rapidly changing economies of the contemporary period; and therefore attempts to reach this pole of the U were virtually certain to fail, leaving such economies with very suboptimal performances. Therefore, it followed, even those countries which once achieved good records of centralization must undertake the difficult and extremely radical task of dismantling labour-market institutions and regulation so that they can join the USA at the free-market pole.

Because the OECD takes neo-classical assumptions for granted, it does not give the same sceptical consideration to the difficulties of achieving pure self-clearing labour markets, and the consequent implications of suboptimal performance in that direction. This is surprising. Self-clearing labour markets are almost certainly incompatible with the existence of trade unions unless these are either totally ineffective or are able and willing to accept market-clearing policies as part of a neo-corporatist deal. Given that by its charter the OECD is committed to accepting the existence of free trade unions, and given that it considers successful neo-corporatist policies to be impossible, this must mean that its model of the economy implicitly assumes surviving but totally ineffective unions.

The OECD has not considered the serious possibility that a country might embark on a strategy of dismantling its labour-market institutions, only to find it can go no further towards maximum performance at the market-clearing pole than it could at the co-ordination pole—unless it is willing seriously to interfere with trade unions' rights to exist and ignore electoral demands for some forms of labour-market security. In democratic societies with complex institutional structures it cannot be assumed that the logic of neo-liberal economic theory can be automatically implemented. Countries may become mired in the trough of the U-curve, and it may be extremely unhelpful to them that the only set of policy prescriptions available from contemporary economic science is a dogmatic insistence on the need to achieve perfectly free-labour markets. This is a highly germane argument for most Western European economies, where unions are important and wage determination heavily institutionalized.

There is a further problem with the neo-liberal argument which is particularly relevant to the question of the relationships between the European Central Bank and labour markets. As Hall and Franzese (1998) have pointed out, the rational expectations theories on which neo-liberal policy arguments depend heavily, assume a capacity of individuals to respond in a highly accurate and well-informed way to the signals given to the labour market by a central bank's monetary stance. However, apart from a small number of expensively and professionally advised wealthy individuals and institutions, the mass of individual persons is in no position at all to make such calculations. The rational expectations model only becomes realistic for ordinary employees if we assume that they belong to organizations (like trade unions) which have a professional capacity to interpret these complex signals for them, and to act strategically on their behalf in relation to them. Ironically, the model which justifies the move to the free-market pole of the U is a realistic representation of human behaviour only under conditions of organized labour markets which contradict other assumptions of the model.

In such a context the exact opposite policy recommendation—the pursuit of wage co-ordination—becomes a possibly more practical proposition for countries within EMU (for very similar arguments see Boyer 1993a; Marsden 1992; Visser 1998). However, this immediately raises a question, which does not have to be asked of policies at the opposite free-market pole: are we talking about co-ordination at national levels, or at the level of the EMU-area itself? It would seem logical that, if a single monetary system and increasingly a single market are being produced at the European level, then wage determination systems should similarly operate at that level. However, industrial relations institutions at this level are virtually non-existent; unions and, in particular, employers' associations are extremely weak, and certainly incapable of exercising authority over their national affiliates for anything like the degree of co-ordination necessary to co-ordinate a neo-corporatist collective bargaining system. There has, it is true, been considerable development of such institutions at the EU level running alongside the process of economic integration in recent years (Dubbins 2000), but only very rarely do they extend to actual bargaining. Similarly, the social dimension of European integration which was intended to proceed alongside the erection of the single market has stalled considerably since it was initiated in the early 1990s. A Europe-wide co-ordination programme is not feasible within the foreseeable future.

However, the situation at individual national levels is more complex. We need to examine both the incentives and the organizational capacities of the main actors involved. For national trade unions it is very bad news indeed if the single currency regime continues as it inevitably started: severely deflationary, monetarist, and neo-liberal. They therefore have a very strong incentive to demonstrate that it is after all possible to assert some basic moderating influence on the labour market through neo-corporatist mechanisms. The situation confronting employers is less clear-cut. They will share unions' aversion to perpetual deflationary policies, but may prefer an attempt to achieve completely unregulated labour markets to a revival of corporatism and its concomitant need for dialogue with organized labour. However, if the past record of neo-corporatism has been reasonably successful and uncostly, and if unions are relatively strongly entrenched, they may prefer this path to one of complete deregulation that could be reached only after prolonged conflict. If unions in such a context make the running in re-establishing corporatist arrangements, employers may not be opposed. Governments too have good reasons to avoid deflation and may baulk at the social conflict likely to be engendered by a major deregulation struggle. They may be suspicious of neo-corporatist devices as rivals to parliamentary rule, but an attempt at using them might appear as the lesser of several evils.

In other words, there are considerable incentives for at least some social partners to strengthen *national* neo-corporatist responses in the face of European monetary union. The main anxieties about adjustment capabilities under the EMU concern national labour markets being forced to abide by a EMU-area mean, rather than by their own national requirements. Therefore, the fact that labour-market organizations capable of some co-ordination will long remain far more effective at national than at European level can be very useful. Such action could provide a functional equivalent of devaluation without many of the latter's negative effects. Therefore, in the foreseeable future we do not look to possibilities of Europe-wide neo-corporatism but at a new lease of life and a new rationale for national responses precisely because of the European development.

A fundamental condition of any form of co-ordination is that it must not merely interfere with or try to prevent the working out of demand and supply pressures; this is especially true of government-imposed incomes policies which have often been temporary alternatives to voluntary cooperation among social partners. Often, incomes policies have simply dammed up pay claims until the policy is removed, creating an inflationary pressure that may well be more intense than the problem the policy was originally trying to resolve.[3] The stream of market forces will insist on flowing. Indefinite damming leads only to disaster, but the course of a stream may be intelligently diverted. Markets must flow; but they might be able to flow through more than one potential channel; and some channels might give outcome mixes that are preferable, both to other available 'artificial' ones and to the so-called 'natural' one that would dominate were organized actors to do nothing at all. Co-ordination institutions must therefore be mechanisms for diverting the channel; they must correspond to, rather than simply attempt to impede, some kind of market force.

But how feasible is such behaviour given the decentralized and globalized markets of the contemporary economy? An important preliminary answer

---

[3] At the same time, of course, firms' attempts to solve labour shortages by increasing wages may also be inflationary and futile if there are no clear mechanisms linking wages with the provision of training for the occupations in which there are shortages.

is the argument of Soskice (1990) already mentioned: the minimum conditions for the success of a neo-corporatist labour-market policy are less onerous than the full co-ordination by encompassing organizations that the Calmfors–Driffill model and the OECD's interpretation of it seem to require. One possibility which has been historically important is where branch-level unions and employers in the export sector within a small open economy and free-trade regime perceive the obvious inability of their national political system to manipulate prices on the world market, forcing recognition of the need for wages to be internationally competitive.[4] This situation has been analysed in detail by Katzenstein (1985), although he tended to see market-conforming behaviour as a kind of *functional* necessity irrespective of the capacity, form, and political will of interest organizations, which underestimates the difficulties of achieving responses of this kind.

Another significant context is where labour-market actors with a capacity for co-ordination face a strong and autonomous central bank. Since this has direct relevance for our current concern we shall pursue it in detail.

German and other National Experiences

Before German unification and the overvaluation of the Deutschmark in the early 1990s imposed severe strains on the system, the West German collective bargaining model had long provided a successful example of such a case. Given that, at least at sectoral level, German collective bargaining was organized in an essentially neo-corporatist way, the actors within this system were able to anticipate the actions of the Bundesbank. Knowing that it would refuse to accommodate itself to inflationary actions but would respond to them by depressing the whole economy, the bargaining partners had a strong incentive to reach deals that would not lead it to do this. They therefore built moderation into their own behaviour (Hall and Franzese 1998; Kloten, Ketterer, and Vollmer 1985; Streeck 1994). It is unlikely that the Bank itself ever really appreciated this fact. If anything, the system suffered from a deflationary excess, as the Bundesbank occasionally underestimated the capacity of the labour market to respond to its signals (Scharpf 1991). Nevertheless, German national experience shows the utility of neo-corporatist institutions as adaptation mechanisms to severe monetary policy.

It is important to recognize—and it emerges clearly from Streeck's (1994) analysis—that the strength of the German system lay in the *combination* of

---

[4] It is not surprising that this possibility is never discussed in OECD or other mainstream economic policy literature. This literature is so tied to a model of the US economy (for which international trade represents an unusually small proportion of GDP) as archetypal that it has no conception of the idea of extreme exposure to export markets and the implications that this has for the behaviour of interest organizations.

a highly corporatized labour market and a central bank that stood beyond the reach of organized interests—*not* in any power of the corporatist actors to influence the Bundesbank's behaviour. This is true *a fortiori* of the Austrian and Dutch cases, whose currencies had for some years been tied to the Deutschmark, which lay beyond the reach of their national political communities. These collective bargaining systems had to accommodate themselves to the German central bank, with no hope at all of influencing its behaviour.

Within both West Germany itself and in Austria and the Netherlands, neo-corporatism and the Bundesbank, far from being mutually contradictory, played complementary roles; organizations within the former, knowing that the latter could not be brought within their influence, accommodated to its requirements. Without the Bundesbank's guaranteed autonomy, it is likely that such a heavily organized economy as the German would have slipped, as did the old Bismarckian one, into protectionism. Full encompassingness or bargaining centralization was not required to give the social partners a sufficient incentive to act in a *marktkonform* manner. The labour-market actors simply needed to have enough organizational capacity to reach, and impose on their members, agreements, which recognized that a powerful third party, outside the framework of negotiation, would behave in certain predictable ways unless they cooperated.

If interest organizations lack the minimal capacity required for co-ordination, there will always be a problem of individual groups breaking rank, on the grounds that the first few to act can make a gain while the punishment will be shared by all. As governments and industrialists, in Germany and elsewhere, today seek to follow the OECD's alternative strategy of ploughing back through the trough of the Calmfors–Driffill U, dismantling labour-market institutions in order eventually to reach the free-market pole, they run the danger of destroying that minimal capacity for strategy —and are forced to rely on disaggregated uninformed individuals responding to the central bank signals rather than professionally advised organizations. The implications of this could be serious. Hall and Franzese (1998) studied a number of cases where governments had increased the autonomy of central banks. Where this took place in a context of co-ordinated collective bargaining, it was associated with a very small rise in unemployment; where the context was one of poorly co-ordinated bargaining, the rise in unemployment was considerable.

Current Capacities for Co-ordinated Wage Adjustment

Co-ordination of collective bargaining, whether through neo-corporatist centralization or other mechanisms, has become very difficult. The prevailing neo-liberal ideological climate discourages it. In a global economy, particularly one with highly mobile finance capital, firms are less tied to individual national economies, and agreements and regulations which stabilize competition among firms at national level achieve nothing for them internationally. Further, the highly competitive international climate requires individual firms to do everything they can to protect and increase their market share. This both makes them resentful of any external constraints (whether from governments, collective agreements, or their own membership associations) and to seek autonomy to shape their own personnel policies, without external interference, as part of the competitive strategy. Finally, the complex occupational structure of the post-industrial economy no longer gives such a dominant role to the organized manual workers in manufacturing industry whose self-discipline made the previous co-ordinated systems possible.

It is therefore remarkable to note that, in a number of countries, there have recently been attempts by governments and/or social partner organizations to revive and reshape the co-ordination capacity of the collective bargaining system. In a recent article, Schmitter and Grote (1997) make good use of the analogy of the labour of Sisyphus[5] to analyse these alternating characteristics of neo-corporatist policy-making. Something about labour markets in many European countries seems to destine their major participants to keep returning to the task of constructing neo-corporatist agreements, even though just as the tiring work seems almost complete, something goes wrong and it crashes again. The impossibility of the opposite task of achieving pure free labour markets may well explain the refusal of neo-corporatist policy attempts to obey predictions of their final demise.

The conclusions of Schmitter and Grote are corroborated by Traxler (1996), in an analysis which, admittedly stopping at 1990, takes a statistical rather than, like Schmitter and Grote, a narrative approach. He concludes that a *polarization* of cases is taking place, rather than a convergence on neo-corporatism, pluralism, or disorganization. This occurs, he argues, because industrial relations systems tend to be embedded in past practices and develop in ways consistent with past trajectories. In a typology related to but different from that adopted here, he distinguishes between inclusive and exclusive patterns of collective bargaining. The former are characterized by multi-employer bargaining with arrangements for extending the scope of bargains to all firms in either a sector or a whole country; this is clearly a heavily organized and co-ordinated form. The latter are characterized by single-employer bargaining with no arrangements for extension; this is a disorganized form. Distinguishing statistically between these forms he

---

[5] The figure in Greek mythology who was destined for ever to push a huge boulder up a steep cliff, only to have it roll back to the bottom as he neared the top, requiring him to start all over again.

is able to allocate countries as follows. In the former category he puts Austria, Australia, Belgium, Denmark, Finland, France, Germany, the Netherlands, New Zealand, Norway, Portugal, Spain, Sweden, Switzerland. In the latter, fall Canada, the UK, Japan, and the USA. (Traxler did not include Greece, Ireland, or Italy because of difficulties with data.)

In more recent work (Traxler 1997) he adds Ireland and Italy and considers the simpler question of whether or not multi-employer collective bargaining predominates within a country, the existence of such non-localized bargaining being a refutation of theories of disorganization. Countries divide as in the bargaining extension analysis, with Italy being added to the multi-employer group and with Ireland having neither form predominant.

While Traxler stresses institutional continuity, this is not the same as rigidity; rather, it is a question of how institutions respond to a need to adapt by changing in ways sympathetic to their existing structure. There has, in fact, been considerable change in recent years in industrial relations systems as various reform programmes have been introduced by social partners and, in some cases, governments. These reforms have nowhere reproduced or even tried to reproduce the tight co-ordination once achieved by Austrian or Norwegian corporatist institutions. The decentralization of labour questions to the individual firm and the failing power of associations has to be accepted. Co-ordination attempts have to be reshaped in the light of this, which means they restrict themselves to certain minimal tasks, which firms and individual unions are prepared to accept as limited restrictions on their freedom, made necessary by some widely accepted common objectives.

In order to distinguish these new approaches within the general neo-liberal scene, one needs first to see the difference between what Traxler (1995) had earlier called disorganized and organized decentralization. In the former category come those countries where decentralization to the firm level took the form of a *collapse* of wider-organized structures; the UK is the clearest example (Purcell 1995). Under organized decentralization in contrast the shift away from centralized bargaining was *managed* by employers' associations and trade unions. They wanted both to reap the benefits of sensitivity to the individual company and to retain a capacity to act more generally if need arose. Organized decentralization might be seen as a type of neo-corporatism, in that representative organizations are accepting a restraining role over their members, but it is a rather new form of it.

There is then another new category: cases where there seems considerable formal evidence of institutions trying to behave in a neo-corporatist or at least co-ordinated way, but where there is varying room to doubt whether they are really engaged in technical tasks of wage adjustment or something more symbolic; this is the phenomenon of 'social pacts'. Some countries seem poised between organized decentralization and social pacts.

Finally, we shall consider two groups of countries where we cannot speak clearly of new patterns of organized industrial relations; in the first of these neo-corporatist arrangements still seem to be immobilized in crisis, so there is little that is new; the second is the single case of the UK, one of disorganized decentralization and therefore virtually no reprise of co-ordination attempts; here there is much that is new, but not much that is organized.

Organized Decentralization

The logical starting points are Austria and the Netherlands, the relationship of which to the Deutschmark provide the purest cases of how co-ordinated national wage-fixing systems might function in relation to the European Central Bank.

Austrian collective bargaining continues to exhibit many of the features of its previous almost pure form of neo-corporatism, but there has been some change. The system has become slightly displaced. Privatization of the state industries that had been important to the manageability of the model has removed an important lever of control from the central actors. Further, the rise in unemployment (though lower than elsewhere) and demands for deregulation have made it more difficult to achieve consensus outcomes; but commitment to sustaining and reforming the model seems widespread among employers as well as unions (Traxler 1998).

Austrian neo-corporatism had always had rather unambitious social goals, certainly in comparison with the Scandinavian cases; the Austrian distribution of income has been among the most unequal in Europe (OECD 1993). A reduction in aspirations towards equality is one of the consequences of combining manual and non-manual bargaining now being faced by the Scandinavian countries; they are entering a path of which Austria already has experience. The kind of loss of control in a context of globalization that is causing disequilibrium for several neo-corporatist cases is therefore already anticipated in the Austrian model. Similarly, decentralization to works councils of several aspects of industrial relations had already, as in Germany and Switzerland, included aspects of articulation and decentralization.

A crisis of the Dutch industrial relations system in the early 1980s had seemed to bring the country close to breaking with neo-corporatism completely (Hemerijck 1995), but eventually the social partners and government reconstructed it, although with a much lower level of cohesion. By the mid 1990s the apparently moribund set of neo-corporatist institutions had been used to negotiate very wide-ranging reforms of the Dutch labour market, introducing elements of neo-liberal deregulation but through consensus and with important security guarantees to workers. The 'old' institutions rediscovered their purpose and significantly changed their structure, and seem to be operating effectively as a case of organized decentralization (Visser and Hemerijck 1997).

The full model of organized decentralization could be seen earliest and most prominently in Denmark (Due *et al.* 1994, 1995), where paradoxically neo-corporatism had been collapsing for a number of years, but where the organized actors implemented a kind of co-ordinated decentralization in the early 1990s. Bargaining is carried out at firm or often industry level, but the national peak organizations continue to watch the outcomes and issue guidance. Also important to the reforms and to improving scope for co-ordination were various associational mergers together with expansions in the scope of bargaining bodies to bring together collective bargaining for manual and non-manual workers, and also the private and public sectors. Earlier patterns based on the dominance of both the trade-union movement and the national economy by 'the three Ms'—Male Manual labour in Manufacturing industry—had ceased to correspond to reality. Embracing manual and non-manual employees in the same bargaining system is closely analogous to the idea of co-ordinated decentralization. On the one hand, there is a decentralization or at least loss of central steering capacity; since there is less consensus between manual and non-manual unions on strategic bargaining goals, these have to be less ambitious when the two are required to co-operate. On the other hand, without some such cooperation there can no longer be any overall co-ordination at all. In the short term, Denmark is not a member of the EMU, so the capacity of its reformed industrial relations system to perform labour-market adjustments in response to its pressures will not be tested for some time, but it seems to have the institutional capacity in place.

Finland had been gradually moving from its earlier contestative system to a set of neo-corporatist arrangements similar to those of its Nordic neighbours throughout the 1970s and 1980s. It anticipated Denmark and Norway in firmly incorporating sectors beyond manual work in manufacturing within the one system—and, of course, is now anticipating the rest of the Nordic region by being among the first to enter EMU. In some ways it had the usual benefits of latecomers, able to design a more up-to-date system than those it was imitating. Paradoxically, Finns were then given an added incentive to achieve cooperative and co-ordinated industrial relations by the extraordinary shocks delivered to their economy by the collapse of the Soviet Union at the end of the 1980s.

Social Pacts

The cases discussed so far have all been examples of where neo-corporatism has been built on a rather *technical* agenda. When the social partners meet they discuss complex documents with statistical projections, detailed policy plans, and often play a role in the implementation of any agreements. It is usually not possible for an organization to participate effectively in this form of dialogue unless it has its own technical experts who can appraise documents and create their own. This technical corporatism is different from that of *social pacts*. Here, the language is often rhetorical rather than professional; documents are concerned with simple strategic goals and moral appeals; technical experts are not much use to the debate, and in any event there are few of them available within the interest organizations. Such pacts are primarily between government and the interest organizations, particularly the unions, whereas a dialogue between employers and unions has been at the heart of the established technical systems.

Soon after they emerged from rule by fascist dictatorships in the late 1970s, Greece, Portugal, and Spain all went through exercises of grand social pact negotiation between governments, unions, and organizations of employers.[6] During the 1980s, these initial pacts began to lose their impetus, but in more recent years they have revived, precisely under the stimulus of preparing weak economies for participation in EMU. Pochet (1998) has analysed their development in all countries in what might be termed the 'periphery' of the EMU-area (Portugal, Italy, Spain, Finland, Ireland) and also in Belgium. If they had earlier often been on essentially rhetorical form of legitimacy exchange between weak governments and weak social partner organizations, they have recently begun to build on that experience and embark on serious technical tasks of co-ordinated wage moderation and labour-market policy-making.

These countries, mainly in Southern Europe, face the most difficult adjustments within EMU once the euro emerges from its difficult infancy, with untrusted and inexperienced institutions, and becomes a strong currency. If this proves an impossible challenge, the only relatively painless way of achieving a downward adjustment of wage costs will be through a capacity for organized restraint. Viewing the matter cynically, it is quite possible for national shells of union (and employer) organizations to play an amicable though important game of social reconciliation with each other and with governments, while at factory level a membership with which they have little real contact either behaves as it likes or is so oppressed by high unemployment that it cannot do anything at all, pact or no pact. However, this can only go so far. Paradoxically, an important test arises if pacts eventually break down because of strains in the labour-market bargain, and there is a subsequent attempt at reconstruction. The fact that breakdown can take place suggests that the social partner organizations possess some real autonomy from government and that their work is genuinely concerned with real

---

[6] A situation very similar occurred during the early 1990s in the Czech Republic, Hungary, Poland, and in some countries further east.

labour-market questions; and subsequent attempts at reconstruction have to address these. This seems to happen in most of these cases.

Spain presents a good example. Conflict over 'normal' industrial relations questions eventually broke the early succession of Moncloa and post-Moncloa Pacts (Maravall 1997). When the actors in the Spanish labour market now try to come together to build new agreements they do so in a more technical manner, although the level of expertise on the union side remains weak. Given the strain likely to be placed on Spanish competitiveness as the euro gathers strength, this is a country where the challenge of seeking a more institutionalized route out of the trough of the U-curve will be severe. In a sense, this was the path trodden by Finnish institutions from the late 1960s onwards—but in this case with strong unions. Moves to erect bargained corporatist central arrangements have also been attempted in Portugal, where there is a strong, orderly union movement. It is, however, divided between Socialist and Communist wings with conflict between the two.

The French union movement has long been weak and divided, and the French state has had a long record of rejecting cooperation with organized interests of the kind under review. Pochet (1998) explicitly excludes France from his survey of pre-EMU social pacts, and predicts difficulties for that country as a consequence. French industrial relations institutions are certainly considerably less well established than those in Italy and possibly even Spain. It would, however, be wrong to ignore important changes in that country. A prolonged response to the disorders of 1968 has meant that not only successive governments but also organized employers have changed their approach to unions and begun to involve them in tripartite actions. The basis of the attempts to build a system therefore lies with concerns over social order, as in other pact cases; and given the weakness of the unions in dealing with technical matters, the content of French *concertation* tends to be more symbolic than actual.

There has also been a sustained programme of legal change designed to give a more orderly place to negotiated relations, trying to replace the classic French combination of state regulation alongside contestation by a degree of pluralist bargaining and certain elements of bargained corporatism. Both forms of these arrangements usually leave out the Communist CGT union which normally refuses to sign agreements. It may also be argued that most of the agreements reached comprise employers taking advantage of union weakness in order to secure commitments from the union representatives that they would not give at times of tighter labour markets. However, while French industrial relations remain relatively weak in their capacity to negotiate major wage adjustments, if our main concern is with capacity for wage restraint in the context of the single currency, that last characteristic is not necessarily a weakness. France is one of a number of countries where unions are formally involved in managing the pensions and social security system. Many of these systems now require urgent reform. A prolonged period of low birth rates combined with a lowering of the age of retirement and increased unemployment has raised the proportion of the population receiving benefits and reduced that making contributions. Meanwhile, the fact that social insurance is funded partly by employers' contributions increases the costs to an employer of taking on workers and is therefore further increasing unemployment.[7] Union cooperation is necessary for the difficult changes which this situation requires. This gives governments a considerable incentive to retain important relations with them. Therefore, despite their past record and weakness, French unions are less likely to be marginalized than their considerably stronger British counterparts. Whether this can have practical consequences in the French case, as in the Italian situation, to be discussed below, remains to be seen.

Between Social Pacts and Organized Decentralization

In several respects Italian industrial relations are a further case of social pacts, but after a number of years of development, the system has demonstrated a capacity to go beyond this and sustain serious agreements and deals—but with some points of serious weakness. In addition to an important strengthening of co-ordinated bargaining in some regions (Regini and Regalia 1996), there have been important changes at national level. Government engages with union leaders in a mutual search for agreement on the main lines of economy policy in order to encourage wage moderation. Union leaderships were fully committed to the country's EMU ambitions, and were willing to make important changes in their priorities to facilitate these. A major starting point was the social accord of 1993 in which the unions exchanged wage moderation for both acceptance of proper bargaining procedures on the part of employers and a commitment to continuing general policy consultation by government.

Even more important, Italy is another case where unions are formally involved in managing the main national pensions and social insurance system. The same general logic applies as was outlined for the French case, but in Italy the greater strength of the unions combined with their commitment to preparing the country for entry into the European Monetary System (EMS) made possible some substantive negotiations. These have been aimed primarily at reducing the very heavy burden of pension costs produced by a disastrous previous policy of encouraging very early retirement. The

---

[7] In a free labour market the level of wages would fall in response to this, leaving the overall effect on labour costs neutral. However, in nearly all Western European countries there are either statutory or bargained minimum wage levels which prevent this downward adjustment from taking place.

Italian story suggests that, while the prevailing neo-liberal orthodoxy pays no attention to the potential capacity for wage restraint of industrial relations systems, it may indirectly facilitate it. The orthodoxy shares, indeed leads, the general concern for welfare state reform, and may therefore accept the political role of unions in this. This can in turn have serendipitous consequences in improving the capacity for co-ordination of the wage bargaining system.

At the same time, highly autonomous local organizations of workers in a small number of Italian industries continue to have the power to conduct a militant industrial relations quite separate from anything the unions wish to do, while in some parts of the south, labour continues to have virtually no representation and, because it is often in the black economy, to lack any occupational citizenship rights at all. The entire variety of possible European forms of industrial relations is contained within this one country.

Ireland, which had previously been part of a pluralist Anglophone world of organized interests, has been developing neo-corporatist arrangements of a social pact form since the 1970s. As in Denmark, the Netherlands, and some other countries, this had been temporarily interrupted in the early 1980s, but by the 1987 flexible co-ordinated agreements of the new 'Danish' kind had become fairly well established. In the context of a small country it was relatively easy to establish understandings between different levels of the system to ensure a reasonable level of co-operation. Ireland now seems to have left the Anglophone belt for one of the more European models, and in particular a northern European one; here, even more clearly perhaps than in Italy, the system is transcending the social pact form to become an example of technically based co-ordination. Ireland has long had a recognized annual bargaining round, whereby the order of contract renewal is well known and the relationship between levels of increase in the various industries is fairly predictable. During the 1960s and 1970s, in a context of shop-floor bargaining initiatives and high inflation, this characteristic became a source of instability and 'leapfrog' bargaining. However, rather than seek to abolish the system, Irish employers, unions, and governments worked to use it as the basis of an orderly and therefore predictable system, almost on a Japanese model of staged bargaining.

Given not only slacker labour markets but also a commitment by all social partners to external wage competitiveness, the change has been relatively successful. On the other hand, many of the US multinationals, which have become an important aspect of the new dynamism of the Irish economy, do not conform to the outcomes of the central bargaining. There is possibly a kind of tacit deal whereby the population employed by Irish firms and public authorities accept restraint, while their colleagues working for multinationals (who are in any case among the higher paid) do not. There are doubts about the long-term viability of this.

In Belgium there have long been important instances of government intervention in wage determination through statutory incomes policies. These are to be interpreted as failures of neo-corporatism rather than of its presence, since they denote a mistrust by government of the capacity of the bargaining parties. However, it is a form of mistrust that nevertheless envisages or at least aspires to a re-establishment of corporatist arrangements. Belgian social partner organizations retain a framework of co-ordination in order to search for consensus and new compromises. These are needed in order to manage the decentralization and the breaking of the boundaries of the former compromise that are certainly taking place. Whereas Italy represents a case of appeals for social pacts enabling the erection of new institutions, Belgium is an instance of such pacts perhaps being used to repair old ones—rather as had happened earlier in the Netherlands.

Neo-corporatism in Crisis

The social pact cases are clearly to some extent rooted in crisis; but today even the more or less stable systems have undergone moments of crisis, leading in most cases to major reform of the system; it is this alternation which gives the neo-corporatist strategy its Sisyphean character. In Sweden, however, the crisis has been engaged but there is to date no clear sign of the character of the system that will eventually emerge from it. In the late 1980s, the main organization of employers (SAF) made it clear, not that they wished to dismantle their associations (as the British seemed to do), but to change their role from bargained corporatist cooperation to a more aggressive, US-style lobbying (Pestoff 1991, 1995; Ryner 1998). This has been very different from the path followed in Denmark, and may partly reflect the different economic structures of the two countries. The Danish economy comprises many very small companies which both need to pool and share resources and which build on informal, or sometimes even formal, cooperative networks with other firms, and local deals with local governments and trade unions. The large and often multinational firms which dominate the Swedish economy do not have the same dependence, either on each other or on the Swedish national economy.

Given the strength of the unions in Sweden, it has proved difficult for SAF to achieve its goal of an Anglo-American system. The employers' bloc is not in fact united over such proposals, several industry associations preferring a decentralized corporatism, and in a few years time this may prove to be important. At present, the country is remaining outside the EMU, and in past years has made considerable use of the devaluation strategy that adherence to monetary union makes impossible; this has been one of the ways in which Sweden has reconciled its exceptionally strong labour movement with its crisis of competitiveness. It is unlikely that Swedish labour markets and Swedes' welfare state expectations will change rapidly to become like those of Britons. Were Sweden eventually to join EMU, it would almost certainly have to do so with an industrial relations regime of the Austrian, Danish, or Dutch kind, and the system would somehow have to change within that perspective.

So far, all the countries discussed have been small in European terms. Obviously, if one is concerned, as here, with changing balances between centralization and decentralization and capacities for co-ordinating the periphery from the centre, the sheer size of the labour market is a highly relevant factor. The only large-country case in Europe of neo-corporatism in the past has been the former West Germany, where again a role for company or plant autonomy—an element of organized decentralization in fact—had always been built into the co-ordination scheme through the works council system. In principle this existing acceptance of the level of the firm should have made it easier for the German system to adapt than the Scandinavians. However, partly for reasons discussed above, the German economy has recently experienced considerable problems of competitiveness. True, the German manufacturing sector continues to be the most exposed to external competition of any large country in the world (i.e. it has the highest per capita level of export production of any such country (Crouch, Finegold, and Sako 1999: chapter 3)). It also has a positive trade balance in manufacturing with the rest of the world. Nevertheless, the relative strength of its performance is declining, and it has experienced a large rise in unemployment, especially in the former Eastern *Länder*.

German employers have responded to these problems with a crisis of confidence in their industrial relations system. As in Sweden, many of them seek the freedom from institutional constraint afforded by the American and British systems (Streeck 1997). There is no complete collapse of the system; its past record of stability and efficiency and its embeddedness in German business life impose some restraint on employers. There are, however, few innovative attempts at *redesigning* it in the manner of the Danes or the Dutch. German policy-makers seem caught between a desire for a more purely neo-liberal model and mere protection of the former system. At present, therefore, there is a kind of *stasis*, with the system remaining in place, performing some functions (especially at the works council or *Betriebsrat* level), but without the dynamism with which it was associated in the 1970s. The main ideas for change among employers seem to be among those firms proposing and engaging in the *Flucht aus den Verbänden* (the flight from the associations). However, governments of any party are restrained from following this lead by the fact that (as in Italy) union cooperation is needed for pensions and other social policy reform.

Given that the euro has started life as a weaker currency than the Deutschmark, German exporters have been offered some breathing space, sparing industrial relations actors in manufacturing from the need to reshape their system. However, this does not encourage policies which might improve employment chances in various non-traded services sectors, whence any future increase in jobs must come and which will depend on a stimulation of internal demand. Further, as the euro strengthens in future years unions and employers in the export sector will have to decide whether restraint is to be achieved by reshaping their system, building on its existing capacity for centralized co-ordination, or by trying to follow the British route. Germans did in fact revise their industrial relations system in a similar way when it faced certain challenges in the 1970s; presentation of German institutions as incapable of flexibility and change are caricatures, not historically based accurate analyses.

Ryner (1998), in a comparison of these two problematic cases, Germany and Sweden, has pointed to the considerable differences in the response of their union movements, but then to subsequent change in both. Initially, the Swedish response was one of hostility to participation in monetary union, while German unions were enthusiastic. More recently, however, the majority of Swedish unions has begun to see a unified European economy as the only means of securing a general recovery—although it would need to be an EMU with rather different policy rules than that which now exists. Meanwhile, some German unions are beginning to revise their initial enthusiasm.

The British Exception

The UK has been a classic Calmfors and Driffill case. Sisyphus' boulder was laboriously pushed up the neo-corporatist hill during the 1960s and 1970s, but in a context similar to the Finnish and Italian ones of that time. When it finally crashed to the bottom in 1979 the country embarked on Europe's most thoroughgoing neo-liberal experiment of all, and the boulder was pushed far up the other, neo-liberal side, needing to make use of very heavy deflation to avoid inflationary pressure while ploughing through the deep trough in the middle of the U-curve. By the mid 1990s there had been considerable labour-market deregulation, unions had become much weaker, employers' organizations weaker still, and virtually all mechanisms for co-ordinating bargaining at anything other than the most fragmented level destroyed, either by direct government action or by the consequences of organizational collapse of the social partners (Purcell 1995). In the early 1990s, deflation was eased by recourse to the other escape route of a heavy devaluation of the currency (a device also used in Italy and Sweden in the mid 1990s).

At the time of writing, the UK stands with the devaluation gains entirely wiped out by subsequent exchange rate changes, with trade unions still relatively strong but now less capable of co-ordination than ever before, and a

Labour government maintaining the main lines of neo-liberal labour-market policy and exclusion of unions and organized (as opposed to individual) employers from detailed involvement in macroeconomic policy. Unlike in France, Germany, and Italy, unions in the UK are not involved in management of the welfare state, and governments therefore do not need their cooperation for reform. Unemployment levels are lower than those in most EU countries—not least because rejection of EMU entry has enabled the country to avoid the fiscal straitjacket of the entry criteria. Demand-led expansion has made possible the growth of jobs in untraded services sectors —something denied to countries following the EMU stability pact—even if the high value of sterling has continued to cause difficulties for the manufacturing sector. In some respects, the UK has become the mirror image of Germany, with appropriately opposite consequences: Germany retains export competitiveness in a way that the UK cannot match, but not much job growth today comes from manufacturing.

Further, re-erecting a neo-corporatism which had in any case never been very successful in Britain would involve first reinstitutionalizing the labour market; there would need to be a descent from a position fairly close to the neo-liberal extreme into the trough of the U-curve before corporatist reconstruction brought results. As in Sweden, the fact that the country has decided to opt out of the initial period of monetary union saves government and others from facing awkward choices of industrial relations design. The currency continues to fluctuate, but its level is no longer available for political manipulation. In a move widely seen as preparing the way for possible accession to the EMU, the Labour government gave the Bank of England autonomous control of interest rate policy. In the absence of any corresponding moves to resume the search for neo-corporatist wage restraint, this implies confidence by government that labour markets in the UK either already are, or soon will become, fully flexible.

Conclusion

It is not the conclusion of this chapter that neo-corporatist wage bargaining institutions are likely to be established at the level of the new single European currency, nor is such a level even posited as desirable. Indeed, it is precisely in the capacity for labour-market institutions to adapt at *national*—and possibly lower geographical[8]—levels that there are grounds for

---

[8] German wage co-ordination was, even at its peak, nuanced by industry and by geographical region. There was always a need to finesse the relationship between the overall solidaristic co-ordination task and the situation in the labour market, which varies mainly by industry

believing that wage determination systems in *some* countries might be able to pay a part in facilitating adjustment to the euro.

Indeed, to the extent that these systems remain among the mechanisms of economic steering left at national level following recent developments in European integration, the general neo-liberal move to the single currency might paradoxically give rise to new institutions for co-ordinating labour markets. And it is the unions, whose normal work is made particularly difficult by such arrangements, who will be the ones to make the running in their establishment. As we have seen, unions are the ones with the strongest *relative* preference for neo-corporatism in the choice between it and either deflation or deregulation. Therefore they are likely to seek this goal wherever the basic institutional design makes it feasible, though this should not be interpreted as some kind of new union 'power'. Their power is only that, as the ones who most need a particular outcome, they will be the ones most willing to make sacrifices to achieve it. And the outcome they seek is mainly negative: avoidance of high unemployment, the right to bargain, and measures of employment security. This logic of the situation and power balance in the new economy explain why the objectives of recent and prospective future revivals of neo-corporatism are not only very limited (e.g. they exclude any attempts at income redistribution), but will usually embody an attempt at reaching neo-liberal goals through the means of corporatist consensus. For example, the recent Dutch agreements involve relaxing forms of labour protection and reducing the generosity of welfare states (Visser and Hemerijck 1997). By participating in discussions about this, unions acquire the chance to make the move to neo-liberalism selective and discretionary, avoiding the wholesale dismantling of social protection that might otherwise occur.

There is little prospect, therefore, that these new initiatives will be used to establish ambitious redistributive social projects of the social democratic kind pioneered by Scandinavian labour-market institutions during the Keynesian period. This is what Streeck (1998) has called the new 'peace formula' between capital and labour, based on sharing risks and responsibilities in a precarious environment. It is primarily defensive, although it does not exclude innovation and the development of new models of employment relations. It may possibly produce new syntheses between workers' desire for security and the economy's need for flexibility by embodying both in forms different from those which are taken for granted in most policy discussion.

---

and geographical area. It is true that some other systems operated at national and interindustry level, but these were all small countries and rarely sustained complete rigidity for more than a few years. It is also true that industrial and in particular regional agreements in Germany did not vary much. But this was mainly because the former Western Federal Republic came to have a very even national spread of prosperity. It always maintained the potentiality for local as well as industrial variation.

Some social learning is also taking place. Most of the new institutions acknowledge that most wage-fixing today takes place at company level; the organized sectoral or national actors merely retain the capacity to exercise a general moderating touch at moments of crisis. In effect, they turn themselves into functional equivalents of devaluation. This is a painful role, as it involves internalizing within the social partner organizations the stress and conflicts that devaluation manages to dump on trading partner nations. It is because European monetary union has made devaluation impossible that it provides a strong incentive to these organizations to be willing to take up the ungrateful task of neo-corporatist restraint.

However, all these developments are taking place at a time when there are several strong pressures towards a loosening of institutional structures. It is therefore likely that attempts to sustain various forms of co-ordinated bargaining will in future need more or less 'artificial' (i.e. state-generated rather than institutional) support. One example are the attempts seen from time to time in the Nordic countries of requiring the major groups who otherwise prefer to negotiate separately (manual employees, non-manual employees, public services, private services) to bargain at the same table. This necessitates, at least in early stages, government intervention.

Against this, the new openness of economies provides an incentive to governments of most colours and to unions, although less so to employers, to develop national restraint packages. We noted vulnerability to external markets as an important factor inducing co-ordinated approaches to incomes in small open economies, provided the organizational structure was appropriate. The rise of the new industrialized countries in the Far East, the growth of 'footloose' multinationals belonging to no one economy in particular and making strategic alliances with other multinationals from various national bases, and the elaboration of the European single market, all increase exposure to international competition and inhibit recourse to protective cartels. All European economies are now subordinate to international markets in a way that has long been the case for the Belgians and Danes.

This has paradoxical consequences. On the one hand it makes national co-ordination far more difficult (Visser 1998). On the other, however, it reinforces the need to co-ordinate and increases the rewards to be gained from it. However international markets become, electorates and union memberships remain almost entirely indigenous. Governments and unions still depend on satisfying the economic aspirations of populations whose lives are more or less bounded by national economies. If tariffs and non-tariff barriers to trade are no longer available to protect these economies, organizational resources can still be sources of national competitive advantage, while the growing openness of economies provides growing sources of discipline.

It may well be, therefore, that economic openness and global competition will have these consequences: those economies that already have effective interest organizations will be able to learn anticipatorily and effect-ively from competition, and will then be able to turn their organizational specificity into a source of comparative advantage; while those that lack such devices will be forced down the Calmfors–Driffill U-curve into suboptimal performance unless and until they achieve 'pure' labour markets, should such be available.

9

Fiscal Federalism and the Reality of the European Union Budget

GABRIELE TONDL

For both political and economic reasons the group of member states entering the European Monetary Union (EMU) in the first round was more extensive than originally considered likely. Those member states which once fell far short from meeting the convergence criteria—mainly the less developed countries of the European Union (EU)—made considerable efforts to stabilize their budgets, asking their populations for heavy sacrifices in turn for the perspective of early participation in EMU.

Hence, EMU consists of members with rather different economic structures and income levels. This raises two problems. First, as the literature on adjustment in monetary unions has pointed out, with the diversity of economic structures (e.g. differing specialization of production), asymmetric shocks will occur (e.g. Bayoumi and Eichengreen 1993c, Krugman 1993). As a consequence, the common monetary policy may come under severe strain if the EU does not possess a policy instrument to assist members affected by an individual shock. This has led to the argument that stabilization policy should be partly effected by the EU's budget (Krugman 1993; Goodhart 1991; von Hagen 1991). Second, within EMU, income disparities may again increase. Once economic barriers are further eliminated among the core rich economies, the advantages of agglomeration will act even more in favour of the centre, and to the detriment of the less developed periphery (Krugman 1987, 1993, Krugman and Venables 1990). (The extent of divergence effects is debatable; but other effects, as suggested by the literature on economic convergence, are also at work.) Consequently, redistribution at EU level to promote economic development will remain an important task or will even become more significant.

However, the present fiscal constitution of the EU budget does not enable it to fulfil either of these two tasks in a satisfactory way. As to stabilization, the Community's budget does not provide a mechanism at all.

This paper was largely written while visiting the European University Institute in 1997/98. The author wishes to acknowledge kind hospitality of the Institute to carry out her research.

Redistribution to less developed regions and member states is the task of structural funds transfers. However, the redistribution effect is not significant and, in the past, it was counteracted by large transfers under the common agricultural policy (CAP), favouring richer member states. Above all, the volume of the EU budget, restricted by the budgetary ceiling of 1.27 per cent of the EU's gross national product, is too small. Hence, to face the requirements of stabilization and redistribution, the EU's budget needs to increase in size, even if—as some authors have shown (Italianer and Pisani-Ferry 1994; von Hagen and Hammond 1995)—it does not necessarily have to reach the level observed in existing federations. A new design of the Community budget would also have to reconsider how revenues are raised, namely to consider the possibility of individual-based contributions.

Since most economists, in line with the suggestions of fiscal federalism theory, consider the lack of a federal budget of the EU as a dangerous impasse of EMU, it is hardly conceivable that the issue of a reform of the Community budget never entered seriously the political agenda. It was not included in the Amsterdam Treaty, and Agenda 2000, the Commission's proposals of EU policy strategies for the next decade, proposes only a change of the expenditure structure, remaining within the current budgetary ceiling. The current paymasters of the EU budget are unwilling to address the issue, as it might impose additional payments on their shoulders. Their budgetary consolidation problems are likely to block any discussion of the topic in the near future. The issue may re-enter discussion either when adverse effects of EMU occur that would call for policy action, or when finally the EU will have moved beyond mere economic integration and will have become a political union, where citizens show more solidarity across national boundaries.

In this chapter I first present some of the arguments why redistribution and stabilization by a central budget may be required within EMU. I then present the arguments of fiscal federalism theory of how the revenue side and the expenditure side of a federal budget should be designed in order to provide adequate stabilization and redistribution instruments in a federation. Finally, I analyse the Community budget, considering revenue-raising, expenditure, and compliance with fiscal federalism arguments. In the course of so doing, I outline the most important points which should be realized with a reform of the EU budget.

Why EMU will require Central Level Redistribution and Stabilization

Already in 1971, when the Community launched its first initiative to progress towards monetary union with the Werner plan, a comprehensive study, the MacDougall Report (EC 1977), was submitted and strongly argued to create a common fiscal policy for redistribution and stabilization. Consequently, the study of Padoa-Schioppa et al. (1987), addressing the issues of integration and equality, advocated a stronger common fiscal policy as well. In a weaker form, in 1989, the Delors Report (1989) advocated an enhanced structural policy in favour of the weaker member states. Surprisingly, the issue of a new EU fiscal policy did not enter the agenda when the Maastricht Treaty was negotiated. Confronting the political constraints, the European Commission has now taken a clear distance from earlier ideas of a strong EU budget that should provide for stabilization (see EC 1997b: 35).

Several authors, mainly referring to the United States, pointed out that a central stabilization instrument would become necessary (Sachs and Sala-i-Martin 1992; von Hagen 1991; Goodhart 1991; Bayoumi and Eichengreen 1993b, von Hagen and Eichengreen 1996). Three main arguments can be brought forward. First, if one subscribes to the prospect of increasing specialization in the course of integration, as argued by Krugman, asymmetric shocks are not likely to disappear in the EU. The stabilization of individual demand shocks then remains a permanent policy topic. Second, as the EU Treaty and the subsequent Stability and Growth Pact[1] imposes a ceiling on possible deficits and debts of the member states, they will not be in a position to apply individual fiscal policies sufficiently large to offset an asymmetric shock. Third, the more economic integration proceeds, the higher will be spill-over effects from fiscal policy action of one member state onto the others. Thus a country will meet overproportionate costs for adjustment policy.

There are also strong reasons why the EU should accept the task of inter-regional redistribution via the common household. As pointed out with respect to the regional effects of the completion of the Single Market (Padoa-Schioppa et al. 1987; Krugman 1993), in a similar way the benefits of the Monetary Union will not be evenly distributed. Those regions, which host industries with economies of scale and innovative sectors, will benefit over-proportionately from further elimination of market barriers in the EMU. Poorer economies may encounter high restructuring requirements. At least in the medium term these forces will prevail (Krugman's U-curve thesis). However, it would have been even more harmful for the weaker EU economies

---

[1] The Stability Pact specifies the excessive deficit procedure set out in the Maastricht Treaty. Automatic sanctions set in if a member state runs a budget deficit of more than 3%, except for the case of a severe recession which would be given if real GDP fell by more than 0.75%. If the member state does not follow the recommendations of the Council to settle the deficit, non interest-bearing deposits, to be converted into a fine after 2 years, are foresee (Artis and Winkler 1997).

if they had remained outside EMU for these reasons.[2] The overall consequence is that in the medium term there will be no forces ensuring that disparities in the EU diminish. Thus, during the next decade, the issue of redistribution policies in favour of the weakest EU members will become even more important.

However, to settle stronger redistribution at the EU level is rather problematic. The reasons why the EU should care about redistribution to its weaker members is not yet the usual one which applies within the national member state. In contrast to the EU, the European nation states are strong political communities. Political identity implies the existence of moral concerns for equal conditions of living of co-citizens and the solidarity to provide personal resources for redistribution. In addition, politicians will lose the support of some voters if they do not care about redistribution (Harrop 1996: 48). But the EU is only at the very start of becoming a political union. A democratic representation of interests in policy decision, fundamental for operating redistributive schemes, is not yet sufficiently established at EU level.

There are, however, different, rather practical rationales for a common redistribution mechanism in the EU. First, in order to enhance the creation of a political entity, social equality has to be created between the regions and between the member states. Second, the EU can only achieve commonly accepted goals on its integration path if its members enjoy approximately equal standards of living. Strong income disparities entail highly diverging interests. Third, redistribution would help prevent major migrations to the economic centres of richer member states (Bayoumi and Masson 1995: 254), which might lead to social tensions in those places. This argument, already put forward in 1989 by the Delors Report in order to strengthen cohesion policy (1989: 22–3), is particularly relevant if the Union encompasses members with much lower standards of living, as it will be the case when . Eastern European countries join the EU.

Despite the above frequently raised arguments for a strengthening of the EU's fiscal policy, the political support for a major reform of the EU household is missing. It seems that as long as the situation of 'a shock but no instrument' does not occur, there will be no discussion of the introduction of a stabilization mechanism. Therefore, the horizon of the discussion presented in this chapter reaches far into the next decade.

---

[2] Several authors have argued that the weaker member states which do not yet strictly fulfil the convergence criteria should become part of EMU as soon as possible. Otherwise, the adjustment processes to meet the criteria would be particularly burdensome (De Grauwe 1995; Vinals 1995; Gros 1996). In addition, the whole integration process would be at risk with 2 blocs inside the EU integrating at different speeds (Artis 1996a: 1011; Breuss 1996).

Fiscal Federalism Theory: Redistribution and Stabilization in a Federation

Once monetary integration has been established, from an economic point of view one may consider the EU as a federation. Hence the fiscal federalism literature becomes highly relevant. In this section, we will look at the proposals of fiscal federalism theory, how stabilization and redistribution are best effected in a federation, why the central government is called upon to act, and which instruments should be applied.

Stabilization and redistribution are the typical fiscal policy issues in federations. In the case of redistribution, one can distinguish interpersonal redistribution, indicating the redistribution of income between individuals, and interregional distribution, where redistribution is effected from wealthier regions to poorer ones. Both tasks can be effected either via the revenue side of the budget (i.e. by taxation), or through the expenditure side (public purchases, transfers to subgovernments or individuals).

Why, in a federation (i.e. a group of economies with free mobility of goods and factors and a single currency) should stabilization and redistribution be settled on the central government level?

Redistribution

In the case of redistribution, the central consideration goes back to Tiebout (1956). He argues that if interpersonal redistribution is exerted on state level—involving tax raising and individual transfers—and the degree of redistribution differs considerably between the single states, migration will occur. While higher income earners will move to those states with a less intensive redistribution, poor people will have an incentive to move to states with higher redistribution (i.e. rich states). As a result, the redistribution scheme on the level of the states will collapse. Therefore, interpersonal redistribution should be settled on the federal level and should be based on equal criteria on the whole territory of the federation.

Further developments of Tiebout's ideas stressed the risk of tax inefficiencies, which would limit the scope of redistribution schemes of individual states in federalist economies (Gordon 1983; Inman and Rubinfeld 1996a). Inman and Rubinfeld (1996a) provide an overview of a number of empirical studies which have shown that in the case of factor mobility, the tax base of the state with higher tax rates is eroded. Capital in particular reacts very sensitively to different tax rates, but higher property taxes as well will induce the emigration of citizens.

While some authors (e.g. Nowotny 1996) have objected that so far factor mobility has remained rather low in the EU (despite very different income and capital taxes), and that it has been basically confined to high income earners and multinational enterprises, one can expect that monetary union and strengthened economic and political integration will substantially increase factor mobility, both of labour and capital. The common currency eliminates risks and transaction costs which have impinged on that mobility. Oates (1972) demonstrated that no central government policy was needed to effect interpersonal redistribution when factor mobility is low, but EU politics now have to accept that the union level increasingly has to assume tasks in the area of fiscal policy. In a first round, harmonization of tax and transfer schemes can be a viable answer when member-state tax systems enter into increasing competition due to higher factor mobility. In a second round, the use of federal taxes and grants will be required to complement the decentralized tax systems. One may consider the case that the EU will provide transfers that assure a minimum social standard.

The introduction of more central level fiscal competences, to design taxes and transfer schemes, which will not only be relevant in interpersonal redistribution but also in interregional redistribution and stabilization will, however, require a significant change in the Union's decision making process of fiscal policies. This will be demonstrated below. As contributions rooted in the literature of political economy have shown, efficient central fiscal policies require a legislature driven by global goals of the Union and not by local or group specific ones (Inman and Rubinfeld 1996b). This is certainly not the case in the present decision-making process within the Council of Ministers, while the European Parliament's approval procedure is driven by the prevailing view of national governments (see the last section below). Decision-making that rests on a broad representation of interests, as one entirely in the European Parliament, could produce the appropriate concern for union goals in fiscal policies.

In addition to interpersonal redistribution, it is a common characteristic of federations that the federal government provides financial mechanisms to shift resources from richer regions to poor ones, with the aim of complementing their inadequate financial capacity. This is referred to as interregional redistribution.

It is effected, first, by the federal taxation and social security contribution system, second, by transfers from the central government to subgovernments. As to the first, income taxation and social contributions levied from the citizens by the central government automatically lead to lower tax charges in less wealthy regions or in an economic downturn, or, similarly, lower social security contributions in the latter situation. This mechanism implies an equalization of primary income between regions with different income levels. On the other hand, in order to equalize standards of living, the central government directly provides public goods and grants to less endowed regions. While in the major federations the redistributive impact[3] of taxation is relatively weak (3.5 per cent), federal expenditures have a strong redistributive effect (e.g. public services provided by the central government have a redistributive effect of 12.4 per cent, general purpose grants of 13.3 per cent, and specific purpose grants of 6.2 per cent; Costello 1993: 272).

Although grants are a widely applied instrument for interregional redistribution, there is considerable discussion in the literature on their implications, which should be taken into account. Grants are provided either as unconditional or specific purpose grants. Unconditional grants are provided to release the subgovernment's own resources, and their use is left at the discretion of the lower tier. If the federal government intends specific allocative effects, it uses specific purpose grants (e.g. to promote investment in specific sectors). Hence, specific purpose grants permit the federal government a control over the use of provided funds, but there is a risk that local preferences are not matched if the central government acts on incorrect information.

There are two critical points with specific purpose grants (Teutemann 1993: 402–7). First, they are paired with high transaction costs, as typically several intermediary agents are involved in the redistributive process. Resources pass several administrative layers until they are in the hands of the recipient. Second, with specific purpose grants there is a risk that rent-seeking specific interest groups (e.g. industry sectors, etc.) exert some pressure on their design. The actual requirements of the region for specific public goods, or of particular social groups, may fail to be considered in the decision process of specific purpose grants, as there is usually a situation of asymmetric information between the federal authority and the lower government. The central authority possesses less information about the real needs in the locality, and hence is open to demands from pressure groups. This phenomenon often seems to occur in the EU when expenditures for specific purposes are fixed (e.g. R&D support for microelectronics, aid for the textile industry). Some of these distortions of specific purpose grants can be avoided if the distribution of the grant is effected on the basis of objective indicators, as applied for example with EU regional assistance. Again: if the decision process of grant schemes involved a broader representation of EU citizens, the problems associated with rent seeking would be much reduced.

On the other hand, one has to consider that specific purpose grants permit the donor party a control over their use. This is at present particularly relevant in the EU, where a pronounced dichotomy between donors and recipients exists. The donor party (i.e. the net contributors to the EU budget)

---

[3] The redistributive effect of taxation is the resulting change of the region's per capita income relative to the average per capita income in the federation.

wishes to ensure that its money is used for a specific purpose, otherwise it would refuse to provide funds to other, far distant EU citizens. As long as the EU has not become a political union, it will lack the solidarity necessary to use general purpose grants.

Finally, interregional redistribution also involves the case that public goods are directly provided by the central government. According to fiscal federalism theory, public goods should be provided by the central government if there exist economies of scale in their provision, if spill-overs among federal states occur, and if local governments cannot provide the goods in adequate quality. The EU is already financing large-scale public goods where spill-over effects among member states occur, namely large-scale European infrastructure for transport and telecommunications (TEN (Trans European Networks), or cohesion fund projects), and R&D programmes. For the weaker member states this means that Community funds compensate for the lack of national finances for their provision.

In summary, with regard to redistribution appropriate to federations, the EU is missing a federal income tax and a federal social security contribution scheme in order to provide redistribution on the revenue side (the GNP-based contributions do not provide for it). There is no interpersonal redistribution at all. Interregional redistribution is effected by grants, but transfers remain far below the level common in federations.

Stabilization

The other major policy task in fiscal federalism is stabilization, effected by the central government. Stabilization policy intends to smooth income fluctuations in the business cycle and to stimulate economic activity by active fiscal policy. In his fundamental work on fiscal federalism, Oates (1972) provided two considerations why, in a federation, stabilization policy should be performed by the central government. First, with regard to active fiscal policy, one has to consider that in a federation each member is a highly open economy *vis-à-vis* the others. Hence, there are large leakage effects of a member's fiscal expenditures. Similarly, if taxes are cut with the intention to raise disposable income for consumption, a considerable part of the additional income would be spent in other regions. Therefore, the multiplier effects of fiscal stabilization are only very small (Oates 1972: 4–5, 21). Second, one has to consider that because of limited own resources an economy has to borrow funds from outside if it wants to expand its fiscal expenditures for stabilization. Future repayment will lead to a transfer of income to outsiders. In contrast, a central government can borrow in a balanced way from the whole federation, and effects on income on repayment are equally spread over the whole territory (Oates 1972: 5). Both of these points appear very relevant for the EU.

Since the work of Oates, it has become a classic argument that in a federation the central government should have automatic stabilizers under its control, which smooth income fluctuations. As such, an automatic stabilizer a progressive income tax is suggested. If there are asymmetric shocks, tax revenues primarily will come from regions in a boom, whereas regions in a slump will deliver fewer tax revenues (Walsh 1993: 46).

Sachs and Sala-i-Martin (1992) have shown that in the United States federal taxes and transfers offset 30–35 per cent of per capita income deviations caused by asymmetric shocks. Bayoumi and Masson (1995: 265) estimated that the stabilization effect of federal taxes in the US amounts to 7 per cent, and reaches 30 per cent if federal transfers are considered as well.

So far, the EU does not have any competence to collect personal taxes which would effect this kind of stabilization. A fluctuation in the gross national product of a member state is hardly reflected in a change of the level of its contribution to the EU budget. This is because a major part of a member state's contribution to the EU household is based on consumption expenditures (contributions of VAT, customs duties), which do not change at the same extent as incomes. The other part of a member state's contributions, which are based on the national GNP, takes account of relative GNP variations between member states, but in total the GNP-based contributions have to reach a volume necessary to reach the fixed ceiling of the EU budget (1.20 per cent in 1993). According to Eichengreen, a variation of the GNP of a member state is passed to its household contributions at only 1.0 per cent (Eichengreen 1990).

There are also no transfers in the EU budget designed to offset temporary income fluctuations. All expenditures of the EU budget based on income differences have long-term redistribution properties.

I shall now look more closely at the empirical evidence on the present EU budget, and propose some points for a reform.

The Empirics of the EU Budget

The Constitution of the Budget: An Impediment to Flexible Policies

The budgetary scheme of the European Union hardly can be compared with a central budget common to federations. Budgetary volume is bound by a ceiling, which is expressed in relation to the EU's GNP. The EU cannot run into expenditures beyond that ceiling as borrowing is strictly prohibited by the Treaty. For the current financial perspective (1993–9), the budgetary ceiling was fixed at 1.20 per cent of EU GNP in 1993, scheduled to rise to

1.27 per cent in 1999 (see Table 9.1). This budget is considerably smaller than the 5–7 per cent of EU GNP considered necessary for EMU by the MacDougall Report in 1977 (Harrop 1996: 68), and is far smaller than a central government's budget in federations, which reaches up to 20–40 per cent of GNP (Costello 1993: 246).

The Union's budgetary decision process involves the Council of Ministers, which has to achieve an unanimity vote on the Commission's proposed budget, and the European Parliament, which can demand changes in the area of non-compulsory expenditures prior to approving it. Budgetary matters are one of the few policy areas where the Parliament was granted relatively large decision power. Since 1975, the Parliament has the right to demand an increase or reduction of non-compulsory expenditures in the budget decision process, and it can thus pursue its own policy preferences regarding expenditure priorities (Laffan and Shackleton 1996; Bladen-Hovell and Symons 1994). However, from the perspective of the literature on fiscal federalism and political economy these competences are not sufficient.

Since 1988 (Delors I package), the EU budget has been operated according to a multi-annual financial perspective, which initially laid down annual budgetary ceilings, but since 1992 (Delors II package) it also fixes the resources reserved for the major expenditure categories (see Table 9.1) (Laffan and Shackleton 1996). Hence, annual budget expenditures have to comply with the appropriations for commitments of compulsory and non-compulsory expenditures agreed in the financial perspective. (Compulsory expenditures refer to those which need to be incurred according to provisions in EU regulations, as e.g. guarantee payments for agricultural products. In contrast, the volume of non-compulsory expenditures is not determined by EU regulations but can be chosen deliberately. Structural Funds expenditures, or R&D expenditures, belong to this latter category.) Annual expenditures may only deviate from the budget guidelines at a very limited margin.

As a consequence of budgetary ceilings and rather fixed expenditure guidelines, the EU has little freedom for short-term policy actions. The household framework does not allow for fundamental policy shifts. Thus, EU budget policies cannot react to sudden structural economic problems or business cycle fluctuations. In the present economic context of major unemployment problems in particular, it would not be possible to implement at short notice important employment initiatives.

For the present constellation of rather diverging budget policy interests between EU members, multi-annual financial frameworks proved to be an adequate instrument to guarantee smooth EU politics. Given the well-known interest conflicts between member states, EU budget negotiations have become a wearisome process. If an agreed budget became subject to debate, politics in the EU would be blocked. Due to very opposite interests and the sensibility of budgetary issues, unanimity voting in the Council will

TABLE 9.1. Revenues and expenditures of the European Union budget

| | Actual own resources | | | | | | Financial perspective |
| | 1980 | | 1990 | | 1996 | | 1999 |
	ECUmn	Share (%)	ECUmn	Share (%)	ECUmn	Share (%)	Share (%)
Structure of own resources							
1. Agricultural levies (incl. sugar and isoglucose)	4,803.2	13.1	2,357.8	4.5	1,854.1	2.6	
2. Customs duties	14,167.2	38.7	12,928.4	24.8	11,972.7	16.7	
3. VAT-based resource[a]	17,642.4	48.2	36,412.5	69.9	36,315.3	50.7	48.0
4. GNP-based resource[b]			357.6	0.7	21,462.4	30.0	34.4
5. *Total revenues from own resources*	*36,612.8*	*100.0*	*52,056.3*	*100.0*	*71,604.4*	*100.0*	
Own resources in % of GNP	0.75		0.87		1.17		1.15

Note: Annual revenues may not correspond to expenditures because total funds available in a financial year may include carry-overs and surplus from previous years, and payments may be transferred into the next financial year.

[a] VAT-based resource introduced in 1979. Until 1986, it was fixed at 1% of the harmonized tax base, thereafter raised to 1.4%. The Delors II package foresaw a reduction to 1%, to be initiated in 1995.

[b] GNP-based resouce introduced by Delors I package in 1988 (mn, million).

Table 9.1 (*Cont.*)

Structure of expenditures	Payments effected						Appropriations for commitments			
	1980		1990		1996		Financial perspective 1999		Agenda 2000 2006	
	ECUmn	Share (%)	ECUmn	Share (%)	ECUmn	Share (%)	ECUmn	Share (%)	ECUmn	
1. Agriculture guarantee	27,097.4	69.4	31,402.4	57.7	39,784.4	50.9	43,300.0	44.3	50,000.0	
2. Structural policies	4,944.8	12.7	15,640.2	28.7	25,057.6	32.1	36,100.0	36.9	42,800.0	
—Agriculture guidance	1,441.1	3.7	2,833.9	5.2	3,850.0	4.9				
—Regional policies	1,762.0	4.5	4,458.2	8.2	6,144.5	9.0				
—ESF, social policies	1,741.7	4.5	6,162.3	11.3	15,063.0	19.3				
3. R&D, energy, other internal policies	882.0	2.3	2,185.8	4.0	2,991.9	4.8	6,100.0	6.2	8,100.0	
4. External policies: Dev. aid, cooperation third countries	1,219.4	3.1	1,540.1	2.8	3,821.0	5.0	6,600.0	6.7	7,600.0	
5. EU administration	1,966.5	5.0	2,889.0	5.3	4,033.8	5.2	4,500.0	4.6	5,500.0	
6. Other (repayments, etc.)	2,929.7	7.5	2,993.1	5.5	2,448.7	1.0	1,200.0	1.2	500.0	
7. Total expenditures	39,039.9	100.0	54,464.8	100.0	78,137.3	100.0	97,800.0	100.0	114,500.0	
Actual expenditures (% GNP)	0.8		0.96		1.21		1.25			
Budgetary ceiling (% EU-GNP)			1.17		1.22		1.27			

Note: Appropriations for commitments cover all legal expenditure obligations to be entered into, but activities usually extend into the next financial year. Actual payments arise from commitments entered into in the current financial year or in previous ones (mn, million; ESF, European Social Fund).
Source: author's calculations based on data from: EU Court of Auditors, Eurostat, OECD, European Commission.

also persist for a while. With deepening integration and more equal distribution of its economic benefits, the interests of member states may approach each other. Eventually, the EU may once decide on its budget only in its Parliament, by majority voting and on a one or two year basis. (See Table 9.2.)

The Financing of the EU Budget viewed under Stabilization and Redistribution Requirements

The EU budget is financed by the so-called four budgetary own resources: customs duties, agricultural levies, a proportion of VAT, and the GNP-based component. In 1996, the budgetary contribution of customs duties and agricultural levies emanating from imports from third countries accounted for 19.3 per cent of revenues (see Table 9.1). Due to tariff dismantling, both on industrial and agricultural goods, imposed by subsequent GATT rounds, these revenue sources have been significantly diminishing. Gradually until 1989, the major share of budget revenues had been raised from the VAT-based own resource, which then accounted for about 70 per cent of revenues. With the introduction of the GNP-based resource in 1988, which should introduce more progressivity in revenue raising, VAT-based revenues fell to 54.5 per cent in 1993, and were scheduled to be reduced to 48 per cent at the end of the current financial perspective in 1999 (Harrop 1996: 65). The VAT-based contributions of the member states are calculated on a harmonized VAT base. Originally fixed at 1.0 per cent of the harmonized VAT base, this fraction was first raised to 1.4 per cent in 1986, and then, since 1995, lowered again, in order to come back to 1.0 per cent in 1999. The fourth own resource, GNP-based contributions, are calculated on the residual revenue requirements (considering available resources from surpluses of previous years) necessary to reach the budgetary ceiling (1.27 in 1999). Thus, GNP-based contributions accounted for 21.4 per cent in 1993 and should rise to 34.4 per cent in 1999 (Harrop 1996: 65).

EU budget revenues are primarily regressive, even if not as much as in the past. The revenues from VAT are regressive, as poorer member states typically spend a higher fraction of their income on consumption than on savings or investment compared to richer members (Biehl 1992: 57). The same is partly true for customs duties, as lower income countries are more import-dependent.[4] At present, a limited progressivity is only given in the case of the GNP-based contributions; however, at the end of the present

---

[4] Of course, revenues from customs duties are also distorting in the case of small and peripheral countries with higher import propensity from bordering third countries (e.g. Austria, Finland, or Greece), not to mention the Rotterdam Effect.

TABLE 9.2. European Union budget: member states, contributions and receipts (1996)

| | G | F | I | UK | B | Nl | L | Dk | Cohesion countries | | | | Entrants 1995 | | | Total |
									Sp	P	Gr	Irl	A	Fin	Sw	
Payments to the EU budget																
ECUmn	20,766.9	12,410.9	8,935.2	8,227.1	2,743.0	4,435.7	163.2	1,359.9	4,538.9	906.1	1,107.1	710.2	1,872.6	961.3	1,957.4	71,095
Share MS	29.2	17.5	12.6	11.6	3.9	6.2	0.2	1.9	6.4	1.3	1.6	1.0	2.6	1.4	2.8	100
Net position: Receipts minus payments, in % of GDP																
1990	−0.47	−0.19	−0.05	−0.44	−0.51	0.16	−0.74	0.42	0.44	1.14	3.84	5.35	−0.27	−0.12	−0.46	
1996	−0.59	−0.04	−0.15	−0.25	−0.36	−0.79	−0.57	0.14	1.30	3.38	4.06	4.09				
Receipts from the EU budget (CAP guarantee)																
ECUmn	6,050.4	9,572.1	4,231.1	3,470.1	1,152.8	1,536.2	20	1,358.4	4,054.6	646	2,801.7	1,700.1	1,214.2	649.3	624.1	39,081.1
Share MS	15.5	24.5	10.8	8.9	2.9	3.9	0.1	3.5	10.4	1.7	7.2	4.4	3.1	1.7	1.6	100.0
% of GDP																
1990	0.33	0.53	0.46	0.23	0.56	1.18	0.06	1.08	0.52	0.40	3.02	4.36	0.68	0.66	0.32	
1996	0.33	0.79	0.44	0.38	0.55	0.50	0.14	0.99	0.88	0.79	2.89	3.07				
% of agriculture gross value added (GVA)																
1990	22.5	15.7	14.2	15.8	30.0	29.3	3.7	27.9	11.2	6.5	22.8	59.4	45.1	18.4	16.6	
1995	35.3	30.0	14.3	22.8	41.0	20.6	10.7	28.4	36.5	22.8	22.4	50.7				

Structural funds (EAGGF guidance, ERDF, ESF)

	G	F	I	UK	B	NL	L	Dk	Sp	Gr	P	Irl	A	Fin	Sw	EU
ECUmn	3,435.4	1,938.8	3,016.4	1,961.1	327.7	268.7	14.6	104.6	6,234.1	2,961.5	2,122.9	1,206.4	235.9	135.2	94.6	24,057.9
Share MS	14.3	8.1	12.5	8.2	1.4	1.1	0.1	0.4	25.9	12.3	8.8	5.0	1.0	0.6	0.4	100.0
% of GDP																
1989–93 avg.	0.04	0.13	0.23	0.16	0.09	0.06	0.15	0.07	0.64	2.4	1.84	2.15	0.13	0.14	0.05	
1994–96 avg.	0.14	0.13	0.24	0.18	0.12	0.08	0.12	0.09	1.06	3.1	2.16	1.96	0.13		0.05	
of which ESF																
ECUmn	869.8	650.7	332.2	913.4	129.2	177.5	3.9	53.4	1,789.6	538.2	120.4	306	93.9	34.4	23.3	6,035.9
Share MS	14.4	10.8	5.5	15.1	2.1	2.9	0.1	0.9	29.6	8.9	2.0	5.1	1.6	0.6	0.4	100.0
% of GDP																
1990	0.02	0.05	0.05	0.08	0.03	0.03	0.04	0.04	0.16	0.13	0.47	0.58	0.05	0.04		
1996	0.05	0.05	0.04	0.10	0.06	0.06	0.03	0.04	0.39	0.66	0.12	0.55	0.05	0.04	0.01	
Receipts per unemployed, in ECU, 1990 prices																
1990	99	202	160	391	142	133	1,259	158	260	315	1,068	1,142	376	73	45	
1996	221	167	90	370	191	322	526	224	410	236	1,248	1,424				

Abbreviations: G, Germany; F, France; I, Italy; UK, United Kingdom; B, Belgium; Nl, the Netherlands; L, Luxembourg; Dk, Denmark; Sp, Spain; P, Portugal; Gr, Greece; Irl, Ireland; A, Austria; F, Finland; Sw, Sweden.

MS, member state; CAP, Common Agriculture Policy; mn, million; –, net payer; +, negative payer.

EAFGF, European Agriculture Guarantee and Guidance Fund; ERDF, European Regional Development Fund; ESF, European Social Fund.

Source: author's own calculations based on data from: EU Court of Auditors, Eurostat, OECD.

TABLE 9.3. How much does European Union budget revenue-raising account for income progressivity?

Possible relationship of member-state payments (PAY) to GDP and GDP per capita (p.c.) if progressivity is given:

(1) $PAY = \mu\ GDP + \varepsilon$	$0 < \mu < 1$	Payments grow at a linear rate with GDP level.
(2) $PAY = GDP^\mu + \varepsilon$	$1 < \mu$	Payments grow at an increasing rate with GDP level.
(3) $PAY = \mu\ GDP + \nu\ GDPp.c. + \varepsilon$ $0 < \nu$		In addition to (1) or (2) differences in national p.c. income determine payments.
(4) $PAY = \mu\ CGDP + \varepsilon$ with $CGDP = (GDP * (GDPp.c./GDPp.c.\ EU))$		Payments determined by GDP corrected by factor of relative GDP p.c. position in EU.

Results of empirical estimates on member states' EU budget payments 1975–95

EU budget revenue raising is predominately determined by equation (1).
Equation (4) achieves equal explanatory power since the early 1990s.
Equations (2) and (3) are not significant.

Conclusions
Payments are determined by GDP level and no other factors. Slight evidence to use GDP levels corrected by above/below average income position. Payments do not grow at an increasing rate with raising income.

Estimated parameters
Equation estimated for single years by LS (1975–95).
Characteristic results for subperiods grouped together.

Period				Significant equation		
	Equation (1)	SE	R^2	Equation (4)	SE	R^2
1993–6	PAY = 0.011 GDP	0.0003	0.98	PAY = 0.0100 CGDP	0.0003	0.97
1988–92	PAY = 0.010 GDP	0.0003	0.96	PAY = 0.0090 CGDP	0.0003	0.966
1986–7	PAY = 0.0092 GDP	0.0003	0.98			
1982–5	PAY = 0.0083 GDP	0.0004	0.96			
1978–81	PAY = 0.0074 GDP	0.0003	0.96			
1975–7	PAY = 0.0052 GDP	0.0002	0.96			

LS = Least Squares

financial perspective they will already constitute more than one-third of the EU budget revenues.

By their very nature, the EU budget revenue instruments do not comply with the taxation principles of fiscal federalism to guarantee redistribution and stabilization. As to redistribution, richer member states do not necessarily pay an equivalent or even a higher proportion of the EU budget than poorer members. As to stabilization, fluctuations in GNP of a member state will not be fully transformed into variations of its budget contributions. Certainly, revenues from the first three own resources will vary with economic activity and so would GNP-based contributions. However, as the GNP-based contributions need to reach the residual necessary to achieve a certain fraction of the EU budget—a share which refers to EU–GNP as a whole—stabilization may not be met. Both hypotheses were analysed more formally, looking at data of member-state budget contributions over the past twenty years. The results are as follows.

First, I wished to investigate whether member-state payments to the EU budget exhibit some characteristic of income progressivity. Table 9.3 summarizes the analysis and its results. We start with some relationships between payments and GNP which capture progressivity. Each of the equations (1)–(4) in Table 9.3 was estimated for the annual payments of member states. The estimation results suggest that members' payments are a simple fraction of their GNP level. This fraction does not increase with higher per capita income. However, in recent years, payments follow a calculus based on the GNP level corrected by a member's relative income position. The results over consecutive periods show that budget payments increased from 0.5 per cent of GNP on average in the period 1975–7 to 1.1 per cent in 1993–6. The estimation's results are illustrated by Figs 9.1 and 9.2. Figure 9.1, which picks out the year 1996, shows that member-state payments quite neatly follow a linear relationship with GNP level. Figure 9.2 shows that a member's payment in GNP share does not necessarily increase with raising national per capita income. The arrows underline that among the fifteen member states in 1996, the fraction paid into the EU budget partly decreased, partly increased with rising per capita income.

Next, I wish to address the issue whether the development of member states' household contributions satisfy stabilization criteria. How does the behaviour of contributions react to GNP variations? In order to account for stabilization, members' payments should only grow in line with their GNP growth, and they should decline in slumps. In a weak form, stabilization would at least require that growth rates of payments and GNP move into the same direction. Table 9.4 presents the investigation on stabilization properties. The basic equation entering into the estimation with budget payments data, states a simple relationship between a member's i payments growth rate at time t and its GNP growth rate. The coefficient linking payments growth to GNP growth should be positive and smaller than 1. The equation is estimated on a panel of EU members' real growth rates of payments and GNP over the past twenty years. The series are corrected for time-specific means to eliminate period-specific effects. For estimation, panel data estimation with fixed effects were chosen (country-specific effects not reported). The hypothesis that payments would not fulfil stabilization criteria was confirmed by the poor results of the estimation. Member-state payments growth did not fit

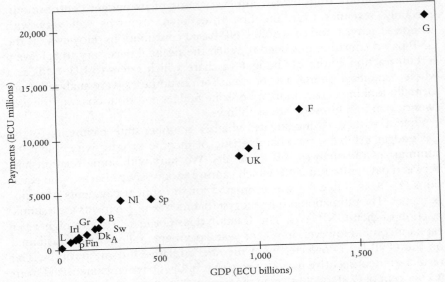

FIG. 9.1. Payments into the European Union budget and GDP level (1996).
(Abbreviations: see Table 9.2.).
Source: based on data from EU Court of Auditors, Eurostat, OECD.

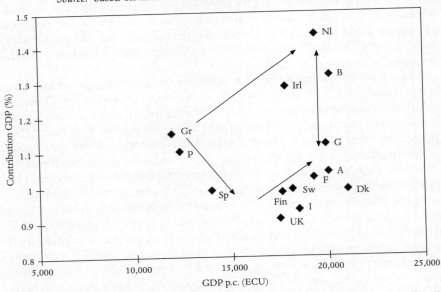

FIG. 9.2. European Union budget contribution as percentage of GDP and per capita (p. c.)
income position (1996). (Abbreviations: see Table 9.2.).
Source: based on data from EU Court of Auditors, Eurostat, OECD.

Table 9.4. Do member states' contributions to the European Union budget fulfil
stabilization criteria?

Stabilization condition

γ PAY $< \gamma$ GDP
where γ PAY, GDP are real growth rate of payments to EU budget and GDP

To account for stabilization, growth of a member's budget payments must not exceed GDP
growth. If GDP declines payments must do so the more.
A weak condition to fulfil stabilization properties is that both growth rates move in the same
direction, have the same sign (positive or negative rate).

Empirical results for EU member budget payments (1974–95)

1. Econometric estimation

$GPAY_{it} = \alpha \, GGDP_{it} + u_i + v_{it}$ $0 < \alpha < 1$

   $GPAY_{it}$ = growth rate of payments country i at time t
   $GGDP_{it}$ = GDP growth rate country i at time t
   (values of both variables corrected by time-specific mean to eliminate time-specific effect)
   u_i country-specific effect

Estimation method: fixed effects

Estimation results

Period	α	SE	R^2	Sample
1974–81	−0.29	0.33	0.29	EU-9
1982–6	+0.35	0.50	0.15	EU-10
1987–95	+0.56	0.38	0.08	EU-12

Conclusion from estimation
There is no significant evidence that payments to the EU budget satisfy stabilization criteria:
(a) empirical estimates fail to prove that growth rates of payments are within GDP growth rate
    bounds;
(b) empirical estimates do not confirm that payment and GDP growth rates move in the same
    direction.

2. Coefficients of correlation $GPAY_i - GGDP_i$ (1974–95)

Group A Weak stabilization fulfilled		Group B Destabilizing effect		Group C No joint pattern	
Spain	0.42	Luxembourg	−0.54	Greece	0.17
Denmark	0.39	UK	−0.33	Italy	0.11
Germany	0.37	Ireland	−0.31	Belgium	0.11
				Netherlands	0.04
				France	0.002
				Portugal	−0.09

Conclusion from series diagnostics
(a) with a small group of members, growth rates of payments and GDP move in the
    same direction. However, payment growth rates are generally above GDP growth;
(b) for a group of members EU budget payments exert destabilizing effects, payment growth
    moves in the opposite direction to GDP growth;
(c) for the majority of member states the development of budget payments' growth and GDP
    growth are not linked.

the relationship, indicated by the low R^2 values and the large standard errors of coefficients. In a less sophisticated way, the coefficient of correlation between a member state's payments growth rates and its GNP growth rates shows that members' payment patterns can be divided into three groups. For a small group, payments fulfil stabilization criteria, in so far as they move at least in the same direction as GNP growth. With a second group, household payments have an absolutely destabilizing effect. Finally, for a third group, the majority of EU members, payments do not follow a joint pattern with GNP growth. Hence, we may conclude that at present EU budget contributions do not support any stabilization of economic activity.

Today, as described above, a part of the EU budget revenues is based on the income level of a member state. One may go further and adopt the argument of fiscal federalism that revenues should be based on individual incomes. This would assure stabilization at the time shocks occur, and also a better match of redistribution. If the national GNP is used as a basis for progressive contributions, the interregional and interpersonal income distribution of a country are neglected. The equivalence principle would be better obeyed if contributions were based on personal incomes or regional incomes. In poorer economies, income distribution is usually rather unequal, hence there is a considerable tax base of high income groups. In contrast, richer member states in general have a larger share of middle income earners. Evidence from the important Luxembourg Income Study, assessing income inequality within European countries in the late 1980s/early 1990s, shows that the income ratio of highest to lowest income is 4.02 in Spain and 4.23 in Ireland, while 3.01 in Germany and 3.05 in the Netherlands (Gottschalk and Smeeding 1997: 661). Similarly, the distribution of households on the income scale is much broader in Ireland (Gini coefficient of 40.3) than in Germany or the Netherlands (Gini coefficient of 29.9) (OECD 1995b: 87).

One may consequently consider an EU personal taxation scheme where the individual is charged according to a national progressivity scale (reflecting the range of intracountry income disparities). The basic tax rate, applying to a median income, would have to consider cross-country per capita income disparities. For example: assume an EU tax for the average EU per capita income of 2 per cent. In Ireland, the median income tax rate would be 1.96 per cent, as the country's per capita income reaches only 98 per cent of the EU average. Suppose further that the intracountry tax progression mirrors exactly income differentials. In that case, the calculation of tax rates may be effected as follows. When the highest Irish income level is 2.86 times the Irish median income level, then the tax rate of the top earners should also be 2.86 times the one of the median income earner. The EU tax rate of the Irish top level income earner would then be $1.96 \times 2.86 = 5.6$

per cent of personal income. In contrast, in Germany, the median income level tax rate would be 2.2 per cent according to relative national per capita income. When the highest German income is 2.1 times the German median income, then the EU tax rate of the highest income group would be $2.2 \times 2.1 = 4.62$ per cent of personal income.

This tax rate calculus gives an important message. There would be hardly any taxation for low income groups in poorer countries, while the average prosperous person of a rich member state would pay less taxes than a rich person from a poor member state. The application of a personal progressive income tax for contributions to the EU household would be considered much more just by citizens of richer EU member states. The same would be true in a weaker form if contributions based on regional incomes were applied. Even in the poorer EU member states some regions are very well off. If income-related contributions were based on a lower level than at present, the permanent net payer dilemma, which is the key obstacle to achieve consensus among EU members for an expansion of the budget, may partly be solved.

In addition to personal or regional income based taxation, a share of individual social security contributions would be an appropriate revenue source of the EU budget under stabilization criteria. Revenues from social security contributions could be used to finance minimum social standards and unemployment benefits throughout the Union. In this case the, employed, irrelevant of which country, would pay to assist the unemployed, whether in their own country or in another member state. This scheme would contribute as well to disentangle the present rigid relations between paymaster and recipient. Individuals in richer member states would have equal chances to benefit as people from cohesion countries. This follows the idea of an insurance scheme where each citizen in the EU is a potential beneficiary (Masson 1996).

To summarize, revenues levied from the individual EU citizen, instead of contributions based on national income, would alleviate the sole function of the rich EU countries as paymasters. Individual based revenue raising would be perceived as much more just and equal. The present problem of a lack of transnational solidarity, preventing any increase of the Union's budget, could be solved, and properties of redistribution and stabilization would be better fulfilled. Such an important change of the EU financial constitution would, however, require major developments of the EU political constitution. While today national-based contributions are subject to a voting process of national representatives in the Council of Ministers, individual-based contributions would require the democratic legitimation of decisions taken by a broad representative institution of European citizens, which means the European Parliament.

The Redistributive Impact of Current EU Budgetary Expenses

On the expenditure side, the largest part of budgetary expenses is devoted to guarantee payments under the Common Agricultural Policy (CAP), and the second largest to transfers under the structural funds. In 1992, CAP expenditures claimed 5 per cent of Community budgetary resources, the structural funds 31.5 per cent (Court of Auditors 1992). In the Community budget of 1996, CAP subsidies still accounted for 51 per cent of expenditure, transfers through the structural funds and the cohesion fund for 32 per cent, and R&D financing, and other internal policies for only 4.8 per cent (see Table 9.1).

The large proportion of agricultural expenditures significantly restricts the scope of the Community budget which is already limited by its small size. Moreover, price support payments have destabilizing effects.

The overproportionate role of spending on the CAP is the result of well-organized, steady lobbying of European farmer's unions since its creation in 1962. In absolute figures, the major share of CAP expenditures traditionally goes to rich member states: France, Germany, Italy, the Netherlands, also now the UK (Table 9.2). However, partly because of a stepwise creation of support schemes for Mediterranean products, allocations to cohesion countries, such as Spain and Greece, have become substantial. Ireland has also received significant CAP payments ever since its Community accession. In terms of contribution to GNP the cohesion countries, above all Ireland and Greece, have become most reliant on CAP receipts. In 1996, CAP payments to Ireland reached 3.1 per cent of its GNP (4.4 per cent in 1990), those of Greece 2.9 per cent of GNP (3 per cent in 1990). Spain and Portugal managed to approach their receipt share to those of high recipient Northern member states, initially relying on little CAP support on their Community entry. For the richer, Northern member states CAP payments constitute an important return flow from the EU budget, the loss of which would seriously worsen their net payer position. For the Netherlands and Denmark receipts from CAP always were significant and once amounted to more than 1.0 per cent of GNP, before declining in recent years. For other richer member states as well (France, Austria, Belgium, Italy, etc), the return flow of EU funds through CAP is significant. However, it is no longer the case that rich members are the only party interested in a maintenance of CAP support schemes. Cohesion countries have acquired similar interests.

For agricultural production the role of CAP price support differs considerably between member states, without any correlation with income level (see Fig. 9.3). Relative to agriculture gross value added (GVA), Ireland, the Netherlands, Denmark, Belgium, and recently also Austria, have enjoyed the highest aid intensity through CAP price support, reaching more than 40 per cent of GVA. Aid intensity has been also high in France and Germany. In contrast, aid intensity for agricultural production has remained low in

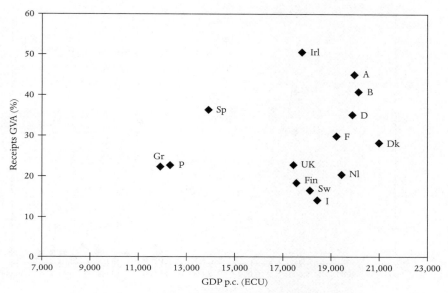

FIG. 9.3. Member states' receipts under CAP guarantee
(percentage of agriculture gross value added, GVA) and per capita (p. c.)
income position (1996). (Abbreviations: see Table 9.2.).
Source: based on data from EU Court of Auditors, Eurostat, OECD.

Mediterranean countries, except for Spain, which also has a large agricultural area with similar conditions for production as in Northern member states. Following the McSharry reform of 1992, CAP support has declined. The Uruguay Follow-up negotiations, which start in 1999, will require further reduction of CAP price support in future. A crucial point for future survival or decline of CAP support will, however, come from a more closely perceived event, namely Eastern European enlargement. Given the large share of agriculture in Eastern Europe and a price level below those in the EU, an extension of present CAP support to new entrants would overwhelm the financing capacity of the EU budget. However, the actual costs of current CAP policies for a new Eastern member state are hard to estimate precisely. Agricultural restructuring and convergence of price levels might happen very rapidly but might take decades (Baldwin, François, and Portes 1997). Because of these uncertainties, any proposals of the Commission to reduce CAP expenditures are prone to meet resistance of the major beneficiary countries.

That only an abolition of present CAP price policies can free the necessary resources for new important EU policies for redistribution and stabilization, is undeniable.

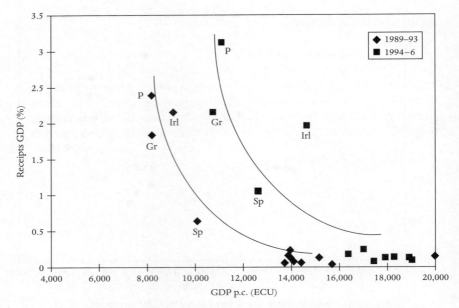

FIG. 9.4. Member states' receipts from structural funds (percentage of GDP) and per capita (p. c.) income position (1989–96). (Abbreviations: see Table 9.2.). *Source*: based on data from EU Court of Auditors, Eurostat, OECD.

At present, the structural funds (EAGGF guidance, ERDF, ESF), and the cohesion fund perfectly generate interregional redistribution in the EU, and thus respond to persistent income differentials. The contribution of structural funds transfers in relation to GNP exhibits a strong progressivity in favour of member states with weak per capita income (Fig. 9.4). Redistribution by the structural funds has significantly increased between the first regional support programme (1989–93) and the second (1994–9) (see Table 9.2 and Fig. 9.4). In the two weakest cohesion countries, the annual contribution to GNP of structural funds receipts has attained 3.1 per cent in Portugal, and 2.2 per cent in Greece (cohesion fund not included) in the period 1994–6. Ireland ranks next with 2 per cent and Spain, a not entirely objective 1 area, has received 1.1 per cent in terms of GNP. One should, however, consider that in Greece, Spain, and Ireland the CAP receipts exceed those of the structural funds. Significant resources for real structural policies could be released if CAP guarantee expenditures were renounced (see Table 9.2).

One should note that structural funds transfers are not used to support incomes in the weaker regions, but to finance public investment and business investment in order to improve the conditions for long-term development (Delors Report 1989: 22). As in federations, Community funds are assigned to weaker member states for public investment (infrastructure, education, and social services), which, in view of limited financial capacity, otherwise would not take place. The assignment of financial transfers is effected on the basis of matching grants (i.e. Community funds are only provided if supplemented by national funds), which according to fiscal theory is optimum to prevent fiscal illusion and to assure spending according to local preferences (Costello 1993). However, a principal weakness in the structural funds grants, namely the non-existence of conditionality (i.e. freezing of payments if macroeconomic policy deviates from an agreed programme—like the convergence programmes), resulted in a loss of efficiency of the structural funds programmes in the past. The importance of sound macroeconomic policies for the efficiency of economic development programmes has often been pointed out (e.g. World Bank 1997). Recent changes of macroeconomic policy and government practices (e.g. in Greece), driven by the concern to participate in EMU, promise to raise the efficiency of structural funds spending.

Among the structural funds, the present role of the European Social Fund (ESF) is particularly interesting under the perspective of establishing a socially oriented stabilization mechanism, as discussed above. At present, the ESF provides funds for professional training schemes to reintegrate unemployed people into the labour market, to combat youth unemployment, and to prevent unemployment by active labour market policies. The ESF is designed to provide funds for employment policies to all member states, with no restriction to specific regions. As shown in Table 9.2, besides significant transfers to the cohesion countries, important ESF volumes are also received by richer member states. Reflecting the increase of unemployment problems in Europe, funding by the ESF has significantly increased in many member states between 1990, when major unemployment problems had not yet started, and 1996, when unemployment reached a peak. The contribution of ESF transfers relative to GNP doubled in several member states, including Spain, Germany, Belgium, and the Netherlands. However, when comparing GNP ratios of ESF transfers one has to consider the double task of the ESF of financing unemployment measures on the one hand, and supporting training measures in general on the other. The cohesion countries, which—except for Spain—need to overcome major deficits in education and professional skills enjoy much higher ESF support in terms of GNP (see Table 9.2).

The same picture appears if ESF transfers are regarded in relation to unemployed persons. Cohesion countries employ more than ECU1,000 of ESF transfers per unemployed, whereas that amount is ECU200–300 in richer member states. In general, member state's funding by the ESF neatly corresponds to their unemployment level, as shown in Fig. 9.5, if accounting for the particular policy content in the smaller cohesion countries. Hence, the ESF can be already considered as a policy instrument which provides

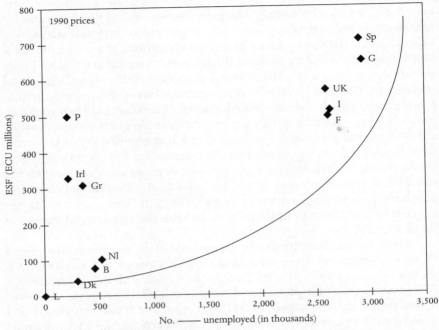

FIG. 9.5. Member states' receipts from the Europen Social Fund and unemployment levels (1991–3, average). (Abbreviations: see Table 9.2.)

Source: based on data from EU Court of Auditors, Eurostat, OECD.

for interpersonal redistribution in the Union, shifting funds from the EU level to disadvantaged persons in the member states. Moreover, ESF spending satisfies also stabilization criteria. If one examines ESF annual transfers since the late 1980s it shows that transfers per unemployed rose with economic stagnation and high unemployment in the period 1991–3 compared to previous years. When economic activity again accelerated, ESF transfers per capita again dropped. In future, the ESF could not only serve to finance labour market restructuring measures, but it may also provide minimum unemployment benefits, as a part of stabilization. In that case, the ESF would have to be funded by individual social security contributions.

The reforms suggested in this chapter to achieve redistribution and stabilization necessary in a European wide monetary union, can be summarized in the scheme shown in Table 9.5. The central points are the introduction of individual EU taxes, social transfers to individuals, and a sharp reduction of CAP guarantee payments in favour of other expenditure items. The management of interregional redistribution, now operated by several funds, could be effected by a single, new cohesion fund.

TABLE 9.5. Proposed modifications to the European Union budget to fulfil fiscal federalism criteria

Present revenue sources	Modifications	Functional characteristics	Financial impact
Revenue			To be calculated
1. Customs duties	Reduction		
2. Agricultural levies	Reduction		
3. VAT	Introduction of formula to assure Income progressivity		
4. GNP-based contributions	Replaced by:		To be calculated
	4.1. regional income based	Redistr. & stabiliz.	
	4.2. personal income taxation	Redistr. & stabiliz.	
	4.3. social security contributions	Redistr. & stabiliz.	
Expenditure			To be calculated
5. CAP guarantee	Phasing out		
6. EAGGF guidance	6–8 combined as a	Economic	
7. ERDF	new 'Cohesion Fund'	development:	
8. Cohesion fund		vertical grants for public expenditures (interregional redistribution)	
9. ESF	New ESF	Social transfers for minimum standards Employment initiatives (stabilization and interpersonal redistr.)	
10. R&D, TEN	Expenditures on public goods of Community interest: R&D, TEN, security, defence	Provision of large scale public goods with strong national external effects	

In July 1997, the European Commission presented its proposals for the next financial perspective 2000–6 in Agenda 2000 (EC 1997a) (see Table 9.1). The proposed changes are rather modest compared to the requirements advocated in this chapter. Given member states' fiscal constraints, Agenda 2000 did not propose an increase of the EU budget volume, which from the beginning would have had no chance of becoming reality. Under the restricted budget ceiling of 1.27 per cent of EU–GNP, and financial requirements to finance pre-accession structural policy measures for Eastern European applicants and to phase in new members in structural policy aid schemes most likely after 2002, interregional redistribution for existing EU members will not increase as in the past, but rather decline. The financial perspective for structural policies, proposed in the Agenda 2000, foresees a drop of structural policy spending for EU-15 from ECU34.3 billion in 1999 to ECU30.2 billion in 2006 (1997 prices). The document proposes structural policy pre-accession aid of ECU1 billion for Eastern applicants and expects structural policy funding requirements for new members to start with ECU3.6 billion in 2002 and mount to ECU11.6 billion in 2006.

To create some room for financial manoeuvring, the Commission proposes significant reductions of CAP guarantee spending, which, however, will only free ECU4.5 billion per annum in 2006. In contrast, the Commission expects rather modest agriculture payment requirements for new entrants of ECU3.9 billion by 2006. However, the actual costs for Eastern European countries and their timely incidence are rather vaguely assessed, as underlying economic developments and the progress of accession negotiations are uncertain. Relatively modest costs of Eastern enlargements in the financial period 2000–6 rest on the assumption of gradual phasing-in into EU structural policies of new members, a significant reduction of the EU's CAP payment scheme with very limited payments for new members, and a maximum of two to three new member states by not earlier than 2002. With the exception of the CAP, Agenda 2000 does not address any major budget policy reforms.

The gradual application of structural policies to new entrants was advocated by several economists, stressing the limited absorption capacity of a transition country for transfers. Transferring the present aid intensity of structural policies (structural funds spending per capita) to Eastern European countries, would require an absorption ratio of 9–12 per cent of GNP and cost the Union ECU26.6 billion for the Visegrad-5 countries (Baldwin *et al.* 1997). Baldwin *et al.* demonstrate that limiting transfers to 5 per cent of GNP would cut structural funds spending to ECU12.8 billion. The Commission proposes to restrict aid intensity to 4 per cent of a country's GNP and assesses payments for new members at ECU11.6 billion in 2006.

The Commission's plans to reduce CAP price support payments by 20–30 per cent have been considered already before by many experts (see Baldwin *et al.* 1997) as essential for financial management of the accession of Eastern European countries. Without any reduction of the present price support schemes, a transfer to the Visegrad countries alone would cost the EU between ECU5 billion and ECU15 billion ECU (Breuss and Schebeck 1996; Baldwin *et al.* 1997). However, the start of the Agenda 2000 discussions has already shown that reduction of CAP policy measures meets heavy resistance, not only from Northern member states but also from the cohesion countries. The often experienced difficulties of the EU to effect any reform of its budget will appear once again in the political discussion of the Agenda 2000 budgetary plans. Interest groups, not only of the Northern member states, can be expected to resist a reduction of CAP expenditures.

Agenda 2000 has failed to propose fundamental reforms of the EU budget, such as the introduction of a personal EU tax. Individual contributions and transfers are not envisaged. Under the effects of EMU, a number of attempts at reforms and policy debates will arise, which may ultimately lead the EU to a new fiscal constitution containing the proposed elements.

Conclusion

The European Monetary Union comprises eleven EU member states, much more than the small group of homogenous members originally considered to qualify. However, it cannot be assumed for certain that weaker member states will benefit from EMU in the same manner as the core European members. Hence, diverging forces on income disparities may rise again for some time. In addition, it is most likely that asymmetric supply and demand shocks will occur within EMU. Both call for a more profound settlement of redistribution and stabilization policies in the framework of the EU budget.

The fundamental issues of fiscal policy within federations with a common currency have been addressed by fiscal federalism theory. Transferring its arguments to the European Union, a reform on the revenue side, as well as of the expenses of the EU budget, appears inevitable. To ensure stabilization under a central monetary policy and restricted national fiscal policy (stability pact and growth pact), the European Union needs automatic stabilizers at the central level. A progressive income tax and social security contributions seem appropriate. Thus, member states suffering an economic stagnation should make lower contributions to the budget. These revenue sources, levied at the individual level and not at the member-state level, would also match the requirements of redistribution. Further, the introduction of personal taxation should be perceived as more just by European citizens than national contributions. As the equivalent of stabilization on the expenditure side would be individual transfers of a social fund, each citizen would potentially benefit. Redistribution is a most common task performed by federal budgets, but still effected at a negligible extent in the EU. Stronger interregional redistribution should be more acceptable to EU citizens once the EU has formed a stronger political union, which might be assisted by the use of a common currency. Interregional redistribution, operated by specific purpose and matching grants, as currently practised in the EU, provides appropriate control over expenses, and therefore may facilitate political acceptance. Moreover, redistribution of this type is not a mere income support, but aims at improving conditions for long-term economic development.

The proposals outlined in this chapter would constitute a fundamental reform of the European Union's fiscal constitution. Although from an economic point of view there are clear arguments in favour of more fiscal policy competence at EU level, in the practical political context those reforms constitute a remote prospect.

References

Aeschimann, E. and Riché, A. (1996), *La Guerre de Sept Ans: Histoire Secrète du Franc Fort 1989–1996* (Paris: Calmann-Lévy).

Aglietta, M. (1995), *Macroéconomie Financière* (Paris: La Découverte).

—— and de Boissieu, Ch. (1998), 'La responsabilité de la future Banque centrale européenne', *Conseil d'Analyse Economique*, 5 (Paris: La Documentation française), 49–59.

Akhtar, M. A. and Howe, H. (1991), 'The Political and Institutional Independence of US. Monetary Policy', *Banca Nazionale del Lavoro Quarterly Review*, **178**: September.

Albert, M. (1991), *Capitalisme contre Capitalisme* (Paris: Seuil).

Alogoskoufis, G. and Portes, R. (1997), 'The Euro, the Dollar and the International Monetary System'. Paper for the Seminar on EMU and the International Monetary System, Fondation Camille Gutt/IMF, Washington DC, 17–18 March.

Amin, A. and Thrift, N. (eds.) (1994a), *Globalization, Institutions, and Regional Development in Europe* (Oxford University Press).

—— —— (1994b), 'Holding Down the Global', in Amin and Thrift (1994a), q.v.

Aoki, M. (1996), 'Towards a Comparative Institutional Analysis: Motivations and Some Tentative General Insights'. Mimeo for the Annual Meeting of The Japan Association of Economics and Econometrics, Tokyo, 23 September.

Artis, M. (1996a), 'Alternative Transitions to EMU', *The Economic Journal*, July: 1005–15.

—— (1996b), *The UK Economy* (Oxford University Press).

—— and Winkler, B. (1997), 'The Stability Pact: Safeguarding the Credibility of the European Central Bank'. Centre for Economic Policy Research. Discussion Paper No. 168 (London: CEPR).

Artus, P. (1998), 'Une "Guerre des Productivités" après l'Unification Monétaire?' Document de travail, 98–22/EI, Juin, Service des Etudes Economiques et Financières (Paris: Caisse des Depôts et Consignations).

Atkinson, A. (1998), 'Pauvreté et Exclusion', *Conseil d'Analyse Economique*, 6 (Paris: La Documentation française).

Auschuss für Wirtschaft des Deutschen Bundestages (1990), *Stellungnahme des Bundesverbandes der Deutschen Industrie zur Öffentlichen Anhörung*, 16 May.

Baldwin, R., François, J., and Portes, R. (1997), 'EU Enlargement. Small Costs for the West, Big Gains for the East', *Economic Policy*, April.

Balkhausen, D. (1992), *Gutes Geld und schlechte Politik*, Düsseldorf, Capital.

Bank of England (1996), *Practical Issues Arising from the Introduction of the Euro* (London: Bank of England).

—— (1997), *Practical Issues arising from the Introduction of the Euro* (London: Bank of England).

Bauer, M. (1988), 'The Politics of State-directed Privatisation: The Case of France 1986–88', *West European Politics*, **11**: 49–60.

Bayoumi, T. and Eichengreen, B. (1993a), 'Monetary and Exchange Rate Arrangements for NAFTA'. Working Paper (Washington DC: International Monetary Fund).

—— —— (1993b), 'One Money or Many? On Analysing the Prospects for Monetary Unification in Various Parts of the World'. Working Paper C93–03 (University of California at Berkeley).

—— —— (1993c), 'Shocking Aspects of European Monetary Integration', in Torres and Giavazzi (1993), q.v. 193–229.

—— and Masson, P. R. (1995), 'Fiscal Flows in the United States and Canada: Lessons for Monetary Union in Europe', *European Economic Review*, **39**: 253–74.

BBA, APACS, LIBA (1996), *Preparing for EMU: the Implication of European Monetary Union for the Banking and Financial Markets in the United Kingdom*. Report of the EMU City Working Group (London: BBA, APACS, LIBA).

Bélanger, D. and Gutierrez, S. (1990), 'Impact de la variabilité des taux de change sur le commerce international: un survol critique de la littérature', *L'Actualité Economique*, **66**: 65–83.

Bellon, F. (1980), *Le Pouvoir Financier et l'Industrie en France* (Paris: Seuil).

Berger, S. and Dore, R. (eds.) (1996), *National Diversity and Global Capitalism* (Ithaca/London: Cornell University Press).

Biehl, D. (1992), 'Structural Funds and Budgetary Transfers in the Community', in A. Hannequart (ed.), *Economic and Social Cohesion in Europe. A New Objective for Integration* (London: Routledge), 53–64.

Blackburn, K. and Christansen, M. (1989), 'Monetary Policy and Policy Credibility: Theories and Evidence', *Journal of Economic Literature*, **29**: March.

Bladen-Hovell, R. and Symons, E. (1994), 'The EC budget', in M. Artis and N. Lee (eds.), *The Economics of the European Union* (Oxford University Press), 368–87.

Blank, S. (1995), 'U.S. Firms in North America: Redcefining Structure and Strategy', *North American Outlook*, **5**: 5–72.

Bonin, H. (1989), *L'argent en France depuis 1880: Banquiers Financiers Epargnants* (Paris: Masson).

Bourlanges, J.-L. (1998), 'L'Union européenne au lendemain d'Amsterdam: Une évaluation politique', *Pouvoirs*, **84**: 133–61.

Bowles, S. and Boyer, R. (1995), 'Wages, aggregate demand, and employment in an open economy: an empirical investigation', in G. A. Epstein and H. M. Gintis (eds.), *Macroeconomic Policy after the Conservative Era* (Cambridge, MA: Cambridge University Press), 143–71.

Boyer, R. (ed.) (1988), *Labour Market Flexibility in Europe* (Oxford: Clarendon Press).

—— (1993a), 'D'une série de National Labour Standards à un European Monetary Standard?', *Recherches Economiques de Louvain*, **59**: 119–53.

—— (1993b), 'The Economics of Job Protection and Emerging New Capital-Labor Relations', in C. H. Buechtemann (ed.), *Employment Security and Labor Market Behavior* (Ithaca, NY: Cornell University Press), 69–125.

—— (1996), 'State and Market: A new engagement for the twenty-first century?', in Boyer and Drache (1996), q.v. 84–114.

—— (1997), 'Les mots et les réalités', in *Mondialisation au-delà des Mythes*, '*Les Dossiers de l'Etats du Monde'* (Paris: La Découverte), 13–56.

—— (1998), 'The Changing Status of Industrial Relations in a More Independent World: An interpretation and Agenda for further Research', in Wilthagen (1998), q.v. 35–65.

—— (1999), *Le Government Economique de la Zone Euro* (Paris: La Documentation française).

—— and Coriat, B. (1985), 'Innovations dans les Institutions et l'analyse monétaires américaines: les greenbacks "revisités"', *Annales—Economies, Sociétés, Civilisations*, **6**: 1330–59.

—— and Didier, M. (1998), 'Innovation et croissance: Relancer une dynamique de croissance durable par l'innovation', *Conseil d'Analyse Economique*, 9 (Paris: La Documentation française).

—— and Drache D. (eds.) (1996), *States Against Markets: The Limits of Globalization* (London/New York: Routledge).

—— and Orléan, A. (1992), 'How do Conventions Evolve?', *Journal of Evolutionary Economics*, **2**: 165–77.

—— and Saillard Y. (eds.) (1995), *Théorie de la Régulation. L'Etat des Savoirs* (Paris: La Découverte).

Brash, D. T. (1993), 'The New Zealand Experience of Organising a Central Bank to Control Inflation'. Address by the Governor of the Reserve Bank of New Zealand to the European Policy Forum, London, 17 June.

—— (1997), 'The Reserve Bank of New Zealand's New Inflation Target, and New Zealand's Expectations About Inflation and Growth'. Address by the Governor of the Reserve Bank of New Zealand to the Canterbury Employer's Chamber of Commerce in Christchurch, 23 January.

Breuss, F. (1996), 'Die Wirtschafts- und Währungsunion. Abschluß oder Ende der Europäischen Integration?', Wifo Working Paper No. 86 (Vienna: Österreichisches Institut für Wirtschaftsforschung).

—— and Schebeck, F. (1996), 'Ostöffnung und Osterweiterung der EU', *WIFO Monatsberichte*, No. 2, 139–51.

Briault, C. (1995), 'The Costs of Inflation', *Bank of England Quarterly Bulletin*, February.

British Invisibles (1996a), *Key Facts about the City of London* (London: British Invisibles).

—— (1996b), *Invisibles Facts and Figures* (London: British Invisibles).

—— (1996c), *The City Table 1995* (London: British Invisibles).

—— (1999), *Key Facts about the City of London* (London: British Invisibles).

Bundesverbandder Deutschen Banken, Cologne (1990), *Supervisory Board Mandates in the Largest German 100 Corporations in 1988*, 4 April.

Burrin, P. (1995), *La France à l'Heure Allemande, 1940–1944* (Paris: Seuil).

Busch, A. (1994), 'Central Bank Independence and the Westminster Model', *West European Politics*, **17**: 53–72.

Calmfors, L. and Driffill, D. G. (1988), 'Bargaining Structure, Corporatism and Macroeconomic Performance', *Economic Policy*, **6**: 14–61.

Calmfors, L. *et al.* (1997), *EMU: A Swedish Perspective* (Boston: Kluwer).

Campbell, D. (1998), 'Labour Standards, Flexibility, and Economic Performance', in Wilthagen (1998), q.v.

Capie, F., Goodhart, C., and Schnadt, N. (1994), The Development of Central Banking. Monograph prepared for the Tercentenary of the Bank of England Central Banking Symposium, 9 June.

CEPR (Centre for Policy Research) (1995), 'Flexible Integration: Towards a More Effective and Democratic Europe. Monitoring European Integration', *6* (London: CEPR).

Clarkson, S. (1997), 'The Global-Continental-National Dynamic: Hypotheses for Comparative Continentalism'. Paper presented to the International Studies Association, Toronto.

Cohen, B. J. (1996), 'Phoenix Risen: The Resurrection of Global Finance', *World Politics*, **48**: 268–96.

—— (1998), 'How will the Euro behave?', in *The Euro and the Future of International Monetary System* (Washington DC: International Monetary Fund).

Coleman, W. D. and Porter, T. (1993), 'Regulating International Banking and Securities: Emerging Cooperation among National Authorities', in R. Stubbs and G. Underhill (eds.), *International Political Economy* (Toronto: McClelland & Stewart), 190–203.

Commission Bancaire (1993), Rapport. 'La Bancassurance en France'.

Corby Report (1995), The Pension Time Bomb in Europe, Rapporteur: Dick Taverne. Report of a study group chaired by Sir Brian Corby (London: The Federal Trust for Education and Research).

Costello, D. (1993), 'The Redistributive Effects of Interregional Transfers: A Comparison of the European Community and Germany', in *The Economics of Community Public Finance, European Economy*. Reports and Studies No. 5 (Brussels: European Commission), 269–94.

Côté, A. (1994), 'Exchange Rate Volatility and Trade: A Survey'. Working Paper No. 94–95 (Ottawa: Bank of Canada).

Court of Auditors, *Report on the Community Finances*, various years.

Crouch, C. (1993), *Industrial Relations and European State Traditions* (Oxford: Clarendon Press).

—— (1994), 'Incomes Policies, Institutions and Markets: An Overview of Recent Developments', in Dore, Boyer, and Mars (1994), q.v.

—— and Streeck, W. (1997), *Political Economy of Modern Capitalism: Mapping Convergence and Diversity* (London: Sage).

—— and Traxler, F. (eds.) (1995), *Organized Industrial Relations in Europe: What Future?* (Aldershot, UK: Avebury).

—— Finegold, D., and Sako, M. (1999), *Are Skills the Answer? The Political Economy of Skill Creation in Advanced Industrial Countries* (Oxford University Press).

Cukierman, A. (1994), 'Central Bank Independence and Monetary Control', *The Economic Journal*, November.

Davies, S. and Graham, G. (1998), 'Europe's Big Bang', *Financial Times*, 8 July: 15.

DeBlock, C. and Rioux, M. (1993), 'NAFTA: The Trump Card of the USA?' *Studies in Political Economy*, **41**: 7–44.

Deeg, R. (1998), 'What Makes German Banks Different?', *Small Business Economics*, **10**.

De Grauwe, P. (1995), 'Monetary Union and Convergence Economics'. Paper presented at the Annual Congress of the European Economic Association, Prague, September.

Dehove, M. (1997), 'L'Union Européenne inaugure-t-elle un nouveau grand régime d'organisation des pouvoirs publics et de la société internationale?', *L'Année de la Régulation 1997*, 1 (Paris: La Découverte), 11–83.

—— (1998), 'Les institutions de l'Union européenne. Problématique introductive'. Mimeo 16 May (Paris: Commissariat Général du Plan).

Delors Report (1989), *Report on Economic and Monetary Union in the European Community*. Committee for the Study of Economic and Monetary Union. (Luxembourg: Office for Official Publications of the European Communities).

De Ménil, G. (1996), 'Les politiques budgétaires en Europe à la veille de l'Union Monétaire: Les effets des anticipations', *Economie Internationale, La Revue du CEPII*, **68**: 31–56.

de Silguy, Y.-Th. (1998), *L'Euro* (Paris: Livre de Poche).

Dore, R., Boyer, R., and Mars, Z. (eds.) (1994), *The Return to Incomes Policy* (London: Pinter/Paris: La Découverte).

Dornbush, R., Favero, C., and Giavazzi, F. (1998), 'Immediate Challenge for the European Central Bank', *Economic Policy*, **26**: 17–52.

Drago, M. E. (1998), 'The Institutional Bases of Chile's Economic "Miracle" '. Ph.D. thesis (Florence: European University Institute).

Dreze, J., Malinvaud, E. *et al.* (1994), 'Growth and Employment: The Scope for a European Initiative', *European Economy, Report and Studies*, **1**.

Dubbins, S. (2000), 'The Growth of European Industrial Relations'. Ph.D. thesis (Florence: European University Institute).

Due, J., Madsen, J. S., and Strøby, J. C. (1994), *The Survival of the Danish Model* (Copenhagen: DJØF).

—— —— Petersen, L. K., and Strøby, J. C. (1995), 'Adjusting the Danish Model: Towards Centralized Decentralization', in Crouch and Traxler (1995), q.v.

Dumez, H. and Jeunemaitre, A. (1994), 'Privatisation in France', in V. Wright (ed.), *Privatisation in Western Europe, Pressures, Problems and Paradoxes* (London: Pinter), 83–104.

Eastman, H. (1971), 'Canadian — USA Financial Relationships'. Proceedings of a conference held at Melvin Village New Hampshire, September.

Eichengreen, B. (1990), 'One money for Europe? Lessons from the US Currency Union', *Economic Policy*, **10**: 119–86.

Eijffinger, S. and Schaling, E. (1993), 'Central Bank Independence: Theory and Evidence'. Discussion Paper 9325, April (Center for Economic Research, Tilburg University).

Ergas, H. (1986), *Does Technology Matter?* (Brussels: Centre for European Policy Studies).

ERT (European Roundtable of Industrialists) (1997), *Benchmarking* (Brussels: ERT).

Esser, J. (1990), 'Bank Power in West Germany Revisited', *West European Politics*, **13**: 17–32.

EC (European Commission) (1970), 'Economic and Monetary Union in the Community' (Werner Report), *Bulletin of the European Communities* (Suppl. 7).

—— (1977), *Report of the Study Group on The Role of Public Finance in European Integration* (Brussels: European Commission).

—— (1990), 'One Market, One Money. An Evaluation of Potential Benefits and Costs of Forming and Economic and Monetary Union', *European Economy*, **44**.

—— (1993), 'Stable–Sound Finances. Community Public Finance in the perspective of EMU', *European Economy*, **53**.

—— (1997a), 'Agenda 2000. For a Stronger and Wider Union', COM (97)2000 final (Brussels: European Commission).

—— (1997b), 'Economic policy in EMU, Part A: Rules and adjustment', *Economic Papers*, No. 124, November (Brussels: European Commission).

—— (1997c), 'Economic Policy in EMU. Rules and Adjustment. Specific Topics'. Mimeo, Directorate General II Economic Papers, 124–5, November (Brussels: European Commission).

—— (1998a), 'Euro 1999. Report on the Convergence and Recommendations for the Third Phase of the EMU', 25 March, Brussels.

—— (1998b), 'Commission's Recommendation for the Broad Guidelines of the Economic Policies of the Member States and the Community'. Mimeo, Directorate General II, 13 May (Brussels: European Commission).

European Council (1996), 'Dublin European Council 13 and 14 December 1996: Presidency Conclusions'. European Commission Press Release.

European Monetary Institute (1997), *The Single Monetary Policy in Stage Three: Specification of the Operational Framework*, January (Frankfurt: EMI).

Fair, R. C. (1998), 'Estimated Stabilization Costs of the EMU'. Mimeo (New Haven, CT: Cowles Foundation).

Farrell, V. S., DeRosa, D. A., and McCown, T. A. (1983), 'Effects of Exchange Rate Variablility on International Trade and other Economic Variables: A Review of the Literature', *Staff Studies*, No. 130 (Washington DC: US Board of Governors of the Federal Reserve System).

Favereau, O. (1989), 'Marchés internes, marchés externes', *Revue Economique*, 2 March: 273–28.

Fenton, P. and Murray, J. (1993), 'Optimum Currency Areas: A Cautionary Tale', *The Exchange Rate and the Economy* (Ottawa: Bank of Canada), 485–531.

Ferner, A. and Hyman, R. (eds.) (1998), *Changing Industrial Relations in Europe* (Oxford: Blackwell).

Fischer, A. M. and Orr, A. B. (1994), 'Monetary Policy Credibility and Price Uncertainty: The New Zealand Experience of Inflation Targeting', *OECD Economic Studies*, 22: Spring.

Fitoussi, J.-P. (1998), 'Une politique de croissance combattrait beaucoup plus efficacement le chômage', *Le Monde*, 27 January: 15.

Flassbeck, H. (1998), 'L'Allemagne menace l'Union monétaire en faisant baisser les coûts salariaux', *Le Monde*, 27 January: 15.

Forder, J. and Oppenheimer, P. (1996), 'The Fluctuating Rationale of Monetary Union', in J. Hayward (ed.), *Élitism, Populism, and European Politics* (Oxford: Clarendon Press), 220–37.

Fortin, B. (1978), *Les Avantages et les Coûts des Différentes Options Monétaires d'une Petite Economie Ouverte: Un Cadre Analytique* (Ottawa: Gouvernement du Québec).

Fratianni, M., von Hagen, J., and Waller, C. (1993), 'Central Banking as a Principal–Agent Problem'. Discussion Paper No. 752, January (London: CEPR).

Friedmann, W. (1992), 'German Monetary Union and Some Lessons for Europe', in R. Barrell (ed.), *Economic Convergence and Monetary Union in Europe* (London: National Institute of Economic and Social Research).

Froud, J., Haslam, C., Johal, S., Leaver, A., Williams, J., and Willams, K. (1998), 'Accumulation Based on Inequality: A Keynesian Analysis of Investment for Shareholder Value'. Mimeo (Manchester, UK: Manchester University Press).

Genscher, H. D. (1989), 'Die Rolle der Bundesrepublik Deutschland bei der Vollendung des Europäischen Währungssystem', in *Ergebnisse einer Fachtagung, Strategien und Ergebnisse für die Zukunft Europas* (Gütersloh: Bertelsmann).

German Monopolies Commission 1973–1983 (1987), *Summaries of the First Five Biennial Reports* (Baden-Baden: Nomos), 15.

Gill, S. (1997), 'An EMU or an Ostrich? EMU and Neo-Liberal Economic Integration; Limits and Alternatives', in Minkkinen and Patomäki (1997), q.v. 207–31.

Gil-Robles, J.-M. (1997), 'The New Treaty Must Display an Important Social Component', *Seven Days in Europe*, May.

Goldfinger, C. (1986), *La Géofinance* (Paris, Seuil).

Goodhart, C. A. E. (1991), 'Fiscal Policy and EMU', in J. Driffill and M. Beber (eds.), *A Currency for Europe* (London: Lothian Foundation Press), 157–74.

—— (1995), 'The Political Economy of Monetary Union', in P. B. Kenen (ed.), *Understanding Interdependence: The Macroeconomics of the Open Economy* (Princeton, NJ: Princeton University Press), 448–505.

Goodman, J. (1992) *Monetary Sovereignty: The Politics of Central Banking in Western Europe* (Ithaca, NY: Cornell University Press).

Gordon, R. (1983), 'An Optimal Taxation Approach to Fiscal Federalism', *Quarterly Journal of Economics*, 95: 567–86.

Gormley, L. and de Haan, J. (1996), 'The Democratic Deficit of the European Central Bank', *European Law Review*, April: 95–112.

Gottschalk, A. (1988), 'Bankeneinfluss und Depotstimmrecht', *WSI-Mitteilungen*, 5: 294ff.

—— and Smeeding, T. (1997), 'Cross-national Comparisons of Earnings and Income Inequality, *Journal of Economic Literature*, **25**: June, 633–87.

Granovetter, M. (1985), 'Economic Action and Social Structure: The Problem of Embeddedness', *American Journal of Sociology*, **91**: 481–510.

Grilli, V., Masciandaro, D., and Tabellini, G. (1991), 'Political and Monetary Institutions and Public Financial Policies in the Industrial Countries', *Economic Policy*, **13**: October.

Gros, D. (1996), 'Towards Economic and Monetary Union: Problems and Prospects'. CEPS Papers No. 65, Brussels.

—— and Thygesen, N. (1992), *European Monetary Integration: From the European Monetary System to European Monetary Integration* (London: Longman).

Guitian, M. (1995), 'Central Bank Independence: Issues and Diversity of Models'. Paper prepared for a workshop on 'Independence and Accountability: the Role and Structure of the South African Reserve Bank'. Organized by the Centre for Research into Economics and Finance in South Africa, the London School of Economics and the South African Reserve Bank, January.

Hall, P. (1986), *Governing the Economy: The Politics of State Interventions in Britain and France* (Oxford: Polity Press).

Hall, P. A. (1994), 'Central bank interdependence and coordinated wage bargaining: their interaction in Germany and Europe', *German Politics and Society*, **31**: 1–24.

—— and Franzese, R. J., Jr. (1998), 'Mixed Signals: Central Bank Independence, Co-ordinated Wage-bargaining, and European Monetary Union', *International Organization*, **39**:

Hamilton, A. (1986), *The Financial Revolution* (London: Viking).

Harden, I. (1992), 'The European Central Bank and the Role of National Central Banks in Economic and Monetary Union'. Draft in mimeo.

Harris, R. G. (1992), *Exchange Rates and International Competitiveness of the Canadian Economy* (Ottawa: Economic Council of Canada).

Harrop, J. (1996), *Structural Funding and Employment in the European Union* (Cheltenham, UK: Edward Elgar).

Harvard Business School (1996), *Governance at Metallgesellschaft* (A), (B).9–495–055.

Hasse, R. H. (1990), *The European Central Bank: Perspectives for a Further Development of the European Monetary System* (Gütersloh: Bertelsmann).

Helleiner, E. (1998), 'Denationalizing Money? Economic Liberalism and the 'National Question' in Currency Affairs'. Paper presented to the International Studies Association, 17–21 March.

Hemerijck, A. (1995), 'Corporatist Immobility in the Netherlands', in Crouch and Traxler (1995), q.v.

Henning, C. R. (1994), *Currencies and Politics in the USA, Germany, and Japan* (Washington DC: Institute for International Economics).

Hoffman, S. (1963), 'Paradoxes of the French Political Community', in *In Search of France* (New York: Harper).

Hollingsworth, R. and Boyer, R. (eds.) (1997), *Contemporary Capitalism: The Embeddedness of Institutions* (Cambridge, UK: Cambridge University Press).

—— Schmitter, P., and Streeck, W. (eds.) (1994), *Governing Capitalist Economies* (New York: Oxford University Press).

House of Commons (1997), Bank of England Bill, House of Commons Internet Publications, Session 1997–8.

—— Treasury and Civil Service Select Committee (1993), *The Role of the Bank of England*, First Report, Vol. 1, Session 1993–4, July (London: HMSO).

House of Lords Select Committee on European Communities (1996), *An EMU of ins and outs* (London: HMSO).

Hughes Hallett, A. J. and Ma, Y. (1996), 'Changing Partners: the Importance of Coordinating Fiscal and Monetary Policies Within a Monetary Union', *Manchester School of Economics and Social Studies*, LXIV: 2 June.

InfEuro (1998), 'Finland: An Original Social Agreement'. *Information Letter of European Commission*, March.

Inman, R. P. and Rubinfeld, D. (1996a), 'Designing Tax Policy in Federalist Economies: An Overview', *Journal of Public Economics*, **60**, 307–34.

—— —— (1996b), 'The Political Economy of Fiscal Federalism', in D. Mueller (ed.), *Perspectives of Public Choice* (New York: Blackwell).

Italianer, A. and Pisani-Ferry, J. (1994), 'The Regional-Stabilization Properties of Fiscal Arrangements', in Jorgen Mortensen (ed.), *Improving Economic and Social Cohesion in the European Community* (New York: St. Martin's Press), 155–94.

Jacquet, P. (1998), 'L'Union monétaire et la coordination des politiques macro-économiques', *Conseil d'Analyse Economique*, *5* (Paris: La Documentation française), 35–46.

Jenkinson, T. and Meyer, C. (1992), 'The Assessment: Corporate Governance and Corporate Control', *Oxford Review of Economic Policy*, **8**, 3.

Johnson, H. (1970), 'The Case for Flexible Exchange Rates', in George N. Halm (ed.), *Approaches to Greater Flexibility* (Princeton, NJ: Princeton University Press).

Katzenstein P. (1985), *Small States and World Markets* (Ithaca, NY: Cornell University Press).

Kaufmann, H. M. (1995), 'The Importance of Being Independent: Central Bank Independence and the European System of Central Banks', in C. Rhodes and S. Mazey (eds.), *The State of the European Union. Building a European Polity?* (Boulder, CO: Lynne Rienner), 267–92.

Kenen, P. B. (1995), *Economic and Monetary Union in Europe* (Cambridge, UK: Cambridge University Press).

Kennedy, E. (1991), *The Bundesbank: Germany's Central Bank in the International Monetary System* (London: Royal Institute of International Affairs/Pinter).

Keohane, R. O. and Milner, H. V. (1996), *Internationalization and Domestic Politics* (Cambridge, UK: Cambridge University Press).

Kloten, N., Ketterer, K.-H., and Vollmer, R. (1985), 'West Germany's Stabilization Performance', in L. N. Lindberg and C. S. Maier (eds.), *The Politics of Inflation and Economic Stagnation* (Washington DC: The Brookings Institution).

Krugman, P. (1987), 'Konzepte der wirtschaftlichen Integration in Europa', in Padoa-Schioppa *et al.* (1987), q.v. 113–42.

—— (1992), *Economic Geography* (Boston, MA: MIT Press).

—— (1993), 'Lessons of Massachusetts for EMU', in Torres and Giavazzi (1993), q.v. 241–60.

—— and Venables, A. (1990), 'Integration and the Competitiveness of Peripheral Industry', in C. Bliss and J. Braga de Macedo (eds.), *Unity with Diversity in the European Economy* (Cambridge, UK: CEPR/Cambridge University Press), 56–75.

Laffan, B. and Shackleton, M. (1996), 'The Budget', in H. Wallace and W. Wallace (eds.), *Policy-making in the European Union* (Oxford University Press).

Lafrance, R. and van Norden, S. (1994), *To Fix or Float? A Review of Issues Related to Canada's Exchange Rate* (Ottawa: Bank of Canada).

Laidler, D. E. W. and Robson, W. B. P. (1990), 'The Fix is Out: A Defence of the Floating Canadian Dollar', *Commentary*, July (Toronto: C. D. Howe Institute).

Lalonde, R. and St. Amant, P. (1995), 'Optimum Currency Areas: The Case of Mexico and the USA', *Money Affairs*, July–December.

L'Année Politique, Economique, Sociale et Diplomatique, 1987 (Paris: Editeur du Moniteur).

La Revue du CEPII (1996), 'L'Europe entre marché unique et tensions monétaires', *Economie Internationale*, **65**: 1st quarter.

Laskar, D. (1993), 'Union monétaire: differences structurelles et assymétrie des chocs', *Revue Economique*, **44**: 1045–69.

Levitt, M. (1996*a*), *European Monetary Union—The Impact on Banking* (London: Royal Institute of International Affairs).

—— (1996*b*), 'EMU: A View from the Banking Sector', *Journal of European Public Policy*, **3**: September.

LIBA (1996), *Non Participation in EMU: Possible Consequences for the City of London* (London: LIBA).

Lipsey, R. R. (1992), 'Global Change and Economic Policy', in N. Stehr and R. Ericson (eds.), *The Cultural and Power of Knowledge* (New York: de Gruyter).

Lohmann, S. (1996), 'Quis Custodiet Ipsos Custodes', in H. Siebert (ed.), *Monetary Policy in an Integrated World Economy* (Kiel/Tübingen: Institut für Weltwirtschaft an der Universität Kiel/Mohr), 139–60.

Lordon, F. (1997), *Les Quadratures de la Politique Économique* (Paris: Albin Michel).

Loriaux, M. (1991), *France after Hegemony: International Change and Financial Reform* (Ithaca, NY: Cornell University Press).

Louis, J.-V. (ed.) (1989), *Vers un Système Européen de Banques Centrales. Projet de Dispostions Organiques*. Rapport du groupe présidé par Jean-Victor Louis. Institute d'Etudes européennes (Brussels: University of Brussels).

McNamara, K. R. and Jones, E. (1996), 'The Clash of Institutions: Germany in European Monetary Affairs', *German Politics and Society*, **14**: 5–30.

Majone, G. (1996), 'Temporal Consistency and Policy Credibility: Why Democracies need Non-Majoritarian Institutions'. EUI Working Papers, RSC 96/57.

—— (1997), 'From the Positive to the Regulatory State: Causes and Consequences of Changes in the Mode of Governance', *Journal of Public Policy*, **17**: 139–67.

Maravall, J. M. (1997), *Regimes, Politics and Markets* (Oxford: Clarendon Press).

Marks, G., Scharpf, F. W., Schmitter, P. C., and Streeck, W. (1996), *Governance in the European Union* (London: Sage).

Marsden, D. (1992), 'Incomes Policy for Europe? Or Will Pay Bargaining Destroy the Single European Market?', *British Journal of Industrial Relations*, **30**, 587–604.

Marsh, D. (1992), *The Bundesbank. The Bank that Rules Europe*. London: Mandarin.

Martin, P. (1995), 'Free Riding and Two Speed Monetary Unification in Europe', *European Economic Review*, **39**: 1345–64.

Masson, P. R. (1996), 'Fiscal Dimensions of EMU', *The Economic Journal*, May: 996–1004.

Matzner, E. and Streeck, W. (1991), *Beyond Keynesianism: The Socio-Economics of Production and Full Employment* (Aldershot, UK: Edward Elgar).

Mazier, J. (1997), 'L'Europe: enlisement ou transition vers un nouveau régime de croissance?' *L'Année de la régulation 1997, 1* (Paris: La Découverte).

Meade, J. and Weale, M. (1995), 'Monetary Union and the Assignment Problem', *Scandinavian Journal of Economics*, **97**: 2.

Milesi, G. (1998), *Le roman de l'Euro.* (Paris: Hachette).

Minkkinen, P. and Patomäki, H. (eds.) (1997), *The Politics of Economic and Monetary Union* (London: Kluwer).

Minsky, H. P. (1982), *Can it Happen Again?* (Washington DC: Congress Hearings).

Mitchell, A. (1997), 'It's Official: Quebec falls below 25 per cent of population', *Globe and Mail*, 16 April: A1.

Monti, M. (1996), *The Single Market and Tomorow's Europe* (Luxembourg: Office for Official Publications of the European Communities).

Moses, J. (1998), 'Finland and EMU', in E. Jones, J. Frieden, and F. Torres, (eds.), *Joining Europe's Monetary Club. The Challenges for Smaller Member States* (New York: St. Martin's Press), 83–104.

Muet, P. (1998), 'Deficit de croissance européen et defaut de coordination: une analyse rétrospective', *Conseil d'Analyse Economique, 5* (Paris: La Documentation Française), 13–34.

Munchau, W. (1998), 'The International Impact of EMU is anyone's guess', *The JapanTimes*, 20 August.

Mundell, R. A. (1961), 'A Theory of Optimum Currency Areas', *American Economic Review*, **51**: 657–67.

Murray, J., van Norden, S., and Vigfrisson, R. (1996), 'Excess Volatility and Speculative Bubbles in the Canadian Dollar—Real or Imagined?', *Bank of Canada Technical Report*, No. 76.

Neumann, M. J. M. (1991), 'Central Bank Independence as a Prequisite of Price Stability', in Commission of the European Communities, *European Economy: the Economics of EMU*, Special Edition, No. 1 (Luxembourg: Office for Official Publications of the European Communities).

Nowotny, E. (1996), 'Zur regionalen Dimension der Finanzverfassung der EU—gegenwärtiger Stand und Perspektiven'. Unpublished manuscript, Vienna.

Oates, W. E. (1972), *Fiscal Federalism* (New York: Harcourt Brace).

OECD (Organization for Economic Cooperation and Development) (1993), *Employment Outlook* (Paris: OECD).

—— (1994a), *Statistics of Foreign Trade*, Series A (Paris: OECD).

—— (1994b), *The OECD Jobs Study: Evidence and Explanations. Part II. The Adjustment Potential of the Labour Market* (Paris: OECD).

—— (1995a), *Etudes Economiques de l'OECD: France 1995* (Paris: OECD).

—— (1995b), *Income Distribution in OECD Countries*, Social Policy Studies, No. 18 (Paris: OECD).

Ohmae, K. (1995), *The End of the Nation State* (New York: The Free Press).

Olson, M. (1982), *The Rise and Decline of Nations: Economic Growth, Stagflation and Social Rigidities* (New Haven, CT: Yale University Press).

Padoa-Schioppa, T. *et al.* (1987), *Effizienz, Stabilität und Verteilungsgerechtigkeit* (Brussels: European Commission).

Palan, R. (1998), 'Les Fantômes du Capitalisme Mondial: l'Economie Politique Internationale et l'Ecole Française de la Régulation', *L'Année de la Régulation 1998*, 2 (Paris: La Découverte).

Palombarini, S. (1997), 'La Crise Italienne de 1992: une Lecture en Termes de Dynamique Endogène', *L'Année de la Régulation 1997*, 1 (Paris: La Découverte).

—— (1999), 'Vers une Théorie Régulationniste de la Politique Economique', *L'Année de la régulation 1999*, 3 (Paris: La Découverte).

Pastré, O. (1992), 'Le Reveil des ZINvestisseurs', *La Tribune de l'Expansion*, 7 September.

Patomäki, H. (1997), 'EMU and the Legitimation Problems of the European Union', in Minkkinen and Patomäki (1997), q.v. 164–206.

Peet, J. (1998), 'EMU: An Awfully Big Adventure' (Survey), *The Economist*, 11 April: 1–26.

Pestoff, V. (1991), 'The Demise of the Swedish Model and the Resurgence of Organized Business as a Major Political Actor'. University of Stockholm, Department of Business Administration, 2.

—— (1995), 'Towards a New Swedish Model of Collective Bargaining and Politics', in Crouch and Traxler (1995), q.v.

Picchi, F. (1991), Economics and Business: dizionario enciclopedico economico e commerciale inglese-italioino, italiano inglese (Bologina: Zanichell).

Pochet, P. (1998), 'Les Pactes Sociaux en Europe dans les Années 1990', *Sociologie du Travail*, 2: 173–90.

Posen, A. (1993), 'Why Central Bank Independence does not cause Low Inflation: There is No Institutional Fix for Politics', in R. O'Brien (ed.), *Finance and the International Economy*, vol. 7 (Oxford University Press).

Posner, R. A. (1981), *The Economics of Justice* (Cambridge, MA: Harvard University Press).

Purcell, J. (1995), 'Ideology and the End of Institutional Industrial Relations: Evidence from the UK', in Crouch and Traxler (1995), q.v.

Purvis, D. (1992), 'Economic Integration, Currency Areas and Macroeconomic Policy', in J. Murray and B. O'Reilly (eds.), *The Exchange Rate and the Economy* (Ottawa: Bank of Canada), 541–79.

Reid, M. (1988), *All-change in the City* (London: Macmillan).

Regini, M. (1997), 'Still Engaging in Corporatism? Recent Italian Experience in Comparative Perspective', *European Journal of Industrial Relations*, 3: 259–78.

—— and Regalia, I. (1996), *Italia Anni '90: Rinasce la Concertazione* (Milan: IRES).

Risse, T. (1998), 'To Euro or Not to Euro? The EMU and Identity Politics in the European Union' (with Daniela Engelmann-Martin, Hans-Joachim Knopf, and Klaus Roscher). Unpublished manuscript, 16 March 1998 (Florence: European University Institute).

Rogoff, K. (1985), 'The Optimal Degree of Commitment to an Intermediate Monetary Target', *Quarterly Journal of Economics*, **100**: November.

Roll Committee (1993), 'Independent and Accountable: a New Mandate for the Bank of England'. Report of an independent panel chaired by Eric Roll, October (London: CEPR).

Rousseau, H.-P. (1978), *Unions Monétaires et Monnaies Nationales: Une Étude Économique de Quelques Cas Historiques* (Ottawa: Gouvernement du Québec).

Ryner, M. (1998), 'Neo-Liberal Globalization and the Crisis of Swedish Social Democracy'. Working paper SPS 4/98 (Florence: European University Institute).

Sabel, C. F. (1997), 'Constitutional Ordering in Historical Context', in F. W. Scharpf (ed.), *Games in Hierarchies and Networks*.

Sachs, J. and Sala-i-Martin, X. (1992), 'Fiscal Federalism and Optimum Currency Areas: Evidence for Europe from the United States', in M. Canzoneri, V. Grilli and P. E. Masson (eds.), *Establishing a Central Bank: Issues in Europe and Lessons from the US* (Cambridge, UK: Cambridge University Press), 195–219.

Salvati, M. (1997), 'Moneta Unica, Rivoluzione Copernicana', *Il Mulino*, **369**: 5–23.

Scharpf, F. (1991), *Crisis and Choice in European Social Democracy* (Ithaca, NY: Cornell University Press).

—— (1996), 'Negative and Positive Integration in the Political Economy of European Welfare States', in Marks *et al.* (1996), q.v.

Schmitter, P. (1997a), 'Political Europe and Social Europe'. Seminar on Social Europe. Gulbenkian Foundation, Lisbon, 5–7 May.

—— (1997b), 'Citizenship in an Eventual Euro-Democracy'. Paper presented at the Austrian Civil Dialogue on Fundamental Rights in European Union, Vienna, 23–24 May.

—— (1997c), 'The Emerging Europolity and its Impact upon National Systems of Production', in Hollingsworth and Boyer (1997), q.v. 395–430.

—— and Grote, J. R. (1997), 'The Corporatist Sisyphus: Past, Present and Future'. Working paper SPS 4/97 (Florence: European University Institute).

Schokker, E. (1980), *The Central Bank and the State in the Light of European Integration*, SUERF Series 34A (Tilburg University for Société Universitaire Européenne de Recherches Financières).

Shapiro, M. (1997), 'The Problems of Independent Agencies in the United States and the European Union', *Journal of European Public Policy*, 4: 276–91.

Shaw, E. R. (1981), *The London Money Market* (London: Heinemann).

Sinclair, P. and Horsewood, N. (1996), 'Has the Phillips Curve Been Reborn?'. Paper for the conference on 'European Unemployment: Macroeconomic Aspects'. Organized by the European University Institute, Florence, 21–23 November.

SOFRES (1997), *Un Sondage de l'Opinion Publique française* (Paris: SOFRES).

Soros, G. (1997), *Le Vertige de la Finance Internationale* (Paris: Flammarion).

Soskice, D. (1990), 'Wage Determination: The Changing Role of Institutions in Advanced Industrialized Countries', *Oxford Review of Economic Policy*, 6: 31–61.

—— (1997a), 'German Technology Policy, Innovation and National Institutional Frameworks', *Industry and Innovation*, 4: 75–96.

—— (1997b), 'The Future Political Economy of EMU. Rethinking the Effects of Monetary Integration on Europe', *Yearbook of the Freidrich Erbert Stiftung* (Berlin: Friedrich Ebert Stiftung).

—— and Iversen, T. (1997), 'Central Bank—Trade Union Interactions and the Equilibrium Rate of Employment'. WZB Working paper, FS 1 97 308 (Berlin: Wissenschaftszentrum).

Stanford, J. (1995), 'The Impact of Real Competitiveness on Monetary Policy and Exchange Rates in an Open Economy'. Unpublished paper, 27pp.

Stern, F. (1990), *L'Or et le Fer: Bismarck et son Banquier Bleichröder* (Paris: Fayard)

Sternhell, Z. (1978), *La Droite Révolutionnaire: 1885–1914. Les Origines Françaises du fascisme* (Paris: Seuil).

Story, J. and Walter, I. (1997), *Political Economy of Financial Integration in Europe: The Battle of the Systems* (Manchester, UK: Manchester University Press).

Streeck, W. (1994), 'Pay restraint without incomes policy: institutionalized monetarism and industrial unionism in Germany', in R. Dore, R. Boyer and Z. Mars (eds.), *The Return to Incomes Policy* (London: Pinter).

—— (1996), 'On the Beneficial Role of Constraints', in Boyer and Drache (1996), q.v.

—— (1997), 'German Capitalism: Does It Exist? Can It Survive', in Crouch and Streeck (1997), q.v.

—— (1998), 'The Internalization of Industrial Relations in Europe. Prospects and Problems'. Discussion Paper 98/2 (Cologne: Max-Planck Institut für Gesellschaftsforschung).

Sturm, R. (1989), 'The Role of the Bundesbank in German Politics.' *West European Politics*, 12(2): 1–12.

Swinburne, M. and Castello-Branco, M. (1991), 'Central Bank Independence: Issues and Experience'. International Monetary Fund Working Paper, June (Washington DC: IMF).

Talani, L. (1997), 'The City vs the Continent: Social Origins of British Hostility to EMU'. Paper presented to the International Studies Association, Toronto. 30pp.

—— (1998), 'Interests or Expectations? The Problem of Credibility of the Exchange Rate Policy: An IPE Approach. The Case of Italy and the UK and the Departure from the ERM of the EMS'. Ph.D. thesis (Florence: European University Institute).

Teichman, J. (1997*a*), 'Neoliberalism and the Transformation of Mexican Authoritarianism', *Mexican Studies/Estudios Mexicanos*, **13**: 121–47.

—— (1997*b*), 'Democracy and Technocratic Decision Making: Mexico, Argentina and Chile'. Paper presented to the Latin American Studies Association, Guadalajara, April 1997.

Teivainen, T. (1997), 'The Independence of the European Central Bank: Implications for Democratic Governance', in Minkkinen and Patomäki (1997), q.v. 164–206.

Teutemann, M. (1993), 'Interpersonal versus Interregional Redistribution at the European Level—As Seen from the Perspective of Fiscal Federalism and Public Choice Theory', in *The Economics of Community Public Finance, European Economy, Reports and Studies*, 5 (Brussels: European Commission), 39–411.

The Economist (1998*a*), 'Under Starter's Orders. Britain's Referendum Campaign over the Euro May Not have Been Announced Yet-But it has Already Begun', 8 August: 29–30.

—— (1998*b*), 'Follow the Money. Remember Monetarism? It May be Coming Back into Fashion', 18 August: 68.

Théret, B. (1992), *Régimes Economiques de l'Ordre Politique* (Paris: PUF).

—— (1997), *Du Fédéralisme et de la Protection Sociale en Amérique et en Particulier au Canada* (Paris: IRIS—Commissariat Général du Plan).

Thygesen, N. (1989), 'Decentralization and Accountability Within the Central Bank: Any Lessons from the US Experience for the Potential Organization of a European Central Banking Institution?', in P. De Grauwe and T. Peeters (eds.), *The ECU and European Monetary Integration* (London: Macmillan), 91–115.

—— (1992), 'Coordination of National Policies', in P. Newman, M. Milgate, and J. Eatwell (eds.), *The New Palgrave. Dictionary of Money and Finance*, vol. 1 (London: Macmillan), 458–61.

Tiebout, C. M. (1956), 'A Pure Theory of Local Expenditure', *Journal of Political Economy*, **64**:

Tinbergen, J. (1991), *Techniques Modernes de la Politique Économique* (Paris: Dunod).

Torres, F. and Giavazzi, F. (eds.) (1993), *Adjustment and Growth in the European Monetary Union* (Cambridge, UK: CEPR/Cambridge University Press).

Traxler, F. (1995), 'Farewell to Labour Market Associations? Organized versus Disorganized Decentralization as a Map for Industrial Relations', in Crouch and Traxler (1995), q.v.

—— (1996), 'Collective Bargaining and Industrial Change: A Case of Disorganization? A Comparative Analysis of Eighteen OECD Countries', *European Sociological Review*, **12**: 271–87.

—— (1997), 'Collective Bargaining in the OECD: Developments, Preconditions and Effects'. Mimeo. European Sociological Association Conference, Colchester, UK.

—— (1998), in Ferner and Hyman (1998), q.v.

Treaty on European Union (1992), Council of the European Communities/ Commission of the European Communities (Luxembourg: Office for Official Publications of the European Communities).

Trigilia, C. (1991), 'The Paradox of the Region: Economic Regulation and the Representation of Interests', *Economy and Society*, **20**: 306–27.

Van Apeldoorn, B. (1998), 'Global Capitalism and the Struggle for Europe's Socio-economic Order'. Ph.D. thesis (Florence: European University Institute).

Verdun, A. (1995), *Europe's Struggle with the Global Political Economy. A Study of How EMU is Perceived by Actors in the Policy-making Process in Britain, France and Germany*. Ph.D. dissertation (Florence: European University Institute).

—— (1996), 'An "Asymmetrical" Economic and Monetary Union in the EU: Perceptions of Monetary Authorities and Social Partners', *Journal of European Integration* **20**: 59–81.

—— (1998*a*), 'The Institutional Design of EMU: A Democratic Deficit?', in M. Artis and R. Marimon (eds.), *The Political Economy of an Integrated Europe* (Florence: European University Institute).

—— (1998*b*), 'The Logic of Giving up National Currencies: Lessons from Europe's Monetary Union', in E. Gilbert and E. Helleiner (eds.), *Nation-States and Money: The Past, the Present and Future of Currencies* (London: Routledge).

Vernet, D. (1998), 'Divergences entre Paris et Bonn sur la Monnaie Unique, Tensions sur la Pologne', *Le Monde*, 30 July: 10.

Vinals, J. (1995), 'European Monetary Integration: A Narrow or a Wide EMU?' Paper presented at the annual congress of the European Economic Association, Prague, September.

Visser, J. (1998), 'EMU and the Art of Making Social Pacts'. CESAR mimeo. University of Amsterdam.

—— and Hemerijck, A. (1997), *A Dutch 'Miracle'* (Amsterdam: Amsterdam University Press).

von Furstenberg, G. M. (1995), 'Winning Support for Price Stability: How Governor Crow Did It'. Working Paper. (Toronto: Centre for International Studies), 34pp.

—— (1996), 'Monetary Union: Still Coming in Europe and North America?' *Challenge*, **39**: July–August.

von Hagen, J. (1991), 'Fiscal Arrangements in a Monetary Union. Evidence from the US'. Indiana University School of Business, Discussion Paper No. 58.

—— and Eichengreen, B. (1996), 'Federalism, Fiscal Restraints, and European Monetary Union', *American Economic Review*, **86**: 134–8.

—— and Hammond, G. W. (1995), 'Regional Insurance Against Asymmetric Shocks. An Empirical Study for the European Community'. Discussion Paper No. 1170, May (London: CEPR).

Walsh, C. (1993), 'Fiscal Federalism: An Overview of Issues and a Discussion of Their Relevance to the European Community', in *The Economics of Community Public Finance, European Economy*. Reports and Studies No. 5/1993 (Brussels: European Commission), 25–62.

Weintraub, S. (1997), *NAFTA at Three: A Progress Report* (Washington DC: Center for Strategic and International Studies).

White, H. (1998), 'A Theory of Markets'. Mimeo (New York: Columbia University).

Wilthagen, T. (ed.) (1998), *Advancing Theory in Labour Law and Industrial Relations in a Global Context* (Amsterdam: Elsevier).

Wincott, D. (1992), 'The European Central Bank: Constitutional Dimensions and Political Limits', *International Relations*, **11**: 111–26.

Winkler, B. (1996), 'Towards a Strategic View on EMU: A Critical Survey', *Journal of Public Policy*, **16**.

Wolfe, D. (1997), 'The Emergence of the Region State'. Paper presented to the Nation State in a Global Information Era conference, Queen's University, 35pp.

Wood, G. E. (1994), 'Central Bank Independence in New Zealand: Analytical, Empirical and Insitutional Aspects'. Paper for a conference on 'Central Bank Independence and Accountability', Universita Bocconi, Milan, March.

World Bank (1997), 'The State in a Changing World', in *World Development Report 1997* (Washington DC: World Bank).

Wyplotsz, C. (1997), 'EMU: Why and How it might Happen', *Journal of Economic Perspectives*, **11**: Autumn.

Ziegler, R., Bender, D., and Biehler, H. (1985), 'Industry and Banking in the German Corporate Network', in F. N. Stokman, R. Ziegler and J. Scott (eds.), *Networks of Corporate Power: A Comparative Analysis of Ten Countries* (London: Polity Press).

Zysman, J. (1983), *Governments, Markets and Growth: Financial Systems and Policies of Industrial Change* (Oxford: Martin Robertson).

Index